TOLERANCE

Imprimi Potest.
    ÆMILIUS THIBAUT, S.J.,
            PRÆPOSITUS PROVINCIÆ BELGICÆ.

Imprimatur.
    EDM. CAN. SURMONT,
            VICARIUS GENERALIS.

WESTMONASTERII,
    Die 8 Augusti, 1912.

Nihil Obstat.
    REMIGIUS LAFORT, S.T.D.,
            CENSOR.

Imprimatur.
    JOHN CARDINAL FARLEY,
            ARCHBISHOP OF NEW YORK.

NEW YORK,
    October 21, 1912.

TOLERANCE

BY THE
REV. A. VERMEERSCH, S.J.
DOCTOR OF LAWS AND POLITICAL AND ADMINISTRATIVE SCIENCE
PROFESSOR OF MORAL THEOLOGY AND CANON LAW

TRANSLATED BY
W. HUMPHREY PAGE, K.S.G.
PRIVY CHAMBERLAIN TO H.H. PIUS X.

R. & T. WASHBOURNE, LTD.
PATERNOSTER ROW, LONDON
AND AT MANCHESTER, BIRMINGHAM, AND GLASGOW
BENZIGER BROTHERS: NEW YORK, CINCINNATI, CHICAGO
1913
[*All rights reserved*]

PREFACE

THE *question of intolerance occupies the attention of Europe and the New World; and those who are accused of intolerance to-day retort upon their accusers with complaints of their intolerance in the past.*

What is meant by tolerance and intolerance? How are we to judge of one or the other? On what grounds are we to approve or to condemn either? Is Catholicism intolerant? Is free thought tolerant?

These are important and practical questions, complex and much debated, and interesting to all. We propose in this work to discuss these questions candidly and dispassionately; not superficially, but comparing doctrines with facts, and principles with their applications.

In the fulfilment of this task we shall have to review the past, though we do not profess to write history. Our arguments are founded on facts; but our object is neither the narration of facts nor the description of manners and customs. Our study is not so much historical as moral and social.

We desire to be perfectly just; if our language appears sometimes to be severe, it will never be rancorous or vindictive. We write for all, whether Catholic or non-Catholic, who wish to form an impartial judgment of the present conjunction or of the institutions of the past; in short, to all who desire to be just and well-informed.

The author has had occasion to speak strongly on the subject of the intolerance shown in England at the time of the Protestant Reformation; but in offering to the public an English translation of his work, he feels it to be his duty as well as his pleasure to acknowledge the courteous and respectful consideration shown to Catholicism in England at the present day.

TABLE OF CONTENTS

	PAGE
PREFACE	V
THE TOLERANCE OF JESUS CHRIST	1
PRELIMINARY: DEFINITIONS AND DIVISIONS	5

FIRST PART

TOLERANCE IN PRIVATE LIFE

CHAPTER I. ITS OBJECT, VALUE, AND CONDITIONS	13
CHAPTER II. APPLICATIONS	20

SECOND PART

TOLERANCE IN PUBLIC LIFE

GENERAL VIEW - 31

FIRST SECTION: ECCLESIASTICAL TOLERANCE.

I. THE FACT OF RELIGIOUS SOCIETY	34
II. DOCTRINAL INTOLERANCE	37
III. DISCIPLINARY INTOLERANCE	40
IV. APOSTOLIC TOLERANCE OR INTOLERANCE	45

EXCURSUS ON THE COERCIVE POWER OF THE CHURCH, AND ESPECIALLY ON THE RIGHT OF THE SWORD.

§ 1. GENERAL STATEMENT OF THE CASE	58
§ 2. THE CHURCH AND THE RIGHT OF THE SWORD	63
I. THE ARGUMENT FROM AUTHORITY	63
II. THE ARGUMENT FROM TRADITION	73
III. THE ARGUMENT FROM REASON	85
§ 3. THE FORMULA OF THE CHURCH'S RIGHT TO PUNISH	100

CONTENTS

SECOND SECTION: CIVIL TOLERANCE.

	PAGE
CHAPTER I. GENERAL PLAN OF THIS SECTION	103
I. DEFINITIONS	103
II. GENERAL VIEW	107
CHAPTER II. CIVIL TOLERANCE DOWN TO THE SIXTEENTH CENTURY	110
§ 1. SUCCESSIVE POLICIES IN THE MATTER OF HERESY	110
§ 2. THE INQUISITION	122
§ 3. WHAT HERETICS WERE PERSECUTED?	155
§ 4. THE REPRESSION OF HERESY CONSIDERED FROM THE TRUE POINT OF VIEW	162
§ 5. WHAT AUTHORITY MADE HERESY PUNISHABLE WITH DEATH?	168
CHAPTER III. CIVIL TOLERANCE FROM THE REFORMATION TO THE FRENCH REVOLUTION	181
ARTICLE I. REVIEW OF THE FACTS OF THIS PERIOD	181
ARTICLE II. DOCTRINES OF THE SAME PERIOD	191
§ 1. DOCTRINES OF INTOLERANCE CRITICIZED	191
§ 2. DOCTRINES OF TOLERANCE	194
I. MOTIVES APPEALED TO IN FAVOUR OF THE DOGMA OF TOLERANCE	195
II. PRACTICAL CONCLUSIONS OF SYSTEMS OF TOLERANCE	207
III. CRITICISM OF DOCTRINES OF TOLERANCE	211
CHAPTER IV. CIVIL TOLERANCE OF THE PRESENT DAY—ORDER OF ARGUMENT	217
ARTICLE I. CIVIL TOLERANCE OF THE FRENCH REVOLUTION: DOCTRINE AND FACTS	218
ARTICLE II. DOCTRINES SINCE THE FRENCH REVOLUTION	221
I. DOCTRINES OF TOLERANCE	221
II. DOCTRINES OF INTOLERANCE	224
ARTICLE III. FACTS SINCE THE FRENCH REVOLUTION	233
ARTICLE IV. CRITICISM OF DOCTRINES AND FACTS	237
CHAPTER V. THE THEORY OF RIGHT CIVIL TOLERANCE	246

CONTENTS

THIRD PART
COROLLARIES AND QUESTIONS

INTRODUCTION - - - - - - 259

FIRST SECTION: DOCTRINAL QUESTIONS.

I. DIFFERENT KINDS OF TOLERANCE AND INTOLERANCE - - - - - - 260
II. THE PENAL REPRESSION OF HERESY - - 268
III. CONSISTENCY AND PROGRESS IN THE THEORY OF TOLERANCE - - - - - 279
IV. RELIGION AND SCIENCE - - - - 283
V. THE GENESIS OF CIVIL TOLERANCE - - 314
VI. WHAT AGREEMENT IS POSSIBLE? - - - 321

SECOND SECTION: HISTORICAL VIEW.

§ 1. THE PAST - - - - - - 329
    I. GENERAL CONCLUSIONS - - - 329
    II. THE INQUISITION IN PARTICULAR - - 338

§ 2. THE PRESENT AND THE FUTURE - - - 340
    I. THE PRESENT - - - - 340
    II. THE FUTURE - - - - 344

CONCLUSION

CHRISTIANITY, THE RELIGION OF LOVE - - - 350

BIBLIOGRAPHY - - - - - - 363

TOLERANCE

THE TOLERANCE OF JESUS CHRIST

IN this Western world, which owes to Christ its civilization, its life, and all its sentiments of charity and generosity, in which His personal character is admired even by those who refuse to acknowledge His divinity, no book has ever been written on tolerance without appealing to the example and the lessons of Jesus of Nazareth.[1]

He is the Peacemaker and the Comforter of all, as He came to be the Redeemer of all; and He has received the loving and fervent homage of Christian piety, and the colder but still sincere homage of respectful indifference. But, alas! He has received also the homage of bigoted schismatics, who have sought in the words and actions of Christ to find the condemnation of His Church; who have laboured to prove that the Church is in opposition to Him who promised to be with her for ever.

As we touch upon the delicate question of tolerance, how can we refrain from invoking the name of Him whom we profess to serve and imitate? If we do not confess Him before men, we must expect that He will deny us in heaven.

---

[1] See even the conferences of Jules Simon on liberty of conscience, Fourth Lesson.

Certainly in the life of Christ we cannot hope to find minute directions for our conduct in circumstances such as did not exist during His earthly life ; and hence the fallacy of the argument used against the Church.

We say, without fear of contradiction, that we Catholics derive our ideas of tolerance in its best and truest meaning from the Heart of Him who united the most loving tenderness with the most transcendent Majesty ; that Heart in which the fullness of human nature is joined to the fullness of the divinity ; in which God and man are loved as they are loved nowhere else ; in the Heart of God made man.

But we must study the character of Christ until we get a complete idea of His perfections ; and we cannot do this by limiting our attention to one or two qualities detached from the rest.

Let us pause for a moment to recall the impressions we derive even from a superficial reading of the Gospel narrative.

The Master, who is truth and holiness itself, has affection and forgiveness for repentant sinners, tears of fatherly affection for the most hardened, miracles for the Gentiles, excuses for Pilate and His own executioners, praise for strangers and schismatics ; while for an example of benevolent charity He points to a Samaritan.

The Gospel must be preached without doing violence to any ; it is by instruction, by persuasion,[1]

---

[1] *Docete omnes gentes*—Teach ye all nations (St. Matt. xxviii. 19).

THE TOLERANCE OF JESUS CHRIST

by virtue,[1] and by meekness,[2] that a way is to be opened for the glad tidings which can never be opened by the sword, the way to the intellects and hearts of men. Resistance may be a cause of sorrow, but it can never justify angry or revengeful feelings. Beware of calling down the fire of heaven on the city that will not receive you : " You know not of what spirit you are."[3]

And yet Christ does not doubt. " Woman," He said, in that gentle voice that won all hearts, " woman, you adore that which you know not : we adore that which we know ; for salvation is of the Jews."[4]

But His voice was terrible as thunder when He rebuked the narrow and arrogant hypocrisy of the Pharisees,[5] and held out threats of divine vengeance over those who obstinately shut their ears to the faith. " He that believeth not shall be condemned. Whosoever shall not receive you, nor hear your words : going forth out of that house or city shake off the dust from your feet. Amen I say to you, it shall be more tolerable for the land of Sodom and Gomorrha in the day of judgment than for that city."[6]

Thus, then, generosity without weakness, con-

---

[1] *Ut videant opera vestra bona, et glorificent Patrem vestrum qui in cœlis est*—That they may see your good works, and glorify your Father who is in heaven (St. Matt. v. 16).
[2] *Ecce mitto vos sicut agnos inter lupos*—Behold, I send you as lambs among wolves (St. Luke x. 3).
[3] St. Luke ix. 55.
[4] St. John iv. 22.
[5] St. Matt. xviii. 17.
[6] St. Mark xvi. 16 ; St. Matt. x. 14, 15.

stant restraint of the passions, patient but not doubtful preaching, the awakening of responsibility and appeal to good-will, and, above all, love and the desire to save souls[1]—these are the characteristics and summary of the tolerance of Christ.

They teach us our duty, too. The life of Christ, which reveals the true principles of life, will serve as our guide and light in our arguments. Our conclusions would be false, if they were contrary to the teaching and example of Christ.

[1] The Son of man came not to destroy souls, but to save (St. Luke ix. 56 ; St. John xii. 47).

PRELIMINARY VIEW

SUMMARY: The object of tolerance; an evil.—Subjects of tolerance; private individuals and public authorities.—General definition.—Three kinds of tolerance, according to the subjects.—Religious tolerance and religious liberty.—Tolerance of the true religion.

THE first thing necessary is to endeavour to form such a general idea of the meaning of the word " tolerance " as will enable us, in spite of its imperfections, to measure the extent and understand the complexity of our subject.

Strictly speaking, tolerance has always some evil for its object, such as a physical defect, an intellectual error, or a moral deformity. As Trautmansdorff remarks, we approve only that which is good; we tolerate what is evil.[1] Balmes goes farther, and says: " It is a monstrous absurdity to speak of tolerating goodness or virtue;"[2] and long before Balmes, St. Augustine had made this just observation: " There is no such thing as tolerance except in connection with evils."[3] We tolerate an affront or an injury, but not a favour; and even in speaking of physical sensations, it is not pleasure, but pain, that we describe as tolerable or intolerable. It is

[1] *De tolerantia ecclesiastica et civili*, initio.
[2] *Le protestantisme comparé avec le Catholicisme*, c. 36.
[3] "*Tolerantia quæ dicitur non est nisi in malis*" Enarrat. in Ps. xxxii., (M.P.L., t. 36, col. 271).

true that opinions furnish matter for tolerance, but what sort of opinions ? Evidently those which are opposed to our own, and which, therefore, we consider erroneous. " The opinion of another person is, in our judgment, an error."[1]

In matters of public interest, tolerance is exercised in respect of vices and abuses against which the authorities consider it impossible or unadvisable to take legal proceedings ; as, for instance, in the case of houses used for immoral traffic not punished by the law. St. Thomas also expressly recognizes the necessity imposed upon human legislators of allowing many things to be done which are repugnant to natural law, and restricting their repressive action to those graver excesses from which it is possible for the majority of the multitude to abstain.[2]

Tolerance, then, denotes an attitude towards evil, and the very word describes that attitude as characterized by caution and deliberation. We may say, then, that tolerance consists in a certain patience of evil, a forbearance which restrains us from showing anger or inflicting punishment.

Experience tells us that tolerance may be shown by individuals or by public authority : we may be tolerant or intolerant in our private relations, or in the exercise of official functions.

We distinguish between two kinds of authority, as we distinguish between two kinds of society : religious society and civil or political society.

Tolerance, then, resides in the individual, the Church, or the State. In the first it is *private*

[1] Balmes, *op cit.*, chap. xxxiv.
[2] *Summa Theologica*, 1, 2, Q. 96, Art. 2.

PRELIMINARY VIEW

tolerance, in the second *ecclesiastical* tolerance, in the third *civil* tolerance. There are essential distinctions between the three kinds of tolerance, and they must be looked at from different points of view.

Let us first consider private tolerance. What is the position of a private individual towards his fellow-men according to both human and divine law? Except the right to resist violence, and to defend himself against injustice, he has no control over the acts of another, and no right to constitute himself a judge in respect of such acts; he is bound to respect the liberty of his fellow-man as a right, even if that liberty be improperly granted. He may endeavour to dissuade another from a particular line of conduct, or blame him if he persists in it; but he has no power to prevent or to punish. If he is compelled to listen to language of which he may disapprove, or to be a passive witness of acts which he may deplore, he must exercise all his patience, so as to avoid any untimely exhibition of anger or disgust, and refrain from expressing his opinions in a manner which may offend against charity. This prudent self-control, much more than the occasion which has called for its exercise, draws attention to the tolerance of the individual, and makes him respected accordingly. Balmes says very justly: "A man is called tolerant when he is habitually in a state of mind which allows him to endure the existence of opinions contrary to his own without any feeling of vexation or irritation;"[1] and we may accept the definition given in a lexicon of great

[1] *Op. cit.*, chap. xxxiv.

repute :[1] " Tolerance is a willingness to permit in others a way of living, thinking, and acting, different from our own."

The consideration of tolerance, which is subjective in the private individual, becomes objective in public authorities. Men who are invested with authority are equally bound by the obligation of self-restraint, personal moderation, and respect for others—in short, of all the duties incumbent on private individuals ; but they have the power by their official acts to extend or restrict the liberty of others, and their liberality and strictness are appreciated according to the principles by which they are dictated, and the good order they establish.

The mission, the competence, and the purpose of the civil authority are one thing ; the mission, the competence, and the purpose of the religious authority, another. Religious society derives its reason for existence from the teaching and diffusion of speculative and practical truths, which have only an indirect interest for civil society, constituted for the purpose of insuring temporal prosperity. These differences have an influence on the purpose, the extent, and even the form of tolerance ; and it may be added that the State, as such, is tolerant, or intolerant, only within its own territory, while ecclesiastical authority shows tolerance, or intolerance, in the manner in which it treats other religions, and persons who are not its own subjects.

Finally, private tolerance, considered in the person who practises it, is patience ; civil tolerance, con-

[1] *Dictionnaire Universel* of Hatzfeld, Darmesteter, and Thomas.

sidered in those who are tolerated, is an impunity;[1] ecclesiastical tolerance is also an impunity, but sometimes also an independence.[2]

*   *   *   *   *

What is good is free; what is evil is tolerated. Edicts of tolerance, as distinct from laws of liberty, tacitly condemn and disapprove the things which they permit, and the idea of disapproval implies that of a temporary and revocable concession.

Tolerance, then, will not content those who assert the right of all opinions and all creeds to be openly preached. Ruffini, imbued with modern political ideas, wrote in this sense: " Tolerance, which is an admirable private virtue, is a word which has a hateful sound when used of the relations of public life."[3] Mirabeau was logical when he said in the National Assembly: " The most unfettered liberty of religion is to my mind so sacred a right, that the word tolerance, when used to express it, appears to me to a certain extent tyrannical, because it implies that the authority which tolerates has the right to refuse to do so."[4] And when Anglicanism was in its most persecuting mood, some fifty years

---

[1] " Civil tolerance, that is to say, the impunity granted by the magistrate to all sects " (Bossuet, *Sixth Warning to Protestants*, Part iii., n. 11).

[2] The independence of those who do not belong to the Church. The simple fact of remaining separated from, and independent of, a universal Church implies an opposition which requires the exercise of tolerance. It is not the same with a stranger's independence of a political society, for as no State has universal jurisdiction, such independence has nothing offensive in it which can be the object of tolerance.   [3] *La Libertà Religiosa*, p. 10.

[4] August 22, 1789, *Discours et Opinions de Mirabeau*, Barthe's edition, vol. i., p. 328.

after the passing of the famous Test Act (1672), Lord Stanhope, the Whig Minister of George I., an advocate of the complete emancipation of all dissenters, Catholics included, foretold three successive stages in the legislation on the subject of public worship : " There was a time," he told the House of Lords, " when the dissenters humbly asked for toleration as a favour ; to-day they claim it as a right ; and the time will come when they will reject it as an insult."[1] He described thus the three stages through which religious liberty was to pass : First appeared edicts of toleration, of which the Christian religion itself has received, and still receives, the advantage in pagan countries ; these were issued as a favour revocable at the will of the Sovereign or the Government. Then, by the side of an official and privileged Church, certain other religious bodies obtained a guarantee for the free practice of their religion, as by the Treaty of Augsburg (1555) and the Treaty of Westphalia (1648). Finally, all religions are placed on the same footing in the eye of the law, whether as regards one another, or as regards irreligion. Such is the tendency of the modern State. Though not yet universal, the principle of the equality of religions in the eye of the law, or religious indifference, is firmly established in the United States of America, and is gaining popularity in European countries

When applied to the true religion, especially in countries in which it is professed by the majority of the inhabitants, the word *tolerance* is simply an insult. Truth and justice demand more than toler-

[1] The quotation is from Ruffini, p. 10 ; the original has not been traced.

PRELIMINARY VIEW

ance; they claim the right to be free and protected.[1] Politicians sometimes, under the influence of modern ideas, speak of showing great tolerance to Catholics, or persons who are attached to some form of religious belief. How is such language to be explained? In countries where unbelievers are in the majority in Parliament, it is the expression of a fact and an intention: the fact that the State has the power to oppress Christians, and the intention not to abuse that power. But generally these words contain either a claim set up by the Government, or a philosophical idea—the claim, very strongly asserted nowadays by those in power, of a supremacy which gives them the right to legislate freely on the fate of the Church or Churches; the philosophic idea which makes irreligion, or even atheism, the goal of contemporary speculation. Under this system the profession of a positive religion is looked upon as a weakness, an old-fashioned notion, which may be suffered to exist for a while, but is bound sooner or later to disappear. The literature of the day repeats this with infinite variety of expression.

*   *   *   *   *

This first general view of the subject shows us that the problem of tolerance in public life is much more complex than in individuals, and that the two kinds of tolerance are quite distinct. For this reason we begin with a few simple observations on tolerance in individuals before proceeding to explain the systems and discuss the principles of tolerance in public life.

---

[1] Béranger's lines may be taken as a jest:
" On peut aller, même à la messe,
Ainsi le veut la liberté."

PART I

TOLERANCE IN PRIVATE LIFE

CHAPTER I

ITS OBJECT, VALUE, AND CONDITIONS

SUMMARY : The precise object of private tolerance, some evil which offends or annoys us.—The virtues exercised in this tolerance.—It is a source of light and progress for the person who practises it.—The words of St. Augustine.—The influence of Christianity on the practice, even the heroic practice of tolerance.—The example of missionary priests and nuns.—All outward tolerance is not virtuous, or even honourable.—The conditions of virtuous tolerance.

ALL tolerance is practised in respect of some evil, or some error; but it is not every evil, or every intellectual error, or every kind of misconduct, that puts our tolerance to the test. There are evils that do not affect us, errors that we share, faults to which we give our consent or in which we participate. Such evils, such errors, such faults as these can neither hurt nor annoy us. If we remark their existence in others, they excite only our compassion; in ourselves we regard them with complacency. Only those acts or conditions are the object of tolerance which affect us disagreeably, which cause us suffering, uneasiness, or displeasure. When we are contradicted in our opinions, opposed in our desires, thwarted in our plans, and, above all, when an adversary insolently attacks our most firmly established convictions, our most cherished beliefs, or the honour and reputation of which we are justly jealous, such conduct causes disgust, depression, fear, impatience, or anger ; and trials of this kind bring out the tolerance of a man who has control over his passions, and remains constant in his own goodness and justice.

Can we wonder that tolerance in individuals is so universally commended ? Self-control and moderation, which tell of strength and victory, are pleasing to all ; and to us, as Christians, this tolerance presents itself with all the charms of three eminent virtues—justice, charity, and humility. It is *justice* because it respects the inviolable rights of man among his fellow-men : persuasion is the only way in which I can legitimately induce my neighbour to share my opinions. It is *charity*, for St. Paul tells us that that queen of virtues " is patient, is kind . . . beareth all things, believeth all things, hopeth all things, endureth all things "[1]—that, in short, it inspires us with all those sentiments from which the most perfect tolerance springs as naturally as a flower from the branch that is created to bear it. Lastly, it is *humility*, for a prudent distrust of himself, the consciousness of his own liability to error, the knowledge of his own weakness, keep a man from showing contempt or irritation at the opinions of others.

In tolerance among our fellow-men we recognize a fruitful principle of light and progress. We may

[1] 1 Cor. xiii. 4, 7.

always derive instruction from listening to others, and by allowing them full freedom of speech we learn to know ourselves better, and to correct our own faults. St. Augustine was fully convinced of this when he wrote : " My opinion is not expressed with such authority that it may not be contradicted. I admit that I endeavour to be among those who write in proportion as they progress, and progress as they write ; but if my prudence or my knowledge is at fault, and if capable judges subject me to criticism, whose justice I must sooner or later recognize if I progress, what is there to wonder at or complain of ? Pardon me rather, and congratulate me, not on having fallen into error, but on having my mistakes corrected."[1]

This is what religion enables us to find in tolerance, practised, not as a means of exciting the empty admiration of others, but as a help to a consistent and honourable life. It helps us by the most express and touching exhortations to subject our whole life to the glorious and gentle rule of humble and charitable justice ; it forbids all hatred and pride ; it commands us to love all men, not excepting strangers and our enemies, and *a fortiori* not excepting the guilty—that is to say, the weak, and those who persist in error, that is to say, who have gone entirely astray.

This Christian law would neither approve of the massacre of pagans, nor allow us, like the Mahomedans, to treat those who profess another religion as dogs. The great doctors of the Catholic Church teach us to be kind in our treatment of others,

[1] Ep. 143 (Migne, P.L., t. 33, cols. 585, 586).

generous in our appreciation, ready to make allowances or excuses for them, always willing to help or befriend them; and the best and truest Christians are most generous with their sympathy and their prayers and offers of service, which is the best proof of good-will; they are always ready to believe in the repentance of sinners, and rejoice over it. And how many good Christians sacrifice themselves entirely to their tolerant generosity! In our own cities we see the nursing sisters at the bedsides of the most malignant enemies of their religion, of the most foul-mouthed infidels; and everyone knows that in non-Christian countries the most bigoted Mahomedan is sure to receive the devoted attention of the admirable White Sisters.[1] What tolerance is required in a true Catholic missionary! He refuses to use violence or compulsion; he faces the most repulsive spectacles, making up his mind to endure

[1] Madame Marcelle Tinayre, a woman of letters, who does not profess to be a Catholic, was struck with the difference between the two religions (Christianity and Mahomedanism). She was visiting a hospital in Constantinople shortly after the revolution of the Young Turks, and met with a young lady of good family, named Selika, who was attending some of the wounded from Thessalonica. Madame Tinayre asked her: "Have you attended the reactionaries also?" Selika's beautiful black eyes grew hard as she answered: "No. I had my choice, because I came as a volunteer. I do not nurse any but the *good* men." "Oh, my little Selika!" says Madame Tinayre, "brave and charming as you are, you would be willing to die at once if your death could insure the triumph of the constitution. Little Selika, whom I admire so much, you have no idea what an abyss there is between us! No Christian woman, even if she did not practise her religion, but if she were a Christian by birth and education, would stop to think that there are good and bad among the sick" (*Notes d'une Voyageuse en Turquie. Premiers jours d'un Noveau Règne*, p. 274, sixth edition).

ITS OBJECT, VALUE, AND CONDITIONS

them without irritation or complaint; no rebuffs wear out his patience or his courage; and his hope of making converts does not arise from any desire for power.[1] His desire is to give, not to receive: he willingly gives up health, home, friends, even life itself to gain souls—that is, not to enslave them or exploit them for his own advantage, but to lead them to God, to truth, and happiness.

The Catholic thus finds in his religion all the principles of the best kind of tolerance. What more does he need to be really tolerant? Balmes wisely remarks: "If we have a little experience of men, and are brought into contact with those who differ from us, we shall understand better the prejudices and illusions stored up in the human mind, and shall be less surprised at the resistance offered to faith; we shall mistrust all such things as tempt us from the path of duty; we shall appreciate the influence of environment on principles and action, knowing that, if we were in the unbelievers' place, we should perhaps be more perverse and more sceptical than they; and all these considerations will increase our gratitude to God, the giver of life and grace, and our compassion for the misfortunes of others."

How well Salvian in the fifth century was able to put himself into the place of those in error, and in what modern language is his tolerance expressed!

[1] Among Mahomedans, as an impartial author remarks, " the Holy War is intended not to bring about the conversion of unbelievers, but to destroy their political power. Whether the vanquished embrace Mahomedanism or not is their own affair. Sometimes even the Arab chiefs look with an unfavourable eye upon conversions" (Chantepie de la Saussaye, *Manuel d'histoire des religions*, p. 284).

Speaking of the ignorant Arians, the holy priest excuses them thus : " They are heretics, but without knowing it ; though heretics in our eyes, they are not so in intention ; they think they are such good Catholics that they can call us heretics. What they are in our eyes we are in theirs ; the truth is on our side, but they persuade themselves that it is on theirs ; they are in error, but their error is accompanied by good faith ; what their punishment will be at the day of judgment the Supreme Judge alone can tell."[1]

Are we to infer, from the universal praise bestowed on private tolerance and the Christian inspiration that we recognize in it, that all patience, all indulgence, all insusceptibility to injury from external things, is commendable? No, for in its outward manifestation it is capable of a double explanation. The man who bears pain may be brave, or he may be under the influence of a drug ; ignorance of danger, as well as courage, may make a man face death calmly. The paralytic has no more thought of running away from the enemy than the bravest of soldiers. Similarly, in the moral and intellectual order there are various kinds of blindness and torpor, of paralysis and incapacity, which prevent a man from feeling anger and resentment. The man who does not think at all can never enter into any conflict of ideas with another, for there is no rivalry except between men of the same profession. What does tolerance cost a sceptic, or a man who takes no interest in any great cause? There is a kind of tolerance, induced by weakness or vanity, which is

[1] *De Gubernatione Dei*, l. 5, chap. ii. (M.P.L., t. 53, cols. 95, 96).

ITS OBJECT, VALUE, AND CONDITIONS

merely a distaste for struggles and discussions; for struggles require strength, and discussions expose a man to the risk of being beaten. In short, besides the tolerance which is commendable, there is a tolerance which is entirely vicious; an affectation of good-nature assumed in order to conceal ignorance or carelessness, a selfish love of ease which leads to compromise with error, an indulgence which degenerates into complicity.[1]

Before estimating tolerance at its true value, it is necessary to examine the reasons and motives for it, and even to see who practises it; for it is only in a man devoted to truth and justice that tolerance denotes strength, and may be a virtue; and it will be a virtue when, inspired by noble motives, it displays a moderation that is free from fear or weakness, and placed under the prudent guidance of justice and charity.

[1] Madame de Chantal showed magnanimity when she held at the baptismal font the child of the man who had unintentionally killed her husband; so also did the noble widow of the Governor of Belgian Luxembourg, who, after the assassination of her husband, made her children pray first for the father whom they mourned, and then for the man who had made them orphans. Madame Zola displayed only a contempt for morality when, on the occasion of the marriage of an illegitimate daughter of the deceased novelist, she associated herself with the mother of the girl in issuing the invitations; and certain newspapers only showed their stupidity by going into ecstasies over this deplorable and scandalous compliance, as if it had been an act of tolerance worthy of admiration. Why does a moral abyss separate the actions of the saint and her imitator from that of this other widow? The two great Christian women overcame their own feelings of natural resentment, but they did not approve anything reprehensible. Madame Zola forgot that she represented the rights and the inviolability of the home, and her action ratified a long-continued and shameless contempt of those rights.

CHAPTER II

APPLICATIONS

SUMMARY: The restraint imposed upon the father of a family.—Prudent tolerance of Christian parents towards an erring child.—Assertion of rights to education of children.—Resistance to official interference.—Duties of tutors and educators.—Duties of masters and employers.—Preference shown to honest persons and friends of religion.—Relations with non-Catholics.—Attitude in religious controversies, and towards writers suspected of heterodoxy.

HITHERTO we have dealt with private tolerance as practised among our fellow-citizens, but in private life we have to consider also the family, where the father's authority is sacred. The father of a family is bound to watch over his children as over himself, and is responsible for all that takes place under his roof; and however indulgent he may be to the errors and faults of others, he has no excuse for admitting persons or opinions that he considers mischievous or pernicious. Since there are intellectual and moral perversions as well as organic corruptions, since the soul may be poisoned as well as the body, it is a father's duty to take the same care of the morals of his family as of their bodily health. This obligation, however, is often sadly neglected by timid or injudicious parents. Who can say how much harm is done by this lamentable indifference? But, on the other hand, the obligation is often perfectly understood and scrupulously observed in our country, where parental affection quickens the sense of duty. Hitherto public opinion has always respected and encouraged this prudent severity in the heads of families, for the boldest critic cannot find fault with a wisdom which, while encouraging the utmost freedom of familiar intercourse in the home, is always on guard against danger from without.

Parents, without being considered intolerant, are allowed in the interests of religion to be judiciously strict in the proscription of books and newspapers which endanger the purity of the home, to watch for the first germs of corruption, and, in short, to establish a sort of domestic index or inquisition.

But the most assiduous vigilance is often frustrated. Man's will is always free, and always accessible to temptation, and sometimes even the most carefully brought up children declare for evil. What a period of sorrow and anxiety begins when Christian parents see one of their children lose his faith or fall into evil ways! Their hearts bleed at the sight, and their minds are tortured with anxiety to find a way, while condemning the evil, to bring back the erring one, and preserve the innocent members of the family from corruption. And this trouble may often recur, and sometimes last even during their whole lives. Their Christian profession forbids parents to connive at scandalous conduct;[1] Christian charity discourages excessive severity, but Christian prudence condemns any

[1] Especially such things as debauchery and concubinage, even when they are not condemned by the Civil Law, or even when they receive a legal sanction, as in the case of civil marriage after divorce.

toleration of immorality. The guilty person is a son who has a right to his father's affection and support. If unfortunate, he is to be pitied; but if he is perverse, he deserves punishment; and if he becomes dangerous to others, he must be rendered incapable of doing mischief. What, then, should be the father's ruling principle? When in doubt, he seeks refuge in prayer, that he may have wisdom to do all that duty requires without exasperating the offender. In this analysis of what may be a most cruel trial to a Christian parent, there is nothing to suggest anything like fanatical intolerance; on the contrary, all his actions are prompted by kindness and affection.

Nor can a father be reasonably charged with intolerance because he offers a determined resistance to the invader of his home who attempts to corrupt his children by deceit, threats, or seduction. In an age which boasts of its liberty, attempts have been made, as in the republics of ancient Greece, to claim children in the name of the State, the law, or national unity, and the public funds have been used for the purpose. The parents who dared to assert their independence or their authority, and deny to the State all authority over the soul, or to the human law all power to interfere with the sacred right of a father, were not intolerant, but were resisting the intolerance of others; and in rejecting offers of money, they simply refused to degrade themselves by a shameful bargain.[1]

[1] It is too much, indeed, that, after all the discussions and all the disclosures that have taken place, an attempt should still be made to delude the public as to the meaning of neutral education, secular education, compulsory educa-

APPLICATIONS

The principles by which enlightened parents regulate and measure their tolerance should also guide those who are called upon to take their place or share their authority, such as tutors and instructors. No consideration for the weakness of others should ever make them forget their high and holy mission of keeping safe and sound the souls committed to their charge, in whom they are bound to foster a love of truth and justice. Similarly, it is the duty of persons who have the administration of affairs or the direction of great business undertakings

---

tion. Neutrality is a myth, and secularism means atheism; compulsory education with neutrality and secularism is simple tyranny. There is no such thing really as neutral education, because various branches of study do not lend themselves to neutral treatment, and the great object of education is to elevate and form the mind. Neutral education so-called can only be sceptical, indifferent, and in plain contradiction to religious duties. Secularism closes the school to all supernatural or Divine influence. The compulsory neutral school is an institution forced upon Catholic fathers, the acceptance of which obliges them— the poor especially—to do violence to their consciences. The existence of the free unsubsidized school, supposing it to be tolerated, does not remove the grievance. What would be said of a State which compelled its subjects to attend either a Christian Church or a masonic lodge at their own choice, and which contented itself with building masonic lodges, leaving the people to build churches for themselves? Would it be fair to say that the State was bound to build only a lodge in order to show its impartiality to the different Christian bodies? Would it prove its impartiality by allowing the discontented to build themselves a church? The masonic lodge and the neutral school are as much alike as mother and daughter: their morality is the same. In refusing to build or subsidize any but neutral schools, the Government declares indifference to be the religion of the State. Cicero was very clear-sighted when he congratulated the Roman Republic on having escaped from official teaching and the uniformity of systems of education (*De Republica,* iv. 3).

to exercise a vigilant charity. The influence and authority of masters and employers, though not so sacred as the authority of a parent, are not mere words, and it is right that the servants, even of full age, who submit to that authority, should feel the benefit of it. It is unjustifiable, under pretence of tolerance, to permit in our homes, our offices, or our workshops, language and habits which make these places dangerous for the persons employed therein, while charity obliges us to protect and encourage virtue.

These considerations seem enough to distinguish between the wholesome and the vicious tolerance as practised by superiors to inferiors in private life.

Tolerance among equals, however simple the rules appear, is liable to be misunderstood, and is sometimes called for out of season, for tolerance can never interfere with the demands of charity. Who will blame me for preferring a fellow-countryman to a foreigner? The preference of one involves no hatred or ill-will to the other. Shall we be considered intolerant if we offer help and relief to our comrades in arms before others, especially such help and relief as, if given to our adversaries, would be used to the detriment of religion and virtue? If Catholics unite together to give their patronage or custom to honest people recommended by their religion, is there any reason for calling them intolerant? And are we narrow-minded or bigoted if we take precautions for the future use of our property, to prevent it from being squandered, or used for the purposes of a war against the faith?

We speak here of property which forms our own patrimony, but it is possible that we may be entrusted with the administration of other property. The Catholic statesman is forbidden by his conscience to deal with the funds of the State with the same freedom as if they were his own, or to dispose of public offices as if they were posts in his own household. His appointments and subsidies will be regulated by prudent and impartial justice, according to the government and constitution of the society. The Catholic statesman will take care not to be exclusive, but he must take care also not to be imposed upon. On the contrary, he should be so firm that the fear of reprisals may act as a check on anti-Catholic administrations, and compel them to have some regard for administrative justice and equitable moderation.

If we leave the economic order, and raise our thoughts to consider the interests of religion and morality, we remark that prudence requires each man to show for himself the same care and circumspection that a father exercises over his family. Consideration for others which makes us careless of ourselves, outward indulgence of others which may do us infinite harm, are the result of a vicious tolerance which is not virtue, but weakness of character, cowardice in the face of duty. Let our relations even with those who reject our faith and despise our moral codes be always correct, and even cordial; let our demeanour be always marked by Christian charity. So far, so good ; but how frequent and how intimate should these relations be, and is there any reason for their existence at all ? These questions remain to be answered, for we cannot visit everyone, or be on terms of intimate friendship with the whole world. The true solution is in taking good advice, and endeavouring to fulfil the great Christian commandment : " Be good thyself, and spread all the good thou canst around thee."

It is a delicate question, how we ought to behave in the philosophic or religious controversies in which we take part, and the problem becomes extremely perplexing when our adversary declares that he shares the faith for which we write or speak. This embarrassing subject requires some remarks which will fitly conclude the first part of this work.

A man may err in good faith, or he may make profession of belief without sincerity. Ambiguous or obscure language may be used to conceal a clever trap, or may be the result of ignorance or carelessness. The profession of religious faith reveals the inmost soul, but a false profession of faith may be made to cover the most insidious designs. Freemasonry formerly numbered priests among its members, and not half a century ago it filled the confraternities of Brazil. About 1850 at Brussels it was able to command religious services. If it is wicked to calumniate, or disseminate unjust suspicions, it is necessary at times to have the sense and courage to cry "Wolf !" before it is too late.

A private individual has no right to accuse another of being in error—by which is meant religious error—except after mature deliberation. He has no right to speak in the name of the Church. He is not infallible, and cannot without presumption claim for himself any special orthodoxy. He must avoid the self-conceit which sometimes disguises itself as religious zeal, the attachment to his own opinions

APPLICATIONS

which may be the motive of his ardour in preaching submission. Does it not seem sometimes—in the case of the condemnation of a published work, for example—as if the writer cared less about being on the side of authority than having authority on his side ? On the other hand, it cannot be denied that the decisions of the Church or the Holy See lay down directions which must not be exaggerated or overstrained, but which a loyal Catholic will refuse to evade by quibbles or minimizing interpretations.

In the perplexities which arise in such circumstances, how useful it is to listen to the counsels of toleration ! Be *just*, they say to each of us, and see if the man or the work in which you detect errors does not show too much Catholicism to fall under suspicion. Be *equitable*, and in case of doubt give your brethren the benefit of that presumption of correctness which is laid down in the oldest laws, and of which St. Ignatius writes in these express terms in the beginning of his spiritual exercises : " Every good Christian is more eager to justify than to condemn a statement of his neighbour ; and if he cannot justify it, he asks the author for an explanation. If the author explains it ill, he corrects him with charity ; and when that is not enough, he endeavours to the best of his power to find an acceptable meaning which will save the proposition." History itself attests the opportuneness of this caution : rigorous judgments, though long accepted, are reviewed by the light of fresh study. A more careful examination sometimes shows that timehonoured imputations of heresy rest on expressions badly used, badly understood, or badly translated.[1] Be *kind;* do not seek the malicious satisfaction of having discovered an additional enemy to the Church. The bitterness of some men's writing is very exasperating, and irritation will sometimes bring down a tottering structure which a little kindness might have saved. What would have become of Abelard without the gentleness of Peter the Venerable?[2] Charity has good, not evil, for its object; it would rather win hearts by gentleness than humiliate them by an assumption of superiority. Be *courteous;* in the fight against error treat your adversary with deference. And, above all, be scrupulously *truthful*.[3] To all, friends and foes alike, give that serious attention which does not misrepresent any opinion, does not distort any statement, does not mutilate any quotation.

[1] See, for example, the doctoral dissertation of Professor Lebon on certain Monophysites (*Le Monophysisme Sévérien*, Louvain, 1909). The panegyric dedicated by St. Gregory Nazianzen to St. Athanasius is worth reading. The holy doctor relates how, in the fourth century, the whole world was nearly rent in twain by a quarrel over syllables: the Easterns drew a distinction between substance and hypostasis, while the Westerns used the same word for the two ideas. The dispute was carried on with great bitterness, but St. Athanasius calmly weighed what each side had to say, and showed at the Synod of 362 that both sides were perfectly agreed on the main point. And "at this time of disputes and controversies," said St. Gregory, "it would be a great pity not to draw attention to an example, which our contemporaries would do well to follow" (M.P.G., t.35, cols. 1125, 1126).

[2] See, in the dictionary of Vacant-Mangenot, the article "Abélard," by Father Portalié, S.J.

[3] "Be truthful in all things; be scrupulously sincere. You will deserve to be faithful on important occasions, if you have been faithful in things that seem unimportant, *sinceri filii Dei*. The love of truth is a great grace, only obtained by fervent prayer" (Ruinart, *Abridgment of the Life of Dom. J. Mabillon*, 1709, p. 392).

We need not fear to serve the cause of Christ less efficiently by putting on His spirit. In our own day especially, when men love to make a show of sincerity, and when so many honest but mistaken souls are yearning for the truth, let us count Christian loyalty as one of the most powerful influences to induce men to accept the gift of faith. Defective arguments weaken sound propositions; false statements embitter disputes, perpetuate controversies, multiply misunderstandings, and give an opening for crushing rejoinders. An arrogant and uncompromising tone in an author makes men reluctant to listen to his arguments, and anxious to see him proved to be wrong. We do not establish a truth by showing that there is little evidence to support it; we cannot eradicate error by making it look like truth; and we cannot hope to persuade a reader if we begin by exciting his antipathy. There is much sound sense as well as humour in the words of St. Augustine : " Wolves sometimes disguise themselves in sheep's clothing, but that is no reason why sheep should change their skins."[1] Those victories alone give glory to Christ which are won by the weapons of Christ, for these are the weapons of justice.[2] To wish for no other victory, we need great self-control, perfect confidence in the ultimate triumph of truth, zeal untainted by unworthy motives; and this self-control, this confidence, this zeal, enhance the private virtue of tolerance, and invite the admiration of all men.

[1] *De Sermone Dei in Monte*, l. 1, chap. ii., *n.* 41 (M.P.L., t. 34, col. 1287).
[2] *Per arma justitiæ*—By the armour of justice, on the right hand and on the left (2 Cor. vi. 7).

PART II

TOLERANCE IN PUBLIC LIFE

GENERAL VIEW AND DIVISIONS.

SUMMARY : Unlike tolerance in private life, public tolerance is divided according to the matter, according to the reasons for its exercise ; dogmatic and practical tolerance ; and according to the authority which tolerates religious or civil authority.—Range of ecclesiastical tolerance.

THE tolerance of private life is practised principally among equals, and is summed up in the respect which one person is bound to pay to the rights of another. This right forbids me to regulate the thoughts and speech of another by my own, or to disturb him in the liberty of opinion or worship which is granted to him by Divine or human law. Undoubtedly, when sanctioned by man, liberties may be wisely or unwisely granted, and they extend to all the circumstances of life ; but one private individual is not allowed to restrict the liberty of another, whatever be its origin or the circumstances to which it extends. So far we have treated of private tolerance, without discussing the merits of the liberties which put it to the test, and have not confined ourselves to tolerance in matters of religion, with which we are chiefly concerned.

The Sovereign, on the other hand, must concern himself with all the titles which every liberty can show to justify its existence. There are superior or necessary liberties, which even he is bound to respect; useful liberties, which he sanctions or restricts according to circumstances; and dangerous liberties, which he grants reluctantly, because he cannot do otherwise. While the other liberties are granted as rights, the last-named are only impunities, and they alone, strictly speaking, are the object of the laws of *tolerance*.

Intolerance is twofold in character: it may refuse to recognize an inviolable liberty, or to grant a reasonable indulgence. Oppression or tyranny may be an abuse of power, or only an excess of severity. But tolerance is one: it permits a thing which is disapproved, or is at least looked upon unfavourably. The official grant of any liberty leads naturally to a discussion as to the nature and cause of the concession: is it a right which is intended to be permanent, or is it a necessity of fact to which the authorities think it advisable to bow? And different questions arise according as the liberty belongs to the political, moral, or religious order.

Hence arise distinctions in respect of the source of the tolerance, its purpose, and its object.

According to its *object*, public tolerance is divided into as many branches as there are matters for discussion. We shall be concerned only with tolerance in religious matters.

According to the *reasons* on which it is founded, tolerance is *dogmatic* or *practical*. Dogmatic tolerance is a principle; practical tolerance is an ex-

GENERAL VIEW

pedient. The one claims liberty of opinions and worship as a right which must be respected; the other yields to circumstances so far as is required by social conditions or the common good. To the advocates of dogmatic tolerance, the word " tolerance " seems improper; they would abolish it, and only use it as consecrated by ancient custom. *Religious liberty* signifies for them the liberty of profession of individual belief or unbelief, and sometimes also the liberty of organization granted to religious bodies. The professors of practical tolerance give the word its proper value, and, being accustomed to consider liberty as a function of truth, they define religious liberty as the liberty of the true religion.

Lastly, according to the *authority* which tolerates, toleration is *ecclesiastical* or *civil*. Ecclesiastical tolerance is that of religious authority or the Church; civil tolerance is the act of the civil power or the State. We have already had occasion to state this, and also to draw attention to the following difference in the field of the two kinds of public tolerance:

Many independent States exist simultaneously, and no one questions the lawfulness of their co-existence. From this independence each State derives its sovereign right of internal administration, for which it is not obliged to give an account to any neighbouring State. Civil tolerance, therefore, is only understood as existing within the State, shown by the Sovereign to his subjects. Having no directly religious mission, the State, as such, does not enter into conflict with another State which professes another religion. But the religious society may be one, and obligatory for all : it has therefore a mission of propagation and conquest which puts it in opposition with other religions and false creeds. Hence we have to consider its possible tolerance in a new light, in the attitude which it adopts towards other religions and their adherents.

FIRST SECTION : ECCLESIASTICAL TOLERANCE

I. THE FACT OF RELIGIOUS SOCIETY.

SUMMARY : Social organization of religions.—Hierarchical constitution of the Catholic Church.—The place and mission assigned by Catholic teaching to the Church in the world.

Ecclesiastical tolerance or intolerance presupposes a religious authority. The existence of such an authority is a fact which is necessarily recognizable by the senses. Religions, Divine or human, unlike systems of philosophy, are socially organized ; for it may be said that there is hardly any religious system elaborated by a single individual, and all social organization requires the constitution of a hierarchy.

But if the different religions spread over the globe have a priesthood and principle of authority in common with Christian bodies, nowhere does the hierarchy form such a compact and united assembly, nowhere is authority so strong and active, as in the Catholic Church. We know the famous expression of Guizot : " The Catholic Church is the great school of reverence ; " and Proudhon remarks : " The Catholic Church is the one whose dogmatism, discipline, hierarchy, and progress, best realize the theoretical principle and type of religious society —the one, in consequence, which has the best right to the government of souls."[1]

It is with regard to this Church that we have almost exclusively to consider the different aspects of ecclesiastical tolerance.

Now, what place, according to Catholic doctrine, has God assigned to His Church in the world ? What is the mission she has to accomplish ?

If men consent to leave us really free, if they do not wish by an odious ostracism to practise towards the millions of Catholics the same intolerance that they lay to our charge, and so make us victims and accused at the same time, how can they deny us the right to profess this doctrine, and to regulate our judgments and our acts by our own conception of the Church rather than by that of unbelievers ? And is not every impartial judge bound to consider the arguments by which she explains and justifies her action, if he wishes to form a just estimate of her conduct ?

By the side of the States which are formed and prosper or disappear according to political changes, and of those civil societies which the Author of Nature has created and sanctioned in creating the human race—or, rather, above all these—though their independence in their proper sphere is duly recognized, God has instituted, to last as long as the world shall last, a religious society which traces its origin to Jesus Christ. To that society belong

[1] *De la Justice dans la Révolution et dans l'Église*, Preliminary Discourse, sec. 3, p. 24.

the faithful custody, the infallible teaching, and the zealous propagation, of those truths which are the light and salvation of the human race. As guardian of the inviolable deposit of truth, she is bound to preserve it pure and entire at the price of her blood, and to oppose an unchanging *non possumus* to all attempts at corruption.

Constituted as a perfect society,[1] she has subjects, loyal or rebellious, to lead to a common end, and she possesses all the rights and duties necessary for that end. Called by the express will of her Founder to make spiritual conquests, she acts in constant obedience to the command, " Going therefore, teach ye all nations."[2]

The Church, therefore, has an *exterior* policy towards the religions she wishes to supplant, or the unbelievers she desires to convert ; and an *interior* policy in regard to those who are placed under her rule by faith and baptism. She may show herself tolerant or intolerant in her threefold mission of teaching, administering, and conquering—that is, in her *magisterium*, her *government*, and her *expansion* or apostolate.

---

[1] Juridically, a society is called " perfect " when, being independent of any other of the same order, it is not bound to submit to any other for the attainment of its own end, but possesses in itself, in its resources and its rights, all means necessary for that purpose. A family, a city, a parish, a religious Order, are imperfect societies. The Church and the State are perfect societies.

[2] St. Matt. xxviii. 19.

II. Doctrinal Intolerance.

SUMMARY: Definition.—The uncompromising attitude of the Church in respect of doctrine.—Why it extends to every point of faith.—What liberty of discussion exists in religious matters.

Doctrinal intolerance consists in the rigour with which a Church imposes upon its members the inward acceptance and outward profession of its *Credo*, or its dogmatic and moral teaching.

The Catholic Church, from its very foundation, has presented to the world an unprecedented spectacle, on the austere beauty of which Jules Simon has commented in terms of appreciative admiration.[1] In Greece and Rome there had long been an official religion, without dogma and without morality, which required only an external rite of participation. All that was necessary was to offer incense to the gods of the State, and everyone was in consequence at liberty to believe in the gods or despise them. Peace was offered to all on very easy conditions. To all? Yes, except those who could neither lie nor sell their consciences. Christianity proclaims the inviolable sacredness of the conscience, and offers for its acceptance a positive faith; that faith creates an uncompromising attitude, which is only a claim of liberty. The outward act of adoration which great and learned men of the world offer without scruple and without conviction is, by the authority of the Church, unlawful for those who follow Christ. The incense is refused, and the victim pays for his refusal with his blood. "For three

[1] See his First Lesson on Liberty of Conscience.

centuries the executioners did not cease to strike, nor the victims to suffer; Christianity received its baptism of blood; it gave testimony to liberty of conscience : that was its heroic age." But to what did it owe this heroism and this glory ? To its intolerance, to the intolerance which the Church practises as guardian of the faith, in virtue of which she demands of her subjects a persevering constancy in the faith, admitting no alliance or compromise with error.

On the same grounds the Church requires the acceptance of all that God has revealed; the obstinate denial of a single dogma is equivalent to heresy, and produces apostasy. Many persons profess to be astonished at the severity of laws or ecclesiastical decrees which treat the denial of a single point of faith as severely as positive infidelity. This surprise is intelligible in unbelievers, who are excusable because they discuss the faith as they would discuss some system of philosophy; but how can we account for the same astonishment in certain Catholic writers ? They seem to forget the very nature of the act of faith, and its difference from a simply rational assent. So long as we are concerned with certainties of the same order, springing from the same principles, there may be differences of opinion on every proposition enunciated. But the certainty of reason and the certainty of faith are derived from different sources. By coming to a wrong conclusion on a question of secondary importance, reason does not give up the principles which assist it in the discovery of the more important truths. It is not so with heresy. Without in any way denying the unequal dignity of the truths which God through His Church proposes for our belief, we ought nevertheless to make the value, the merit, the very essence of the act of faith, consist in the fact of believing them all on the Word of God, and in relying more on the Divine truthfulness than on our own lights. We fail to show this confidence if we pick and choose between dogmas, admitting some and refusing to accept others, or if we obstinately reject a single one ; for by so doing we cease to take the Word of God for our guide, and rely simply on our reason. The agreement between my opinions and the dogmas that I accept is only accidental, and almost a matter of chance, like the meeting of two travellers who happen to make part of their journey together, though they are not bound for the same goal ; and, because fortuitous, the agreement loses all consistency. The Protestant Churches were scarcely a year old when Bossuet found materials for writing a history of their variations. Strictly speaking, there is no such thing as partial heresy, for faith is not a thing of shreds and patches.

It is only outside defined dogmas that the Church, according to the gravity and delicacy of the matter, the quality of the authors, and the circumstances of time and place, allows on sacred subjects a greater or less discussion, by reason of what might be called her tolerance ; and even then she reserves to herself the right to close the controversy by a final judgment, to which her children always willingly submit.

III. Disciplinary Intolerance.

SUMMARY: Excommunication of heretics.—In what spirit is it effected?—Other penalties incurred by them.—Power of the Church.

The *magisterium* of the Church condemns all heresy. The government of the Church is concerned with heretics—that is to say, with those who, belonging to her by baptism, openly contradict her teaching; we say *openly* because the secrets of the conscience are necessarily beyond the cognizance of an authority entrusted to the hands of men.[1]

It is the duty of the Church to bring back her erring children first by the gentle ways of persuasion; but if they are obstinate, she must treat

[1] Thus a Christian may be guilty of heresy in the sight of God without having violated any law of the Church. We do not dwell on another difference which seems to exist between guilt before God and guilt before the *forum externum* of the Church. Simple abstention—that is, refusal to give assent to any Divine revelation—is enough to constitute an infidelity which is insulting to God. But would a man who simply confesses his want of faith, without judging of dogmas or contradicting the Church, be liable to outward penalties? According to some modern writers, we ought to answer in the affirmative. But such persons seem to speak of a man who lays down the law for himself, or at least follows those who do so; we know of no case where proceedings have been taken against mere sceptics or freethinkers, so long as they have refrained from open blasphemy. We shall have occasion later to return to this subject, but we can understand how in the age of faith a heretic was considered inexcusable. By a heretic we mean a man who makes public and obstinate profession of an error contrary to faith, and rejects the teaching of the most imposing hierarchy that has ever existed. If simple doubt may seem excusable, it is the grossest presumption for any private individual to set up his own opinion against the teaching of the Church.

DISCIPLINARY INTOLERANCE

them as rebellious subjects, whom, for their own good and the edification of others, she will endeavour to bring back by all the means in her power. This effort shows us a second aspect of ecclesiastical intolerance. The Church, which is the custodian and dispenser of spiritual blessings, will deprive the obstinate of those blessings, and will, in the end, exclude them from her communion. This deprivation involves spiritual penalties, which, in canonical language, are called "censures," and the gravest of all censures is exclusion from the Church, or excommunication, which, when solemnly pronounced, becomes an anathema. What is more natural or legitimate than to refuse the advantages of Christian unity to one who rejects its very principle, to cut off from the vine a branch which refuses to be nourished by the vine? This expulsion, terrible in itself,[1] must have filled the souls of men with holy horror, when the Church, in the solemn assembly of her pastors, uttered those awful anathemas which defined the truth and denounced error.

There are numerous canonical texts which enjoin that obstinate heretics should be cut off from the Church. The integrity of the faith and the preservation of the faithful require this; and it is the

---

[1] We know in what emphatic terms St. Paul described the effects of this penalty when he had occasion to inflict it: "I have already judged . . . to deliver such a one to Satan for the destruction of the flesh, that the spirit may be saved in the day of Our Lord Jesus Christ" (1 Cor. v. 3, 5). For having quoted these words, St. Jerome is accused by Lea (*History of the Inquisition in the Middle Ages*, vol. i., p. 214) of having advocated capital punishment. It is unnecessary to remark how impossible it is for authors like Lea to present in their true light many facts whose real meaning is necessarily not understood by non-Catholics.

most effective means of bringing back to his senses an unhappy person who is hurrying to destruction. "It is said," says Pope Urban,[1] "that excommunication is the plucking up of the cockle, in opposition to the parable in the Gospel; but it is not so. The Apostle tells us that the sentence of excommunication is passed in order that the guilty person may have his soul saved in the day of the Lord. Excommunication is not intended for the destruction of the offender, but for his repentance and amendment."

The use of spiritual sanctions, as practised[2] and enjoined[3] by St. Paul, in order to maintain the purity of Christian faith and morals, has found favour even with liberals. "Religious intolerance," says Jules Simon, "is not only reasonable, but necessary . . . a religion which did not profess it would be condemned by the very fact."[4] And more recently Ruffini writes: "It is impossible to condemn religious intolerance when it employs its purely spiritual weapons to combat and banish all opposition to the fundamental dogmas of a religion, and all persons who contradict them.[5] Moreover, in acting in this manner, the Church only does what the State is constantly doing; she deprives the delinquents of the benefits of religious society, exactly as the State deprives of the privileges of civil life those who offend against its laws.

But besides these spiritual penalties, we find that heretics incur temporal penalties also, though the

[1] Or, rather, the unknown author of the Canon *Notandum*, 37, C. xxiv., Q. 3.
[2] In the case of the incestuous Corinthian, mentioned above. [3] Titus iii. 10.
[4] *Op. cit.*, p. 68. [5] *La Liberta Religiosa*, p. 8.

DISCIPLINARY INTOLERANCE 43

Church has been slow in inflicting them; for, although she legalized temporal punishments as early as the seventh century, she waited until the twelfth before inflicting them on heretics.

The twelfth century gives us an instance of a heretic condemned to suffer temporal punishment. The case was that of the notorious Eon de la Stella, who appeared in 1148 before the Council of Rheims, in which 1,600 Bishops, Abbots, and Prelates were assembled. The case was a very grave one, and Eon, a fanatical disturber of the public peace, might have expected to be treated with the utmost rigour; but, more fortunate than some of his associates, whom the secular arm delivered to the flames, he received the benefit of episcopal clemency. The Bishop who had brought him before the Council interceded for him, and his life and limbs were spared.[1] Thus the first ecclesiastical sentence of temporal punishment inflicted for heresy was the beginning of a series of those effective intercessions which the Church recommends all her judges to make in favour of unhappy persons sentenced to death or mutilation.[2]

In the thirteenth century Innocent III. prescribed confiscation of goods as the punishment for heresy, which was denounced as an infamous crime.[3] Alexander IV. extended this confiscation to the goods of a deceased heretic.[4] The penalties pre-

[1] See Harduin's *Concilia*, vii. 308.

[2] Long before this (in 385) St. Martin of Tours had entreated the tyrant Maximus not to shed the blood of the Priscillianists. Unfortunately, his efforts were not successful. See Sulpicius Severus, *Chronica*, l. 2, *n.* 50 (*Corpus Scriptorum eccl. latin.*, t. 1, p. 103).

[3] Notably at the Fourth Council of the Lateran, from whence comes chap. xiii., *De Hæreticis* (v. 7).

[4] Chap. viii., *De Hæreticis in* 6°.

scribed by Boniface VIII.[1] were confiscation and legal disability for public office. The Clementine legislation[2] forbade excessive severity on the part of Inquisitors, and directed that prisoners should be reasonably treated. The *Extravagantes Communes* provided against other abuses.[3] Such has been the penal legislation of the Church in the matter of heresy, and it does not go beyond the penalties we have mentioned. In the next section we shall speak of the condemnations to death and the stake, and we shall define the part of the responsibility which may have been incurred by the Church in these capital executions.

The excommunication of the heretic furnishes a probable explanation of the Church's slowness in inflicting temporal punishments. As a member cut off from the Church, he ceased to be subject to her, as he ceased to receive life from her. In early times—*i.e.*, during the first three or four centuries—the Church, so to speak, forgot the baptism of those whom she had anathematized; she did not concern herself with them any more than with pagans.[4] Even in the time of Bellarmine and Suarez the objection was still made that heretics were outside the Church, and that, therefore, she had no right to punish them.[5]

[1] Chaps. xv. and xix., *De Hæreticis in* 6°.
[2] Chaps. i. and ii., *De Hæreticis*, Clem. V. 3.
[3] L. 5, t. 3, c. 1 and 3.
[4] See Hinschius, *System des Katholischen Kirchenrechts*, t. 4, p. 749. St. Augustine found it necessary to show the power of the Church over baptized persons. Ep. 185, n. 23 (M.P.L., t. 33, col. 803).
[5] Bellarmine, Controv. I., Cont. 2., *De Membris Ecclesiæ*, l. 3; *De Laicis*, c. 22, Art. 15. Suarez, *De Fide*, d. 20, s. 3, n. 20.

DISCIPLINARY INTOLERANCE

These temporal punishments inflicted for an offence of a spiritual nature astonish us at the present day, though they appeared very natural at a time when the social power was actually divided, according to causes and persons, between the Church and the Sovereign. And what, in fact, is more logical? The heretic committed against the Church, to which he belonged, an offence which might lead to disastrous consequences, and the Church applied to this serious offence the penalties then in her power.[1] No one denied her the right to inflict temporal penalties, and these often had the good effect of making the condemned person understand the gravity of the anathema with which he was threatened, and of leading the way to his conversion. This result was always kept in view in the penal legislation of the Church.

IV. Apostolic Tolerance or Intolerance.

SUMMARY: Nationalism of ancient religions.—Ancient and Modern syncretism.—Lethargy of many religions.—Catholic exclusiveness.—No salvation outside the Church.—Conquest by persuasion.—Respect for the liberty of adults and fathers of families.—Merits of ecclesiastical tolerance.

We have now to consider ecclesiastical tolerance or intolerance in preaching religion and making converts. This missionary propaganda, its energy and its methods, show the attitude which every

[1] As to the coercive power of the Church, see the digression to which a special chapter is devoted. We reserve the discussion of the criminal character of heresy to Part III.

religion and every Church adopts towards other religions and their adherents.

National gods were known in ancient times, conquering or conquered with the nations whose quarrels they espoused, and there was a time when the Israelites themselves gloried in the possession of Jehovah as a national God, more powerful than the deities to which rival nations paid homage. This conception represents gods as well as nations at war with one another.

There are also religious systems which aim at making peace among the different religions; these are the syncretist systems, and they vary in form and extent. The Persian Mani found material for his teaching in the four great religions with which he was acquainted, the Babylonian, Buddhist, Zoroastrian, and Christian,[1] borrowing from each, under the pretext of purifying and perfecting all, and extracting their quintessence. Buddha, or, rather, the religion that bears his name, dispenses with dogmas and insists on morality only, and thus resembles the old Chinese Confucianism and the modern German system of Emmanuel Kant.[2]

In the sixteenth century, Jean Bodin in France[3] preached an alliance among different religions, maintaining that the differences which separated them were of little importance—of so much less importance

[1] De Stoop, *Essai sur la Diffusion du Manichéisme dans l'Empire Romain*, Gand, 1909, p. vii.

[2] With this difference, that Buddhism is pantheistic, while Confucianism is neutral between the affirmation and denial of God, and a personal God is the first postulate of Kantian morality.

[3] *Colloquium heptaplomeres de rerum sublimium arcanis abditis* (*cf.* pp. 129, 133, 174, 351, 354, 356, 358).

because the true religion appeared to him incapable of demonstration. In the following century, Joseph Glanvill, an Englishman, expressed similar views in his *Vanity of Dogmatising*.[1] John Milton desired to unite only those Protestants who were agreed on the rule of faith.[2] Celsus, long before, in arguing against Christianity, had contended that the one God might be recognized in the variety of names and rites under which He was honoured. Maximus of Madaura, in his controversy with St. Augustine, insisted that all religions were mutually complementary of each other, each venerating some special aspect of the Supreme Being. Many centuries later, Bayle wrote in the same sense: " All the religions of the world, fantastic and diverse as they may be, are not incongruous with the infinite majesty of that supremely perfect Being, Who has ordained that all things in nature should glorify Him in His character of infinite perfection.[3]

A Protestant syncretism, that of Jurieu, for example, struggled hard for some time to draw a distinction between fundamental and necessary dogmas on the one hand, and accessory dogmas, to which Christ was supposed to be indifferent, on the other. A certain school of Anglicanism divides the Catholic Church into three branches, legitimately springing from one trunk—the Anglican, the Greek, and the Roman—and so makes it a point of duty for every person to remain faithful to his own com-

[1] Pp. 230, 231.
[2] *Of True Religion, Heresy, Schism, Toleration.*
[3] *Commentaire philosophique sur les paroles de Jesus-Christ, Compelle intrare,* in St. Luke xiv. 23, part ii., chap. vi., p. 418.

munion. A more radical syncretism considers nothing essential except belief in God, around which it hopes to gather all religious-minded men. This syncretism is pushed to its extreme limits in absolute Modernism.[1] Dogmas are deprived of all objective value, and become empty symbols of reality—subjective representations of an Absolute which we do not understand. Religious sentiment is identified with a vague, half-conscious yearning for the Unknowable, distinct or not distinct from ourselves, but to be attained within ourselves; all the merit of faith is reduced to the sincerity of an attitude which pacifies the soul by satisfying its need of a hereafter. These are the means suggested for establishing a brotherly understanding, first among all believers, and then between believers and atheists, while the latter also are allowed to call themselves religious as soon as their aspirations soar beyond mere sensible phenomena.

These ideas of union and brotherhood are attractive enough; but, on reflection, we are bound to see that this imaginary drawing together of men is preached at the cost of our reverence for God. By the mere fact that a religion declares itself to be truly Divine in its source, and obligatory on all, it

[1] See our article on "Modernism" in the *Catholic Encyclopædia*, New York, 1911. Dargaud anticipated Modernism when he sang the praises of a religion embracing all the sects—a philosophical religion but having its philosophy "solidified by faith, fragrant with hope, and burning with the fire of charity," retaining "freely and reverently in its practices of unction and prayer the stamp of the sweet and majestic character of Christ. The sects are to this religion what vigorous but barbarous dialects are to a perfect language" (*Histoire de la liberté religieuse en France et dans ses Fondateurs*, t. 1, p. 371).

clearly imposes upon all men the imperative duty of inquiring into this fact, the most important in history, of verifying its proofs, and, if it is found to be true, of preparing to listen to the voice of God. Certainly there is a good faith which is excusable before God and commendable in men, but a man who is really in good faith will neglect no means of knowledge, and will use all his efforts to arrive at the truth. The tendency of modernism, by the unreserved praise which it bestows upon everything that is not mere dishonest pretence, is to see no difference between a vicious and apathetic indifference and a sincere and honest search for the light; it is insulting to God and baneful to men, for it lulls them into a fatal and inexcusable lethargy.

Finally, without any thought of syncretism or higher principle, there are religions which are content to exist with no more show of life than stagnant water on an extinct volcano. Such are the sleepy religions of India and China.

This torpor and indifference are repugnant to Catholicism; the Catholic Church is essentially active and militant, and for this very reason it admits no truce or compromise with those religions that it hopes and desires to conquer.[1] Paganism insisted only on an outward rite,

[1] Even in China Christianity in this respect contrasts with the other religions which exist within the Empire. Buddhism accommodates itself to the worship of the dead and the honours which the Taoists pay to their numerous divinities. As the proverb goes, "San kiao-i kiao" (The three religions form but one). Christianity refuses all alliance with these. Mahomedanism, it is true, is equally uncompromising, but to its exclusiveness it unites the hatred of the infidel. Christianity alone unites rigour and charity.

Buddhism on morality and respect for the Order;[1] as we come nearer Catholicism, dogma appears—the dogma of one God and one prophet among Mahomedans; mutilated dogmas, only half-believed among Protestants, or, at least, among the more conservative Protestants; ancient dogmas, more completely preserved among the schismatic Christians of the East. The Catholic Church alone possesses a dogma which lives and endures, stable in itself and susceptible of development to us, studied with love and defended with jealous care as a deposit of Divine and indispensable truth left among men.

"Outside the Church there is no salvation" is the translation of what we have just said into ecclesiastical language. This formula scandalizes many people nowadays; but the scandal is the effect of forgetfulness or ignorance. The formula appears presumptuous to those who forget that the Church does not present herself as a human authority, contemptuously superior to other authorities of the same order, but as the Ambassador of Christ, who said: "My doctrine is not Mine, but His that sent Me";[2] and in His name she adds: "He that believeth not shall be condemned."[3]

The formula appears hard to those who are ignorant that it is to be accepted in combination with two other Catholic dogmas: first, that a man may, by charity, belong to the soul of the Church without being in outward communion with her

---

[1] The Order of Monks. See the Buddhist Catechism, published in Ceylon.
[2] St. John vii. 16, xiv. 24.   [3] St. Mark xvi. 16.

visible body; and, secondly, that God never refuses His grace to the man of good-will.[1]

But this uncompromising attitude in the matter of dogma does not transform into a persecutor that Church whose first Apostles were sent as sheep in the midst of wolves. If she cannot enter into any compact with false religions, she is forbidden, on the other hand, to win any victory over them except by the weapons of that charity which becomes all things to all men.[2] What is the commandment she has received from Christ? To teach, to preach, not to do violence. Thus she formally discountenances conversion by the sword. "This society has life in itself; in addition, it requires only liberty of expansion, to enlighten, to quicken, to regenerate the world."[3] From those who do not know her the Church asks one thing only—freedom to speak and to convince. As she has no power to

[1] It is certain that these propositions may be reconciled, though the manner thereof is to some extent veiled in mystery. Charity, or the state of grace which gives to the Church children whom she cannot call by that name on earth, implies faith; and that faith is a supernatural virtue by which we believe firmly, because of the supreme truthfulness of God, all that He has revealed and proposes through His Church to our belief. According to the almost universal teaching of theologians, this faith requires that certain truths shall be presented to the mind as declared by God. Consequently, though faith, which is a condition of charity, may be easy to sincere Protestants and even to Mahomedans, it does not appear to us immediately within the reach of members of other religions. God was not bound to make known to us the secret ways by which His grace operates; it is sufficient for us to know that that grace is never refused to the man who does his best.

[2] "I became all things to all men, that I might save all" (1 Cor. ix. 22).

[3] Mgr. Parisis, *Instruction pastorale sur le droit Divin dans l'Église*, p. 29.

compel men's minds to submit to her, she freely admits that she has no right to exact an outward submission, which might be false and insincere, for she has learnt from her Founder that her heavenly Father seeketh true adorers who shall adore Him in spirit and in truth.[1] This tradition of conquest by persuasion is primitive and constant in the Catholic religion. Excesses may be committed through error or indeliberate impulse; in this matter, as in all others, the perfect agreement between the principle and the application is only reached by slow stages. But the principle is unchangeable, and the persecuted Church of the Catacombs, the Church triumphant under Constantine, the Church reigning with Charlemagne, have but one voice to declare it. When the great Emperor, actuated by political motives, would have left the Saxons no option but that of baptism or death, Alcuin reminded him of this: "Faith," said he, following St. Augustine, "is an affair of the will, not of compulsion. How can you force a man to believe what he does not believe? You may drive him to baptism, but not to faith. Man, as an intelligent being, uses his reason; instruction and zealous preaching should lead him to recognize the truth of our holy faith; and, above all, prayer will bring down upon him the grace of Almighty God, for words are unavailing, unless the dew of grace softens the heart of the hearer."[2] Similarly, the Popes respected, and compelled others to respect, the liberty

[1] St. John iv. 23.
[2] Ep. 37., Edit. Frobenius, t. 1, p. 42. See also p. 51 (M.P.S., t. 100, cols. 194, 205).

of conscience of the Jews. Certainly, to our modern
eyes, especially if we take a one-sided view, and look
at the language of the laws without examining the
reasons for their enactment, the legal treatment of
the Jews, isolated within the narrow limits of the
Ghetto, and compelled to wear distinctive clothing,
will appear humiliating and vexatious ; but, considering the manners of the age, the Jews enjoyed
as much liberty as was possible, and the measures
taken by the Popes to insure and protect that liberty
called forth demonstrations of their gratitude.[1] In
our own day, also, the pioneers of the Gospel, who
follow in the footsteps of St. Francis Xavier, present themselves before the petty chiefs of Indian or
Congolese villages with the same deference and
respect for liberty which their illustrious prede-
cessor and patron showed at the Court of the
Japanese Kings. St. Augustine says : " No one is
to be brought to the faith by force " ;[2] and St.
Athanasius : " It is the part of religion not to
compel, but to persuade."[3] The violent proceedings
of the Arians drew from the great Hilary of Poitiers
an indignant protest, in which he did but echo the

[1] See the testimony of Dr. Gräz, *Geschichte der Juden*,
t. 5, pp. 41, 51 ; t. 6, p. 282 ; t. 7, p. 110. " The successors
of St. Peter," this author is compelled to admit, in spite of
his prejudice against the Church, " made it a point of
honour to protect the Jews from insult " (t. 5, p. 41).
Among their benefactors he specially mentions St. Gregory
the Great, Alexander III.—who on his return to Rome was
made the object of an enthusiastic demonstration—and
Gregory IX.

[2] *Ad fidem nullus est cogendus invitus* (M.P.L., t. 43,
col. 415).

[3] Θεοσέβειας ἴδιον μὴ ἀναγκάζειν, ἀλλὰ πείθειν (M.P.G., t. 25,
col. 773).

opinion of the whole Catholic hierarchy: " God teaches rather than compels men to know Him; He leads men to obedience by admiration for His heavenly works, and He scorns a submission yielded only to compulsion. If we used force for the propagation of the true faith, the whole episcopate would be bound by their principles to forbid it, and would proclaim that God is the Lord of the universe, and has no need of unwilling homage; He asks for no forced submission. We can receive none but those who wish to be received; we can listen to none but those who ask to be heard; we can mark with the Christian sign none but those who make profession of Christianity."[1] The Angelic Doctor speaks in similar terms: " Gentiles and Jews are on no account to be brought to the faith by compulsion, because believing is of the will."[2] Persons of full age, who are free to embrace or reject the faith, have the same freedom to decide for their infant children, and, except in case of extreme necessity, such as danger of death, no child of a Jew or an infidel can be baptized against the will, or even without the consent, of his parents or guardians. St. Thomas declares that " it has never been the usage of the Church to have children of Jews baptized against the will of their parents, for the practice is opposed to natural justice."[3] On February 18, 1705, the Holy Office expressly declared the illegality of baptizing the children of infidels against the will of their parents, and Bene-

[1] M.P.L., t. 10, col. 561.
[2] *Summa Theologica*, 2, 2, Q. 10, Art. 8.
[3] *Ibid.*, 2, 2, Q. 10, Art. 12; and 3 p., Q. 68, Art. 10. See also *De regimine Judæorum*.

dict XIV. repeated the prohibition in his Encyclical *Postremo* of January 28, 1747. All theologians and canonists teach the same, and the instructions of the Holy See have been so distinct that since the declaration of the Propaganda of April 17, 1777, there has been no need to return to the subject.

We see, then, that even the moderate severity, mentioned above, of which the Church makes use against apostate heretics would be unjust and inoperative against those who have not been baptized. Lea is astonished and somewhat scandalized by the distinction which the Church makes between heretics on the one hand and Jews and infidels on the other;[1] and even M. Vacandard sees something illogical in it.[2] And yet there is nothing subtle or mysterious in the distinction, which is observed every day in the civil and political order, in which subjects are not treated in the same manner as strangers. If we look at the matter from the Christian point of view, we shall see that baptism makes a man the subject of the Church, and that heresy constitutes desertion and rebellion, which is a grievous sin in the sight of God, as the result of a voluntary abuse of grace.[3] On the contrary, whether guilty or not before their own consciences, infidels and Jews are not responsible to the Church for their sin, and there can

---

[1] *Op. cit.*, p. 242. [2] *L'Inquisition*, p. 311, *n.* 1.
[3] In the third part we shall examine more closely the object of the sin of heresy. We cannot approve the extravagant language of Jean Jacques Rousseau: " If anyone, after having publicly acknowledged the same dogmas (of a State religion), behaves as if he did not believe them, he should be put to death, for he has committed the gravest of all crimes: he has lied before the law " (*Contrat Social*, l. iv., chap. viii., t. 2, p. 187).

be no question of compelling them to believe, or punishing them for their unbelief; the Church has the right only to defend herself against their calumnious attacks. From this point of view, Jews, whose books give testimony to the Christian faith, have been treated with consideration, as not being dangerous, or even as having rendered service to the Church. We must never forget that the wicked actions and language of Christians exercise a much stronger influence for evil. As to the question of heretics who knowingly abandon the Catholic faith, the distinction between them and infidels is quite clear. But what are we to say of those who have been brought up in schism and heresy, and have never outwardly belonged to the Church? Are they subjects because they have been baptized, or are they strangers because, since the dawn of reason, they have not been in communion with the Church? It cannot be denied that baptism, in giving a soul to Christ, gives it for ever in a certain sense to the Church which represents Christ and continues His work on earth. The non-Catholic Christian is therefore attached to the Church in a manner in which the infidel can never be; he is capable of receiving the other sacraments, and he has a claim to a special care on the part of the Church. The proper answer to this question seems to be that, while they are subjects of the Church, entitled to the benefit of certain favours and privileges, and also of a special solicitude, they are, in consequence of the error of their parents, incapable of contumacy against her, and therefore they ought not to be persecuted or molested in their belief.

In the matter of conversion to the true faith, these heretics appear to us to be in the same position as infidels.[1] It is by gentleness and persuasion, and not by compulsion, that they must be brought within the pale of the true Church.

What we say of adults we think we ought to say of children also ; they belong to their parents, and must ordinarily receive from them the direction they cannot give to themselves. Such is the awful authority with which God has invested parents, and which He leaves to them so long as they are not manifestly unworthy of it.

* * * * *

To sum up : Ecclesiastical tolerance or intolerance is the act of religious authority ; it is shown in doctrine, direction, and propagation of the faith— in other words, in the strictness or latitude with which the religious authority teaches and requires adhesion to its faith, punishes or overlooks differences of opinion, and consents or refuses to enter into any compact with other religions or their professors.

Put away all hatred or contempt for the misguided followers of other religions, otherwise called " unbelievers " ; " ecclesiastical intolerance " may be an unpopular expression, but the reality is in sympathy with all that is most lofty and generous within us. It means assurance and confidence, while tolerance means doubt and despair ; it shows strength, while tolerance implies weakness and failure ; it inspires us with a zeal for the salvation of souls, while

---

[1] We are glad to find our opinion corroborated by that of Father Hugueny, O.P. (see his reply to M. Turmel in the *Revue du Clergé Français*, 1907, t. 50, p. 315).

tolerance leads to selfish indifference; it is a firm attitude which is the logical result of Divine revelation.

The Catholic Church can neither hate anyone nor pass any sorrow by with indifference; her principles do not allow her to neglect any person in need of help, but they forbid her equally to attempt to convert anyone by force. She is the most uncompromising, the most intolerant of Churches; but also the most loving. Her intolerance is the result of her faith, and kindles the flame of her missionary zeal. In the words of a French Archbishop, the Catholic Church has the intolerance which comes of truth and charity, and that intolerance has produced the purest of all her glories during the whole course of her history—her martyrs, whose blood has empurpled the banner of true liberty of conscience, while they have died for their Saviour and their God.

EXCURSUS ON THE COERCIVE POWER OF THE CHURCH, AND ESPECIALLY ON THE RIGHT OF THE SWORD

I. General Statement of the Case.

SUMMARY: Statement of the case.—Interest and importance of the question.—The whole question comprises three points.—Force of the declarations of Pius IX. in the Encyclical *Quanta cura* and the Syllabus.—Common opinion.—Plan of the discussion.

The temporal punishments which the Canons of Councils and pontifical decretals have prescribed against heretics since the twelfth century render a clear understanding desirable on the subject of the right of punishment which admittedly exists in religious society or the Church; a further reason for explanation is suggested by the more severe punishments which have been approved by Popes, if not agreed upon between them and temporal Sovereigns, and of which we propose to treat in the following section.

These extreme measures receive a different explanation, according to the extent which we allow to the coercive power of the Church.

It must be borne in mind, in order to remove any misconception which may prevent us from following the argument, that the explanation offered does not settle the question of responsibility. There are two distinct questions involved. A Church which has not the power to strike with the sword may still be morally responsible for having suggested or counselled its use.

The coercive power of the Church may be original or derivative; given by God as something permanent and essential, or conferred by men, according to the age, the country, and the actual constitution of society. Even when this fullness of power comes from the Sovereign, it is not necessarily granted as a favour; it may be the fulfilment of a promise or a covenant, or, again, an obligation created by circumstances.

The complete question of the Church's right to punish embraces these three points: How far does the *original* right of punishment extend? Does it include absolute condemnations to temporal punishments,—that is to say, such that the guilty person cannot escape from them by leaving the Church and submitting to a spiritual penalty, such as excommunication? Does this original right extend to all temporal punishments that might be inflicted by the State?

Can the Church *demand* from the State the right to inflict effectively certain temporal punishments for which the consent of the Sovereign is materially necessary?

Can the Church *accept* from the State the right of passing all sentences whatever, including sentence of death?

Before discussing the question it is necessary that we should form an opinion as to the force, or rather the meaning, of certain pontifical declarations. Pius IX. says, in the Encyclical *Quanta cura*: "We condemn the error of those who do not hesitate to assert that the Church has not the right to visit with temporal punishments those who offend against her laws"; and, in condemning the twenty-fourth proposition of the Syllabus, *Ecclesia vis inferendæ potestatem non habet*, the same Pope affirms the existence of a coercive power within the Church. According to one interpretation, which, though minimistic, is admissible, the error dealt with in the Encyclical *Quanta cura* is avoided by attributing to the Church the right of inflicting temporal punishments in the sense that we have called "conditional." Expressly or implicitly the judgment takes this form: "Under pain of suspension, or interdict, or excommunication, the accused person is ordered to pay such and such a fine, or to reside in such and such a place."

GENERAL CONSIDERATIONS 61

A Bull of John XXII. similarly prevents us from condemning, as theologically incorrect, the proposition which would limit to the moral order the right of constraint affirmed in the Syllabus. John XXII., in his Bull of 1317 against Marsilius of Padua and Jean de Jeandun, expressly censures the adversaries of the coercive power, and condemns their opinion as at least erroneous. To show the existence of this power he appeals simply to the right of excommunication. We account in this manner for the fact that Don Salvatore di Bartolo, in the corrected edition[1] of his book, *Nuovo esposizione di criteri teologici*, has been able to maintain these two assertions: "The coercion by material force, exercised for the execution of ecclesiastical laws, is derived from human powers. By Divine law, the constraint of the ecclesiastical laws is purely of the moral order."

This interpetation of the decrees of Pius IX. seems a little forced. Don Salvatore di Bartolo finds few supporters, and his voice is almost lost in the chorus of theologians and canonists who assert the innate right of the Church to inflict certain material punishments.[2] We prefer to follow the opinion of Father Choupin:[3] "The universal and firmly established right of the Church in the matter of penalties certainly includes material punish-

[1] The first edition was put on the Index.
[2] The Abbé Vacandard seems to attach too much weight to the work of Don Salvatore. Father Choupin has made it very clear that the opinion of this author cannot claim the authority of Cardinal Soglia, or Pope Celestine III., or Nicolas I., all of whom exclude, as we shall do also, the right of the sword.
[3] *Nouvelle Revue Théologique*, 1910, pp. 82, 83.

ments.[1] . . . To justify the coercive right, the Sovereign Pontiffs have continually appealed to their Apostolic authority and their spiritual and universal primacy of jurisdiction, which is of Divine right."

This point being established, we shall touch upon the very interesting question of the right of the sword, in order to arrive at the formula which accurately describes the repressive right of the Church.

In order to obtain full light on the question submitted to our examination, we shall appeal successively to *authority, tradition, and reason—authority* —that is to say, writers skilled in theological science, who, since the age of the Fathers, have formulated their opinions according to revelation and the study of principles and facts; *tradition*— that is to say, the mind of the Church, as recorded in her ancient doctors and her laws; *reason*—the deductions which are logically drawn from established data concerning the nature and mission of the Church.

---

[1] In proof of this, see the particular Councils of Gaul and Spain, the decretals of Gregory IX. and Boniface VIII., the Clementine decretals, and the Council of Trent; also the fines inflicted and restitutions ordered by existing law, notably in matters of simony.

II. THE CHURCH AND THE RIGHT OF THE SWORD.

1. *The Argument from Authority.*

SUMMARY: Opinions of authors from the sixteenth to the eighteenth century, especially Bellarmine and Suarez.—They are but little supported by St. Thomas.—Different opinion of Bianchi de Lucca.—Contemporary opinions: Cardinal Tarquini, Mazella, Father Lépicier; and on the other side, Cardinal Cavagnis, Vicchiotti, Cardinal Soglia, Cardinal Satolli, Soliera, Lega (afterwards Dean of the Rota), Lombardi, Father Biederlack, Mgr. Douais.—The book of Father de Luca.—Causes of error in the great authors of the sixteenth and seventeenth centuries.—Conflict of opinion between Bellarmine and older authors.

We freely admit that from the sixteenth to the eighteenth centuries theologians and canonists claimed for the Church the right to inflict capital punishment for certain offences in case of necessity. Thus the theory which attributes this power to the Church counts famous and even classical writers among its supporters. Heirs of St. Thomas, they sprang up in an age in which the new social order was taking shape, the development of which has continued to the present day, and they seem to have transmitted to us for our own times the true formula of religious society and civil society. They were the first to state propositions as to the public law of the Church, which are still taught, and which are, to many persons, almost indisputable. Far be it from us to object entirely to the acceptance which they have deserved by their learning and virtue.

We may, however, remark that, while giving the sword to the Church, they hesitate as to the manner in which the Church is to wear it and use it. They instinctively perceive the real contradiction between the maternal spirit of the Church and excessive severity, and are inclined to represent the secular power as a mandatary, bound to obey orders, who will in extreme cases inflict capital punishment on behalf of the Sovereign Pontiff. In the scholastic precision of their formulæ they say that for ecclesiastical criminal cases the right of the sword exists in the Pope, as in one who has the power of ordering punishment, *tanquam in imperante et movente*, and in the Sovereign, as in one who carries out the order of another, *tanquam in exsequente et moto ab alio*. Without making this opinion, even in its modified form, an article of faith,[1] Bellarmine and Suarez give it as that of the schools.[2] Certain authors of repute,[3] such as the late Cardinals

---

[1] Certain expressions may easily be misunderstood. Thus Suarez (*De Fide*, d. 20), after having stated (s. 3, n. 10) that in his opinion the existence in the Church of the power of punishing heretics was an article of faith, subsequently (n. 18) raises this question only, in whom this power resides: for, he observes, there are in the Church temporal princes and ecclesiastical prelates; and although (n. 21) he severely condemns the opinion of those who recognize in the spiritual authority the power only to inflict punishments of the same spiritual order, he does not go so far as to declare that opinion heretical.

[2] Does this include the Angelic Doctor? It may be doubted. Observe the expressions which St. Thomas seems designedly to have chosen; he does not say that the Church condemns heretics to death, but that she leaves them to the secular tribunal (see 2, 2, Q. 11., Art. 3 *c*; Art 4 *c* and ad 1).

[3] Father de Luca was violently attacked by the Catholic *Germania* for having, in a Latin treatise of two volumes on Public Law, devoted four lines to the law and opinions of former times. The book was written in 1901, and the author has been dead several years. Nevertheless, the anti-Catholic Press does not cease to exploit this passage.

Tarquini[1] and Mazella,[2] and Father Lépicier, C.S.M.,[3] share this opinion. The contradiction which it meets with in our own days in the most different

---

After Germany, where the work was even brought up before Parliament, the liberal papers of Belgium had their turn. This year it is the turn of Holland. Under the bombastic heading, "Abominable Doctrines," one of these articles begins thus : " This is how a Jesuit Father, a certain De Luca, Professor of the University of the Vatican (!), *wishes to treat heretics :* ' The civil power may condemn the heretic to death at the order, and on behalf of, the Church.' " The whole is a gross calumny. Speaking of the jurisdiction of the Church over those who have gone astray, Father de Luca divides his answer into two parts. In the first, he makes heretics subject in theory to the Church ; in the second, he declares them in certain cases exempt, by the express will of the Church. With reference to the first part, he quotes the legislation of the earlier Middle Ages, which he sums up according to Tanner, an author of the sixteenth century ; as, later on, when speaking of the exceptions of the present day, he quotes two contemporary authors, Aichner and Ballerini-Palmieri, who declare that in the present day the Church takes no punitive action against heretics. Father de Luca expresses no personal wish ; he simply borrows from an old author the interpretation of a law which is expressly declared to be obsolete. The journal in question has therefore in a few words succeeded (*a*) in raising a dead author to life ; (*b*) in inventing a Vatican University which does not exist ; (*c*) in imputing to one author as his own opinion what is simply a quotation from another ; and (*d*) in falsifying the meaning of the quotation itself. In this connection it is well to take note of the wise words with which Father Brandi concludes one of his articles : " To attempt to treat *ex professo* of delicate questions, without even taking into account the changes which have taken place in the position of the Church, is always useless, and often imprudent and mischievous, by reason of the bitter controversies which are certain to follow" (*Civiltà Cattolica* for June, 1902, series 13, vol. vii., p. 18, *Del potere coattivo della Chiesa*).

[1] *Juris Ecclesiastici Institutiones*, ed. ii., p. 42 *sqq.*
[2] *De Religione et Ecclesia*, d. 4, Art. 6, *n.* 704, 31, *nota* 1.
[3] *De Stabilitate et Progressu Dogmatis*, pp. 174, 175 ; Rome, 1908.

countries and in the most Catholic circles seems to us so much the more significant.

The late Cardinal Cavagnis,[1] who was Professor of Law in the Roman seminary, did not hesitate to say that the great majority of authors deny to the Church the power of the sword—that is to say, the right to inflict capital punishment. Among these authors the celebrated Bianchi de Lucca deserves special mention; he dedicated to the Prince of the Apostles a great work in six volumes,[2] devoted entirely to the defence of the rights of the Church, especially its political rights, against the novel theories of Pietro Giannone. His work was printed and approved at Rome in 1746. In the fourth volume (l. 2, c. 4, sec. 9) he deals with this objection: " In earlier ages the Church had not the power to condemn to corporal inflictions or to exile; still less to mutilation or death." "When, then," asks Bianchi, " did the Church possess this power of punishing by death or mutilation? Whoever pretended that the Church had the power of condemning to a bloody punishment? Does she not expressly forbid it by her Canons, both of modern and of ancient law? Who does not know that the desire of the Church, in punishing delinquents by corporal inflictions, has always been to bring about their repentance and conversion, and never their extermination?"

It would be difficult to answer more categorically than this.

More recently, Vecchiotti,[3] whose lectures at

[1] *Institutiones juris Publici*, first edition; Rome, 1906.
[2] *Della potestà e della polizia della Chiesa;* Rome, 1748.
[3] *Institutiones Canonicæ*, t. 2, l. 4, c. 1, sec. 4, pp. 37, 39 *sqq.*, and 46 *sqq.;* Turin, 1868.

Rome were classical, and the late Cardinals Soglia[1] and Satolli,[2] similarly deny to the Church the power of inflicting capital punishment; and Father Brandi,[3] the editor of the *Civiltà Cattolica*, on the same side, quotes three other courses of lectures on Canon Law delivered at Rome, and published in 1900 and 1901, by Solieri, Lega (afterwards Dean of the Rota), and M. Lombardi; and Mgr. Douais considers it an established truth.[4]

Following so many distinguished authors, we may, then, without temerity circumscribe the coercive power of the Church within limits other and narrower than those laid down by the theologians and canonists of the sixteenth century. The latter were led to their conclusions, perhaps unconsciously, by the bias of preconceived opinions, and we cannot accept their judgment on the point at issue.

Under what influence, then, was the rigorist theory constructed? Under the influence of various factors which made it difficult to grasp the exact truth. We have to consider the psychology of an age which tolerated and applauded the pitiless Calvin—an age wholly given over to the most rigorous ideas. Absolutism reigned in the Courts, and a rigorist current of ideas ran through the Church. The former declared the Divine right of Kings, and the latter was the precursor of the icy blast of Jansenism. A Judaistic method of under-

[1] *Institutiones juris publici*, l. 1, sec. 8, p. 31; Modena, 1850.
[2] *Conferenze storico-giuridiche di diritto pubblico ecclesiastico*, p. 47; Rome, 1889.
[3] Series 18, t. 7, p. 18, June, 1902. *Del potere coattivo della Chiesa*.
[4] *Revue pratique d'apologétique*, January 15, 1909, p. 602.

standing and practising their religion crept into Christian consciences, and one might have thought that the old Mosaic Law had been revived. The same spirit appeared in the highest lyric poetry of France. Moralists and heretics alike took their stand on the antiquated law of Sinai,[1] the former to explain and justify the ecclesiastical observance of Sunday, the latter to excuse themselves for removing the pictures of the Saints and breaking their statues. Even ascetic theology was imbued with an extravagant severity, which preached pure love while sowing the seeds of fear and keeping the soul far from that God to whom it owed all its affection. What wonder, then, if men searched in the institutions of the Jewish people for lessons of religious policy?

We must remember, moreover, that the intimate union which had existed between the Church and the State of the Middle Ages was dissolved, and with the separation began a readjustment of their respective powers—a division of rights never before attempted. Human efforts do not reach perfection except by repeated trials, and we have no right to expect a division of rights so perfect from the first as to require no subsequent amendment.

Should we be rash, then, if we ascribed certain claims to the effect of the shock which a great religious disaster naturally caused to hearts most devoted to the old Christian faith?

---

[1] Even the moral precepts of the old law do not bind by reason of their promulgation by Moses; but their present force comes to them from the natural law, and the positive confirmation given to them by the Gospels. The Mosaic Code is, in fact, entirely abolished.

During the lifetime of Bellarmine and those writers who were the first to claim distinctly for the Church the right to punish with death, the Protestant heresy dealt a deadly blow to Christianity and the religious unity of Western Europe. Religious authorities naturally sought to preserve that unity by enforcing the laws enacted for the punishment of heresy ; it was their duty. The secular rulers gave way, for to make the observance of those laws a matter for their exclusive jurisdiction was only to increase their desire to abolish them. We can easily understand, then, that the theologians of the time, disturbed and agitated by a catastrophe from which Europe has not even yet recovered, in spite of their wide learning, in spite of their excellent intentions, or rather, to some extent, because of those intentions, lacked the calmness and judicial spirit necessary to define precisely the law which had been in force until that time, and trace that law back to its source. The Church pressed for the execution of the old edicts of Frederic II., and had recourse to the secular arm to obtain an effective repression ; therefore, they thought, the Church was competent to regulate that repression herself. The Church, on the other hand, never ceased to make profession of clemency ; therefore, according to their view, the secular arm became the medium, executing purely ministerial functions, by which the Church had to exercise her terrible power. Let us frankly admit it : the argument was faulty, and the expedient only half saved the clemency of the Church ; for it is only common sense that a person is not more merciful merely because he gives effect to his severity through the medium of another.

Moreover, it appeared to these men that every position taken at any time whatever by religious authority was necessarily that of the primitive Church, and must remain that of the future. We ourselves, without seeing shifting sand where our Lord declared that He was building on a rock, have learned, from a more attentive examination of successive theories and facts, to make reasonable allowance for inevitable changes, and to admit that very few ideas and institutions remain for ever unalterable. In the sixteenth century men did not take sufficient account of the fact that, though the foundation was Divinely laid, the superstructure was only human; Catholics and Protestants alike, with an exaggerated horror of any change, condemned a practice as new, or defended it as the expression of an unchanging principle. There was great risk that such a prejudice would distort all their views of history; and, as Gratian, in his *Concordia discordantium canonum*, did violence to the texts in order to reconcile discrepancies which were most simply explained by differences of date, the theologians of the sixteenth and seventeenth centuries gave to earlier events and statements a forced interpretation in order to bring them into agreement with contemporary institutions and opinions. We cannot, therefore, be surprised to see them appeal to the evidence of the Fathers, whose method of reasoning contradicts their own, and who, consequently, instead of strengthening their position, only show its weakness.

ARGUMENT FROM AUTHORITY

Two examples, taken from Bellarmine, will show how remarkable is this contradiction. In support of the argument that the punishment of death should be inflicted on heretics, the illustrious controversialist quotes the severe measures which the Old Testament directs to be taken against false prophets.[1] The Fathers refused to see in the politico-religious organization of the Jewish people the model of the laws which were to govern a spiritual society, thenceforward entirely distinct from the State; and the spirit of the New Testament was to them a reason for not following the Old Testament in this matter. Origen answered Celsus in these terms: "Jews, when they become Christians, are bound no longer to follow the laws of Moses, but those of Jesus.... Christians could not kill their enemies, nor could they burn or stone those who offend against the law, as the Mosaic Law directed."[2] St. Theodore the Studite wrote to Theophilus of Ephesus: "You may quote to me Phinees and Heli a thousand times; Jesus reproved His disciples for using such language to Him, and thus showing themselves destitute of His mercy and His kindness."[3] St. Cyprian draws attention to this contrast between the two Testaments: "Formerly, under the old law of the carnal circumcision, rebels against the law paid for their rebellion with their lives; but now that a spiritual circumcision distinguishes the faithful servants of God, the rebellious and obstinate fall under the edge of a

[1] *Controv. de Laicis*, l. 3, c. 21.
[2] *Contra Celsum*, l. 7, c. 26 (M.P.G., t. 11, cols. 1457, 1458).
[3] Ep. 155 to Theophilus of Ephesus (M.P.G., t. 99, cols. 1481 *sqq.*).

spiritual sword when they are rejected by the Church."[1] And yet Bellarmine appeals to the great Bishop of Carthage ![2] He relies also on St. Jerome, quoting his commentary on that passage from the Epistle to the Galatians[3] which the Canon Law understood as referring, not to the penalty of death, but to separation from the Church.[4] The ancient writers quoted the Parable of the Wheat and the Cockle against the punishment of heretics.[5] This parable becomes an objection in the treatise of Bellarmine.[6]

Great as is the authority of such distinguished writers, they are but human ; and without detracting from the respect which is due to them, we have in the present case very good reasons for declining to follow them.

[1] *Ep.* 62 *ad Pomponium, n.* 4. (M.P.L., t. 4, col. 371).
[2] *Ep. ad Fortunatum de Exhortatione Martyrii,* c. 51 (M.P.L., t. 4, col. 659). St. Cyprian reminds him of the severities of the old law against idolatry ; but when he says that, according to Christ, the precepts concerning the worship of God and contempt of idols ought to be more strictly observed, he means to speak, not of the punishments to be inflicted on idolaters, but of the generosity with which men should be willing to give up their lives rather than deny their God. The context leaves no doubt upon this point. The *a fortiori* argument of St. Cyprian is founded on the example of Christ *suffering,* who exhorts us to suffer and die ; and his conclusion inculcates contempt for death. The whole epistle is an exhortation, not to violence, but to martyrdom, which means death accepted without resistance.
[3] In *Epist. ad Galatas,* c. 5.
[4] Can. 16, *Secundæ,* c. 23, Q. 18. The Eighteenth Canon, *Ecce autem,* speaks more expressly of the amputation of corrupt flesh by the sword of excommunication.
[5] For example, St. John Chrysostom, Hom. 46, on St. Matthew, *n.* 182 ; St. Simeon the Studite, Ep. 155 to Theophilus of Ephesus (M.P.G., t. 99, cols. 1482, 1483) ; Wazon (eleventh century), *Anselmi Gesta Episc. Leodiens.* (*Mon. Germ. Script.,* vii., c. 227, 228).
[6] *Op. cit.,* c. 22.

2. *The Argument from Tradition.*

SUMMARY: Tertullian, Lactantius, St. Cyprian, Origen, St. John Chrysostom, St. Euthymius the Great, St. Theodore the Studite, Alcuin, Rabanus Maurus, Wazon, St. Peter Damian, St. Anselm, Ivo of Chartres, Rupert, Hugo of St. Victor, St. Bernard, Peter the Venerable, Peter Cantor, Gratian.—Canonical legislation does not include capital punishment.—Taparelli's conclusions.

Taparelli says in his *Treatise on Natural Law* (*n*. 1483) : " If I had to decide, as a canonist or theologian, the question of the extreme limits placed upon the coercive power of the Church, I should search tradition or ecclesiastical legislation to see what explanation the Church herself has given on this subject."

We propose to follow this prudent advice, and to take the evidence of ancient writers and ecclesiastical laws as to the mind of the Church.

During the whole of her existence the Church has shown the greatest repugnance to the shedding of blood. Tertullian, naturally somewhat inclined to exaggeration, is disposed to forbid Christians to take any part in war or in the execution of a capital sentence.[1] Lactantius, with greater moderation, expresses the general rule of religious toleration in the antithetical form he was accustomed to use : " Religion should be defended, not by killing, but by dying ; not by cruelty, but by patience ; not by crime, but by faith. . . . If you profess to defend religion by bloodshed, by tortures, by wrongdoing, you do not defend it, you sully it, you violate

[1] *De Corona Militum*, c. 2 (M.P.L., t. 2, col. 92).

it."[1] The testimony of St. Cyprian, the illustrious Bishop and martyr of Carthage, and Origen, the learned doctor of the East, has been quoted above.

In time of persecutions these protests may seem natural, and no special merit attaches to them; but they were repeated with equal energy in the hour of the first excitement of victory. It was at such a time that St. Chrysostom in the East showed his reluctance to have any threat held out over the heads of heretics. "We must not put heretics to death, or we shall have war without quarter throughout the Empire. . . . The Master certainly does not forbid us to restrain heretics, to close their mouths, to reject their oaths; what He does forbid is to shed their blood, and to put them to death."[2]

It was at such a time that St. Euthymius the Great displayed against heretics a zeal which won the admiration of other Saints, both for its ardour and its gentleness.[3] It was at such a time that St. Augustine in the West used all his eloquence to clear the Church from all complicity, even indirect, in sanguinary repression; and yet he was dealing with those very Donatists whose cruelty and excesses he has painted in such vivid colours—vulgar criminals, plundering murderers, who wore out the patience of the imperial power. These are the men whose cause he pleads with the Proconsul of Africa: " There is only one thing I fear from thy justice, and that is that it will consider the enormity of the offences committed without sufficient regard to

[1] *Div. Inst.*, l. 5, c. 20 (M.P.L., t. 6, col. 516).
[2] Hom. 46 on St. Matthew, *n.* 1 and 2.
[3] See his Life by Genier, O.P.; Paris, 1909, p. 172.

ARGUMENT FROM TRADITION

Christian clemency. Do not act in that manner, we beg thee in the name of Jesus Christ. We do not desire to take vengeance on our enemies. . . . We love them, and pray for them. . . . We hope that terror of the laws and judges will enable them to escape from eternal condemnation. We do not desire their death. . . . Forget that thou hast power to kill, but do not forget our prayer. We pray thee not to put them to death, as we pray our Saviour to convert them. . . . Remember, moreover, that these ecclesiastical causes only come before thee for trial on the petition of the clergy. . . . If thou shouldst pass sentence of death, thou wilt receive no more of our complaints. We would rather be killed by these criminals than institute proceedings which may result in their being put to death."[1]

Augustine wrote this letter in 408 or 409, and therefore at a time when experience had already modified his earlier opinions on the treatment of heretics, by showing the usefulness or necessity of some degree of severity. Three or four years later (in 412) he renewed his entreaties in his letters to the Tribune Marcellinus[2] and the Proconsul Apringius.[3] Read, finally, his letter to Count Boniface (417), which contains his "complete theory on the repression of heretics."[4] How can we help being struck by the distress which was caused to St. Augustine by the violent death of certain Donatists? If he rejoices at the deliverance of many Christians who were kept in heresy by terror, he resigns himself

[1] Ep. 100, *n*. 1 and 2 (M.P.L., t. 33, cols. 366, 367).
[2] Ep. 133 (M.P.L., t. 33, cols. 509, 510).
[3] Ep. 134 of A.D. 412 (M.P.L., t. 33, col. 510).
[4] Portalié, *Dict. de Vacant, Augustin*, cols. 2278-2280).

to the temporal loss of a few wicked wretches only because it is rather their own act than that of the law.[1] Again and again he falls back on this same explanation—these heretics have put themselves to death. "Such is their madness," he says, "that they are determined either to kill us in order to satisfy their cruel passion, or to kill themselves to show that they have not lost the power of killing."[2] Such language as this is far from recommending the systematic repression of heresy by blood, and farther still from putting the avenging sword into the hands of the Church. On the contrary, St. Augustine declares that he does not desire the death of any.[3] "The charity of the Church labours to save these heretics from eternal damnation without any one of them being put to death."[4]

We may, then, come to this conclusion: St. Augustine gave up his opposition on principle to measures of severity, it is true; but capital punishment always seemed to him opposed to that Christian rule of mercy from which we may not depart, even with the most unworthy, and he never thought of attributing to the Church the right to punish by death. To the very last he insisted on the distinction between civil and ecclesiastical proceedings which he had laid down in 412: "The mission of the Proconsul is one, that of the Church is another; the former may be accompanied by terror, but the

[1] Observe that these laws did not prescribe capital punishment for the Donatists. See *Code Théodosien*, xvi., 5, l. 54.
[2] Ep. 185, *n*. 11. *Cf. n*. 14, 32, 33, 34 (M.P.L., t. 33, cols. 797, 798, 807, 808).
[3] *Ibid., n.* 11 (col. 797).   [4] *Ibid., n.* 32 (col. 807).

latter must always be recommended by its clemency."[1]

The whole of the West was excited by the news of the punishment which the Emperor Maximus inflicted on the heretic Priscillian and certain of his associates ; and St. Martin, who exerted himself to save them, refused to hold any communication with those who had denounced them. How deeply rooted must be the Catholic opposition to the shedding of blood ! St. Leo the Great had no favour for the Priscillianists, whom he classed with the Manichæans. He denounced their error, as fifteen centuries later Pius X. denounced Modernism, describing it as the common centre of all heresies ;[2] he recognized, moreover, that the imperial severity had served the cause of religion, and induced many persons to return to the faith. And yet how carefully is the office of the Church distinguished from that of the State by that Pope whom Lea[3] accuses of having distinctly pledged the Church to the suppression of heresy at whatever cost ! The Pope declares that the Church is content with an ecclesiastical judgment, and uses these words, which have become axiomatic : " The Church abhors sanguinary vengeance." He calls for prayers on behalf of heretics, for he says : " In this life we must not despair of any, but hope for the conversion of all."[4]

In the eighth century, St. Theodore the Studite, a Greek Saint, devotes the whole of his letter to

[1] Ep. to the Proconsul Apringius (M.P.L., t. 33, col. 511).
[2] Letter to Turribius (M.P.L., t. 54, col. 679).
[3] *History of the Inquisition in the Middle Ages*, vol. i., p. 215.
[4] Sermon 33 (M.P.L., t. 54, col. 249).

Theophilus of Ephesus to the statement and demonstration of the same proposition; his testimony is the more significant because he appeals to the New Testament and the Fathers. He concludes thus: "It belongs to temporal princes to punish material offences, but not offences of the spiritual order; these causes are reserved to those who have the direction of souls, and they inflict excommunications and other punishments. . . . The Church does not take vengeance by the sword. If you have another Gospel of which we know nothing, well and good; but if you have not, remember the teaching of the Apostle."[1]

The question of the right of the sword was not raised for the Church in the ninth and tenth centuries, but there is no doubt as to the answer which it would then have received. At the beginning of the ninth century, Alcuin, who represents the science and theology of his time, had been very energetic in condemning the forced conversion of the Saxons. His words, which we have already quoted, show us what he would have said of the introduction of the penalty of death into the Ecclesiastical Code.

Rabanus Maurus (786-856) complains, as Augustine did, of the violent excesses of heretics,[2] but concludes only that they should be excommunicated. "Let the heretic fall under the sword of the Church, and let his portion be with the unbelievers."[3] Hincmar of Rheims, in his synodal capitula of 881, makes too clear a distinction between the spiritual

---

[1] Ep. 155 to Theophilus of Ephesus (M.P.G., t. 99, cols. 1485, 1486).

[2] Commentary on 1 Kings, c. 13 (M.P.L., t. 109, col. 42).

[3] Commentary on Ezechiel, l. 12, c. 13 (M.P.L., t. 110, cols. 838, 839).

ARGUMENT FROM TRADITION

jurisdiction of the Pontiff and the temporal jurisdiction of the Sovereign ever to empower the Church to inflict capital punishment.[1] In the work known as the *Collectio Pseudo-Isidoriana* no temporal punishment is prescribed against heretics.

In the midst of the popular indignation aroused in many places by the antisocial heresy of the Catharists, Wazon, a great Bishop of Liège, whose voice was listened to even in Rome, expressly denies that the Church has the power to sentence to death. "Let us remember," he writes to the Bishop of Chalons, "that in our episcopal consecration we do not receive the sword of the secular power, and that the Divine unction calls upon us not to kill, but to make alive"[2]—words which are incorporated in the Canon Law; and in the same eleventh century, neither in St. Peter Damian nor in St. Anselm do we find a single word to justify corporal inflictions on heretics.

In the twelfth century a celebrated Canonist, Ivo of Chartres, wrote : "How can that Church which since her birth has never shed any blood but her own come to shed the blood of another ?"[3] The teaching of Abbot Rupert may be summed up in these few words : Heretics must be won by persuasion,[4] and they must be put out of the Church like lepers.[5] Hugo of St. Victor does not threaten heretics with any temporal punishment, and he

---

[1] Cap. I. (M.P.L., t. 125, col. 1072).

[2] See *Anselmi Gesta Episcoporum Leodiensium* (*Mon. Germ., Hist. Scriptorum*, t. 7, c. 227).

[3] Ep. 247 to John, Bishop of Orléans (M.P.L., t. 162, col. 364).

[4] *In Joannem*, l. 8 (M.P.L., t. 169, col. 569).

[5] *De Trinitate, in Leviticum*, l. 11, c. 36, 37 (M.P.L., t. 167, cols. 815, 816).

insists too strongly on the purely spiritual character of ecclesiastical power to think of giving supreme criminal jurisdiction to the Church.[1]

St. Bernard and Peter the Venerable, though not objecting to the repression of heresy by the secular power, were strongly opposed to extreme measures. St. Bernard allows the Church two weapons—viz., preaching and excommunication.[2] Peter Cantor more clearly declares against the sentence of death: "The Apostle St. Paul tells us to avoid a man that is a heretic after the first and second admonition; he nowhere tells us to kill him."[3]

These quotations bring us down to the thirteenth century, and there is nothing of any authority on the other side. If there is anything remarkable in those who attribute to the Church the right of the sword, it is the extreme weakness of their argument from the Fathers, or rather the absence of any such argument. The ancient belief of the Church is, moreover, proved by the Canonical Code, the first book of which was written about 1150. Let us hear its author, Gratian. His collection, as is known, without being authoritatively promulgated, received, from its adoption by the universities and tribunals, a sort of official recognition, analogous to that which the teaching of the schools gave to the *Summa Theologica* of St. Thomas. "Ecclesiastical discipline," he says, "commands that criminals shall be struck, not by the material sword, but by the spiritual sword," and he corroborates

[1] *De Sacramentis*, l. 2, p. 2, c. 7 (M.P.L., t. 176, cols. 419, 420).
[2] Vacaudard, *St. Bernard*, pp. 120, 121.
[3] *Verb. abbrev.*, c. 78 (M.P.L., t. 205, col. 231).

ARGUMENT FROM TRADITION

this assertion by this passage, which he attributes to Pope Nicholas I. : " The Church possesses only the spiritual sword ; she does not kill, but she gives life."[1]

This is the Canon Law of the twelfth century, and it is not altered by any subsequent legislation. Search the whole of the *Corpus Juris*, and in the whole of its provisions you will find nothing to legalize capital punishment ; and Canonists fail so completely to find any such sanction in subsequent legislation that many, including Father Wernz, S.J., consider it unnecessary to discuss the question of law, because it never was a question of fact. Moreover, if capital punishment found a place in Canon Law, would the Church be acting logically in forbidding her clergy under such severe penalties to take any part in a sentence of death or mutilation ?[2] " The sentence of death is on principle odious to the Church ;[3] she does not pronounce it herself,"[4]

---

[1] Can. *Inter. hæc*, 6, c. 33, Q. 2. The passage is taken from a letter said to have been addressed by Nicholas I. to the Bishops of Germany. Mansi fixes the date about the time of the Council of Mayence, 857.

[2] C. *Sed nec*, 4 ; *Clericis*, 5 ; *Sententiam sanguinis*, 9 ; *Ne clerici vel monachi sæcularibus negotiis se immisceant* (iii. 50). The participation in a capital sentence is a cause of irregularity—that is, it puts an obstacle to the reception and lawful exercise of sacred orders. See Gasparri, *De Sacra Ordinatione*, n. 451.

[3] *Hist. du Droit Civil Français*, p. 373.

[4] The Constitution of John XXII., *Dierum*, inserted in the *Corpus Juris*, Extrav. *de Pœnis*, t. 12, is specially significant in this matter. Directed against a populace which was in the habit of assassinating the authorities, it prescribes seventeen punishments for seventeen kinds of offences of which these wretched men were guilty ; and in this list of punishments there is no mention of either death or mutilation. John XXII. adds that he does not prevent the secular power from punishing the miscreants with all the rigour of their laws.

recently wrote M. P. Viollet. Hinschius, so far as we know, is the only person to maintain that certain Popes have used their spiritual authority to pass a sentence of death or mutilation; not for heresy, it is true, but for other offences. These last words refute the argument of Hinschius; the laws he quotes were enacted at a time when the Church was engaged in a fierce struggle with heresy, which she felt to be as dangerous to her as a revolution to an Empire. How could the Popes have shown, against crimes which concerned them far less, a severity which they spared to heresy?[1]

[1] We have taken the trouble to examine one by one the Pontifical letters to which Hinschius appeals, and find that not a single one of them gives him any ground for his argument. Of these letters—

(a) The Const. *Cum primum*, April 1, 1566 (B.R., t. 4, part 2, p. 284), of St. Pius V. is directed against blasphemers, who are threatened with various punishments, including piercing of the tongue; and against sodomites, whom it is necessary to deliver to the secular arm. It is addressed to the feudatories of the Holy Roman Church and to secular princes.

(b) The Const. *Cum sicut* of Julius III., May 29, 1554 (B.R., t. 4, part 1, p. 309), against Jews who obstinately refused to give up their books containing blasphemies against Christ, could not make them amenable to spiritual jurisdiction, according to the well-known maxim, The Church does not judge those who are without.

(c) The Const. *Effrænatum* of Sixtus V., October 29, 1588 (B.R., t. 5, part 1, p. 25), modified by the Const. *Sedes Apostolica* of Gregory XIV., May 31, 1591 (B.R., *ibid.*, p. 275), applies to abortion the ecclesiastical and civil laws against homicide. It cannot, therefore, emanate from the spiritual authority of the Sovereign Pontiff alone.

(d) The Const. *Etsi alias* of Clement VIII., December 1, 1601 (B.R., t. 5, part 2, p. 395), and the Const. *Omnipotentis* of Gregory XV., March 20, 1623 (B.R., t. 5, part 5, p. 97), punish the sacrilegious parody of the Mass, or Absolution by persons not in priests' orders, and the practice of witchcraft, causing death. The guilty were to be

ARGUMENT FROM TRADITION

The ecclesiastical legislator has in later ages been true to his old tradition, and has never made capital punishment legal; and those who attribute to the Church the right to pass such a sentence will find no corroboration of their opinion in the law. Taparelli, whose work suggested this examination

---

made over to the secular arm, *debitis pœnis plectendi*, to be punished according to their deserts.

(*e*) The Const. *Inscrutabilis* of Urban VIII., April 1, 1631 (B.R., t. 6, part 1, p. 288), punishes as guilty of high treason persons who practised astrology on the subject of Christianity, the Holy See, the Sovereign Pontiff, and his relations to the third degree. (Secular princes protected themselves thus against the disturbing effects of astrological predictions.)

(*f*) The Const. *Magnum* of Urban VIII. (1631) directs that certain bigamists shall be punished by the secular arm.

(*g*) The Brief *Cum Super* of Urban VIII. (1643), addressed to the *Auditor Cameræ* (a judge of temporal matters), and directing him, in case of war, to judge the enemy and execute the sentences passed upon them, even *capitalissima*, concerns the Papal States only.

(*h*) Lastly, the Const. of Innocent XI., of March 12, 1677 (B.R., t. 8, p. 23), directs that persons who stole Hosts should, after the first offence, be delivered to the secular arm.

From this short summary it will be seen that these Constitutions apply to offences mentioned in all the criminal codes of the period. The Pope who issues them acts simply as temporal King and Head of Christendom, or, in virtue of his twofold authority (spiritual and temporal), which was recognized at that time in Catholic States, the spiritual and the temporal being often exercised in the same Act. Finally, the infliction of the punishments was not the concern of the ecclesiastical tribunal properly so called.

This, moreover, is the way in which the Constitutions were understood. If any other interpretation had prevailed, the authors who still attribute to the Church the right of the sword without any restriction would not have failed to use against their opponents this conclusive argument from the Canons. The Church is not deceived as to her own competence: what she has done, she has had the right to do.

of the facts, comes to the following conclusion :
" The Church has spoken strongly enough, forbidding
her children to shed blood, and referring always to
the secular arm for the inflicting of the more severe
penalties. Thus she shows what is her spirit as a
Christian Church."[1] We are entirely of the same
opinion as Taparelli. For twenty centuries the
Church has had to deal with heretics and criminals,
and never, even during the thousand years when she
had every facility for doing so, has she passed an
irreparable sentence. This forbearance, maintained
in the most varied circumstances, which seemed
sometimes to render the extreme severity necessary,
raises a strong presumption against her power.
Armed with formidable spiritual weapons to defend
the faithful and preserve them from contagion, she
has the power to punish her guilty children ; but it
is the power of a mother, who never gives up the
hope of a great joy, the joy of converting and saving
them.

Such, in our opinion, is the conclusion to be
drawn from the facts. If since the thirteenth
century some great authors have thought otherwise,
and if the language of the laws themselves (though
containing no mention of capital punishment) is
susceptible of a different interpretation,[2] we desire
to express our opinion with due modesty, but we

[1] *Saggio teoretico di diritto naturale*, n. 1485.
[2] Such, for instance, as the Bull of John XXII. against
Marsilius of Padua, quoted above. Suarez (*De Fide*, d. 20,
sec. 3, *n.* 22) appeals to the famous Constitution of Boniface VIII., *Unam Sanctam*. It is sufficient to remark that,
although the question of the temporal power of the Pope
is discussed in that Constitution, it does not even touch the
special point of the power of sentencing to death.

ARGUMENT FROM REASON

cannot change it without contradicting what seems to us the true tradition of the Church.[1]

We now proceed to consider the argument from reason.

3. *The Argument from Reason.*

SUMMARY: False arguments used for the Church's right of the sword.—Conclusion too easily drawn from the State to the Church.—Too much stress on the Church as a society of natural law.—The concept of a perfect society proves nothing.—Why the State can punish with death.—Different position of the Church.—The mission of the Church, its moral apostolate, the blessings it is intended to procure, the spirit and name which are its glory, the very offences it is called upon to punish, disprove the power of punishing with death.—What is to be said in a case of exceptional necessity?—Divine Providence allows us to put aside the supposition.

The advocates of the right of the sword frequently use an argument which they consider unanswerable. The Church, they say, as a supreme society, is, no less than the State, a perfect society; the State possesses the right of the sword, therefore the Church also possesses it. The argument is fallacious, as Cardinal Cavagnis points out; for what is the major premiss of this ill-constructed syllogism? Will they contend that the Church, because it is a perfect society, can do all that the State can do? The assertion is false, unless we admit that the State is only a province of the Church. Will they argue that every perfect society has the right of the sword? The assumption is gratuitous, unless from the single example of the State they draw an infer-

[1] The direct power of the Pope over temporal affairs has also had its advocates, and more than one law has shown the influence of their opinion.

ence which is evidently vicious.[1] Will they fall back on analogy ? But the point to be considered is not so much the analogy as the difference of two societies, which they compare, the one to the soul, and the other to the body. The only argument that remains for them is that the right of the sword is as necessary to the Church as it is to the State, and that therefore the Church may claim it, because a perfect society has a right to the means which are indispensable to its end. But those who share our opinion deny this necessity ; they see no reason why the Church should be bound to put on a sword which she has never drawn from its sheath ; and Father Biederlack attributes to Cardinal Cavagnis an argument based on the non-necessity of this right.[2] The Church, he says, possesses all the means necessary for her end ;[3] but the penalty of death is not necessary for it : therefore—as his opponents reason *a pari*, and there is no parity— " the argument is a sophism." This is the just conclusion of Father Choupin.[4]

[1] They proceed as if arguing that whatever belongs to a genus belongs also to each subordinate species, whereas in reality there exist also only two species of perfect society— the Church and the State.

[2] Course of lectures delivered at Rome, and autographed under the title, *Institutiones Juris Ecclesiastici* (Rome, 1907). In the original French edition of this work the argument was attributed to Father Biederlack himself, and his own text gives occasion to the confusion ; but, as a matter of fact, he put aside the question as unimportant. We take this opportunity of correcting the mistake.

[3] The Cardinal evidently takes it for granted that necessity is the only reason for attributing to a perfect society means of another order than the end of that society.

[4] *L'Inquisition : La Responsabilité de l'Eglise dans la Repression de l'Hérésie au Moyen Age*, p. 39.

ARGUMENT FROM REASON

This answer enables us to put our finger on the radical defect of so many arguments used in favour of a conclusion opposed to our own. Men reason about the Church too much as if it were a society of natural law; and in this there is a misunderstanding or a misuse of language which it is necessary to point out.

In the case of an institution of the natural order, the argument which proves its existence proves also the existence of all its rights. The same necessary act of the will of the Author of Nature sanctions the institution for the good of mankind, and the rights of the institution which are required by that good; and there is no need for any special economy. But for an institution which is of free Divine creation, the positive will of God decides in the beginning the rights that shall be conferred upon it. We must make a distinction between the powers which are ideally possible and the powers actually bestowed; for Divine Providence, without failing in its wisdom, may well refrain from giving all the powers compatible with the abstract notion of such an institution. Being omnipotent, it has other means for the attainment of its end. Taparelli has well remarked that the repressive measures which are not repugnant to every spiritual society may be entirely repugnant to the Christian Church and the spirit of its Founder. But other contemporary writers have not followed Taparelli's example; their own concepts of perfect society and visible society form the basis of the arguments which they consider conclusive, and they only glance at the texts in order to bring them, at least verbally, into harmony with their own deductions. The reasoning appears to us faulty, for the Church does not become either invisible or imperfect merely because she does not possess all possible outward means of coercion. The character of Christ, His death on the Cross, the testimony given for twelve centuries to the essential clemency of the Church, the Canon Law of the Church, first by its omissions and secondly by its axioms, " the Church does not kill," " the Church abhors bloodshed "—all these things reveal to us the true spirit of the Church, and enable us to draw a correct conclusion as to her powers ; and these things we constantly keep in view in our argument, which is based on the fact of a Church and a religious society very different from the Synagogue and the theocratic organization of the Old Testament.

Our proposition appeals to a sort of moral sense of fitness and propriety ; it invites us to look at the whole subject as made up of a multitude of details whose very complexity excludes the possibility of strict mathematical demonstration. These remarks seem necessary to explain and strengthen the direct arguments which we propose to employ.

Let us go back first to the reason which places the lives and liberties of great criminals at the disposal of the State. This reason is not pure vengeance. Vengeance belongs only to God, who is offended by every transgression, who sees every crime that is committed, and whom no power or cunning can deceive. Man lacks the authority, the competence, and the power required to be a judge in the full sense of the word.

But the State possesses more than the right of

ARGUMENT FROM REASON

self-defence, which is allowed to a private individual. If a private individual is forcibly attacked in his person or property, it is lawful for him to repel force by force. There his right ends, and as soon as the criminal desists from his aggression he recovers, so far as the private individual is concerned, the inviolability which protects him in the possession of his life, liberty, and property. If civil society had no other right than this, it would not be justified in punishing a repentant offender, and could not put a man to death except in order to prevent him from doing harm to others. Capital punishment, which would be legitimate, or at least conceivable, in a nomad population, would be inexplicable in a State provided with prisons protected against sudden attack. But we do, as a matter of fact, recognize in public authorities, even in those of the present day, the right to punish criminals, even when penitent and unarmed.

In the defence of society there are elements which do not exist in the legitimate self-defence of a private person. The punishment which the State inflicts is not only preventive and repressive, but exemplary and retributive. Why? Because it is the duty of the human legislator to establish and sanction effectively a visible order, modelled on that supreme order which is established and sanctioned by God—modelled on it in this sense, that it is the complement of that order in its application to a specified sphere. This human order should give sufficient encouragement to law-abiding persons, and reasonable satisfaction to that sentiment of justice which is offended by the sight of vice triumphant and virtue oppressed. Such is the social necessity which arms the legislator with power to take public vengeance ; and this vengeance may extend to the taking of life when the effective maintenance of order demands such severity.

The right of punishing with death seems to be necessarily attached to the maintenance of an order which the individual has not to dispute but to obey, whatever his personal opinion may be, and which his fear of consequences will compel him to respect.

Unless we identify the Church with the State, we must see that the Church, as such, is not generally concerned in the maintenance of order in any particular territory. She has no geographical limits ; but while it is her mission to penetrate into all countries, imperial or democratic—*docete omnes gentes*—she will not interfere with their interior administration. The higher justice which she preaches does not profess to be imposed by force, but, on the contrary, asks for the free consent of all. The Church fulfils her normal mission by converting all nations, and inducing believers and unbelievers to live peacefully side by side, without disturbing the established order and tranquillity. She does not exist to spread terror, but to disseminate ideas of virtue ; not to satisfy avenging justice, but to develop the higher sentiments of clemency, mercy, and forgiveness. She is visible, no doubt, but for what purpose ? To reach men's souls, and win them by instruction, by preaching, by administration of the sacraments, by gathering men together for mutual edification, by all the outward and visible means which help forward those who have voluntarily entered her communion.

The State has the effective right to take measures for the preservation of visible order, and to use constraint for the purpose, if necessary ; and this right puts into the hand of the State a sword which may be used to take life. The Church has the effective right to save souls, and no force can prevent her from exercising that right. Can such a right as this carry with it that of inflicting a punishment which may risk the eternal loss of the soul ? We must not forget that the Church, brought into existence by the express will of God, is bound to the religious community by other relations than those which exist between the State and the civil community from which it emanates. It is true that both the Church and the State are concerned with men, whose physical existence is not collective, but individual ; and the end and justification of both is the good of those persons who compose the society. But the difference of their objects, their missions, and their duration, involves a corresponding difference in their functions, their duties, and the matters which occupy their attention. Civil society regulates outward acts, as such, and not intentions (*De internis non judicat prætor*), and touches man in the least noble part of him, the body ; for not only is it by the body that all social intercourse is kept up, but, according to the Thomistic philosophy, the necessity for social relations arises from the fact that we have a body. It is by the body that we are many individuals in one species, and humanity finds its perfection and completion in association and union. The Church, on the other hand, regulates outward acts only because they help towards our inward personal sanctification. The State certainly cannot neglect the soul, because without the soul it cannot reach that compound being that we call man. But the Church seeks to make her way through the body or through the compound being to the soul. Moreover, the express will of her Divine Founder gives her, in her sacraments and sacrifices, a directly spiritual action. The attention of the Church, then, is principally directed to that part which in every man is the most worthy, but also the most autonomous and, as it were, the most isolated.[1]

The State, whose function is first of all to maintain that visible order which depends on respect for the rights of others, and then to secure general prosperity by making up for the insufficiency of private initiative, accomplishes its mission when it has sufficiently provided its members with the means of livelihood, and it is not concerned to see how each member makes use of those means. The Church, on the contrary, by preaching and instruction, endeavours to inform every intellect, while her prayers and her sacraments dispose and stimulate every will.

The State is formed for temporal happiness, and has no object beyond the present common good ; the Church, instituted for the eternal salvation of souls, makes use of the present common good in

[1] Is not this, in substance, the argument of the illustrious Cardinal, Robert Pullen ? " Let the State consider that it commands the body, and the Church the soul. Let the former punish the guilty person in his body, and let the latter visit the obstinate with spiritual punishment " (*Sententiarum Libri*, viii., l. 6, c. 56 ; *De duobus Ecclesiæ gladiis* [M.P.L., t. 186, cols. 905, 906]).

order to render easier of attainment the happiness which will follow this life, and which will not come to an end with earthly society.

The special value and independence of the soul, the mission of supernatural sanctification entrusted to the Church, its last end, which every member of the community is bound continually to keep in view, all combine to make the Church much more solicitous than the State for each individual member; and hence arises the difference in the positions of the Church and the State with regard to capital punishment. The State considers this extreme penalty as a means proportioned to its end, which also is outward and visible—the maintenance of public order. Whether the sentence entails the eternal loss of a soul, or whether it is passed on a man who is penitent for his crimes and has once more become worthy to live, these special considerations do not affect the State, and the common good permits it to put them aside. But this severity, on the one hand, has only an accidental effect on the convictions of the intellect and the intentions of the will; and, on the other hand, its consequences are inconsistent with the maternal affection which the Church professes for every one of her children. A mother cannot sacrifice a repentant son, or cause the eternal damnation of an obstinate one, by an act that precludes all possibility of return.[1] The Church,

[1] The advocates of the right of the sword see the force of this argument, and endeavour to escape from the difficulty by the plea that a longer life would only serve to make the eternal punishment of the obstinate person heavier (Bellarmine, *Controv. de Laicis*, l. 3, c. 11). But St. Leo the Great tells us that in this life we must never despair of anyone.

being created to give life, does not put to death ; that is the axiom of Canon Law.

The Church has to act upon superior faculties rebelling against constraint ; there is, therefore, nothing more just or reasonable than to attribute to her a coercive power, appealing, in the last resort, to faith and persuasion, because excommunication is the final sanction. But, if we consider her inherent power, it seems very unlikely that the Church should herself have the right to use violence for the execution of her decrees. "Material violence," writes Father (now Cardinal) Billot, "is one of the means at the disposal of temporal society."[1] This right of exterior constraint, which the Church cannot exercise without the assent of the secular power, she possesses only by her natural and legitimate alliance with that power. It is unnecessary to discuss this matter further, and we need only say that we have no desire to see gaolers and executioners included among the ministers of the Church.

What shall we say of the harm that the exercise of the right of the sword would cause to the Church herself ? On the one hand, there is danger that the use of these violent and summary means would lead her ministers to neglect those means which are more adapted to the end of the Church, but which call for more labour and self-sacrifice—namely, personal edification and amendment of life, the zeal of enlightened and patient preaching, and long-suffering charity. On the other hand, such measures are repugnant to that name of Mother, of which the

[1] *Tractatus de Ecclesia Christi*, t. 2 ; *De Habitudine Ecclesiæ ad Statum*, Q. 19, Art. 1, l. 4, p. 125.

Church is justly proud, and to that clemency which she should always display, as continuing the work of Christ.

But this is not all. We should not think of denying the pernicious effects of the propagation of tenets that corrupt faith and morals, and the necessity of putting a stop to it by efficacious means; but if we consent simply to exclude the irreparable sentence of capital punishment, can we not strengthen the preceding arguments by a secondary consideration drawn from the nature of the offences which the Church has the right to punish?

Offences of the spiritual order are not attended by the inevitable and irreparable consequences of certain crimes, such as murder, which are amenable to the jurisdiction of the secular tribunals. Though voluntary in those who commit them, they hurt none but those who allow themselves to be led away.[1] I may be killed against my will, but I cannot sin against my will; and the will which has grown weak may always receive new strength, and expiate its fault by repentance.

Thus it seems to us that everything points to the same conclusion. The mission of the Church, her moral apostolate, the blessings she is to procure for us, the faculties on which she acts, the spirit and the name in which she glories, the very crimes she is

[1] If a criminal attempt is accompanied by violence, there is always a right of self-defence, and it is the duty of the secular power to interfere when necessary for the maintenance of public order. St. Theodore the Studite explained in this manner the appeal which St. Simeon Stylites addressed to the Emperor against the infidels who were the scourge of some Christian countries (Letter 155, quoted in M.P.G., t. 99, col. 1485).

called upon to punish—all these things tell us to exclude from the coercive system of the Church the disastrous and unnecessary power to punish with death.

It will probably be admitted that the arguments we have adduced prove that the repressive system of the Church does not *habitually* extend to capital punishment. But it may be asked, Does it *never* extend so far ? May we not imagine extreme cases which would compel her to have recourse to it ? Some disturbers of the public peace might go to such lengths that their death would be the only means of preserving the rest of the flock from danger. If the Church has not in such a case the power to cut off a diseased member, would she still be a perfect society ? Would she have at her disposal means sufficient for her end ?

Such is the only specious objection[1] which remains to be examined fairly and without any prejudice. To answer it we appeal first to the testimony given

[1] It is unnecessary to waste time over certain futile objections, invented without any examination of the merits of the question. Some persons, for example, suggest that the Church, as a perfect society, has a coercive power unlimited in principle, and that therefore she must be presumed to possess the right of the sword, unless the contrary is proved ; as if a perfect society could do all that is not proved to be forbidden, and as if the irreparable nature of the punishment and the forbearance of the Church for two thousand years did not at least raise a presumption that she has not the power. Others, who confuse two different orders of things, use this extraordinary argument : The Church has the power of excommunication ; *a fortiori*, she has the power of death, since excommunication is a heavier punishment than death. If this were so, it would be a mitigation of the Canon Law to substitute death wherever excommunication is mentioned, and who would dare to suggest this ?

to the contrary by the first twelve centuries without exception. The great and holy doctors of that long period not only never thought of the possibility of such an emergency, but even when they considered the hypothesis of a diseased member spreading corruption, they contemplated an amputation of the same order as the evil itself—namely, such as is effected by the spiritual sword of excommunication. We have given the texts above. And is it not evident that the excommunication of the guilty is a solemn warning to all the faithful, sufficient to preserve from contagion all men of good-will ?

This is Taparelli's answer to the same objection : " Can implacable severity, and especially capital punishment, ever be *necessary* to a spiritual society ? I have proved elsewhere that a spiritual government, because it penetrates into a man's inmost thoughts, has less need of vigorous measures of coercion. In spite of that, I should not venture to say that the necessity could never present itself. . . . It appears to me clear that recourse to extreme measures is not in its nature incompatible with the idea of a religious society, especially among rude and uncivilized people ; but what shall we say of a Christian society, governed by a God who died for His enemies, and who has given His almighty word as a pledge of the perpetual endurance of His Church ? Certainly this word does not exempt her from using all necessary means ; but it may, on the other hand, diminish the necessity for violent measures, and show that they are inconsistent with the mercy of the Cross."

This is an indirect answer ; but to refute the argument directly, let us observe that the Church is invested with a twofold mission. Unlike the State, she is a perfect society, created to conquer as well as to reign. No one ever thinks of giving her an army, for her conquests must be spiritual ones ; " the right of making war does not belong to her."[1] Why should we give her executioners ? Why set up a contrast between her kingdom and her conquests, instead of trusting to the harmonious designs of God, who can provide as well for the preservation as for the expansion of His Church ?

God, in fact, can secure to His Church a full sufficiency of means in two ways : either by giving her the right and the power, or by preventing the emergency which would make that right and that power necessary.

Whether He confers the power or prevents the necessity for it, is the Church without resources ? The supposition of a problematical necessity need not trouble us, nor make us attribute to the Church a power which is inconsistent with her history and her spirit.

Is it even essential to a perfect society to have at its disposal means sufficient in every case to prevent it from being taken by surprise ? In that case, how many civil societies would lose their claim to be considered perfect societies ! A perfect society may perish ; it is not from its nature as a perfect society, but from the promise of Christ, that the Church derives its assurance of indefectibility. How many perfect societies are unable to withstand the attacks of their more powerful neighbours ! How many empires have fallen in consequence of invasions from without or revolutions from within !

[1] Taparelli, *Saggio*, n. 1487.

How many crimes are there against which every State finds itself powerless ! The Church, therefore, would not cease to be a perfect and supreme society even in the possible, though extremely improbable, case that adequate means of coercion failed her.

This, however, is not our solution of the difficulty. But when our adversaries allege that the Church, in view of such an extreme case, ought to possess the right of the sword, we reply with confidence that God will take care that the Church is never compelled to act in a manner inconsistent with her spirit. Of these two propositions, which at once appears the more probable ?

But there is more to be said. Facts show the falsity of the objection. In a Christian political society true religion becomes a social good which the public authorities are empowered and bound to defend by means appropriate to the customs and circumstances of the time. It is therefore protected against every emergency. But if the political society is not Christian, how can the Church ever take upon herself effectively to order an irreparable punishment ? The power which it is sought to attribute to her would therefore be illusory in the only case in which it might appear to be necessary.

This is all that the Church receives from the theory we are refuting—a sword which she is powerless to wield. And what is the price she would pay for the gift ? The sword, which could never do her any good, would do her infinite harm by destroying her reputation for gentleness, by estranging men's hearts from her, by creating prejudices against her far more injurious than the unpunished propagation of heretical opinions.

No necessity, then, confers upon the Church the right of the sword. Not the necessity of the whole: we may put aside the supposition, for the fate of the Church, which is destined to live and prosper in the midst of persecutions, can never depend on her power to punish. Not the necessity of a part, for the immediate and temporary good of a bloody repression which would be the work of the Church would be outweighed by the general and lasting, if not permanent, harm. A remedy which is worse than the disease is no remedy at all.

Shall we be called upon to explain certain facts—the facts of the Inquisition, to call it by its popular name? We shall refer to them in the second section of this part. For the present it is enough to draw attention to the number of Catholic writers who, without ignoring these facts, share our way of looking at them. This number alone proves that the bloody repression of heresy does not necessarily imply the existence in the Church of the right to punish with death.

III. THE FORMULA OF THE CHURCH'S RIGHT TO PUNISH.

SUMMARY: Originally the Church had at her disposal spiritual punishments, and afterwards reparable temporal punishments placed under the sanction of excommunication.—She may accept, and in certain circumstances demand, the assistance of the State for the reparable temporal punishments inflicted by her.—She cannot, even by consent of the State, inflict irreparable punishments.

"A perfect society," says Cardinal Cavagnis, "possesses *in the order to which it belongs* a plenitude of rights for all the means necessary to its end; but different ends call for different means, and therefore different rights."[1] That is an exact statement of the truth; and if we apply this principle to the Church, it will seem natural that if her children are given to her by an inward and visible grace, they should be cast out of her pale by a spiritual sanction. Thus there is perfect symmetry and consistence between the beginning and the end, between birth and death. In the higher order in which the Church is supreme she possesses a sanction as efficacious as that possessed by the State in the temporal order. She preserves and dispenses spiritual blessings, and deprives the wicked of them, just as the State deprives those who are condemned to death of the exterior goods committed to its care. The State, nevertheless, though not ceasing to be a perfect society, has no power to employ a spiritual sanction. Similarly, without denying the Church's character as a perfect society, tradition, Canon Law, and reason itself, declare that she has not the power to inflict irreparable punishments. We conclude, therefore, that Divine Providence has relieved the Church, which carries on the work of Christ, from the necessity of employing means which are repugnant to the spirit by which Christ desires that she should be animated.

Though it is beyond the exact scope of this chapter, our arguments logically lead us to take this view of the coercive power of the Church—namely, that neither by her own powers nor by concession of the State can the Church, as such, inflict *irreparable*

[1] *Op. cit.*, p. 196.

punishments. She has possessed the power of inflicting all other temporal punishments, and we recognize in her the right to claim the assistance of the State for the application of those temporal punishments which, in view of her spiritual end, she considers it proper in certain circumstances to prescribe or inflict. But if we confine our attention to the inherent power of the Church, that power which she possesses always and everywhere, we consider that her power is limited to those penalties, spiritual or temporal, which find their last sanction in the supreme penalty of excommunication.

SECOND SECTION: CIVIL TOLERANCE

CHAPTER I

PRELIMINARY DEFINITIONS AND GENERAL PLAN OF THE SECTION

SUMMARY: I.—Nominal description of civil tolerance.—In what sense we make it the exclusive work of the State.—What complete civil tolerance would imply.—There are not two schools, to be called, the one the school of tolerance, the other of intolerance.

II.—General views of the subject: its complexity.—Plan and arrangement of this section.

I.

THE effect of religious beliefs and philosophical opinions on the status, the rights, and liberties of citizens, gives rise to the problem of civil tolerance.

Whatever opinion we form on the duties of the State, and the corresponding rights of the Church, it is materially within the discretion of the temporal government to grant or deny to the Church its visible help and support. For this reason, putting aside for the present the question of responsibility, we consider this tolerance as the special work of the civil power.

Civil tolerance may be looked at from many points of view, and lends itself to many divisions.

In regard to its supreme *principle* or its reasons, civil tolerance asserts itself as a permanent, sacred, inviolable institution, which is *dogmatic tolerance;* or it is content to be a concession, a rule of the nature of a compromise, founded on circumstances, which is *practical tolerance*.

The *extension* of civil tolerance may be considered as it is shown to the religions permitted in the State, and to the citizens and their liberties.

With reference to *religions*, civil tolerance may extend to all, or may be restricted to some only—as, for example, to Christian bodies, or religions already established.

It may permit them to make converts, or may simply authorize their existence.

It may grant them public and social life, either in their temples or outside, with liberty to form a hierarchical organization or to possess property ; or it may put certain limitations on that public life by decrees on the subject of associations, processions, and the public exhibition of religious symbols ; or it may even recognize only the individual liberty of conscience of their members.

With reference to *citizens*, tolerance may leave them free choice to continue in their own religion, or pass from one religion to another, or to no religion at all.

It may place all citizens on a footing of perfect equality, or content itself with punishing no one for his religion, while making certain civil rights depend on the profession of faith.

It grants or refuses them the free manifestation and propagation of their opinions and beliefs.

In regard to its *practice*, tolerance of opinions and creeds may be combined with the recognition of a

GENERAL VIEW

State religion, with favours reserved to the true religion, or to religion in general ; or it may observe strict neutrality, giving no preference to one religion over another, or to religion over unbelief. Experience tells us that there are two kinds of neutrality—the one sympathetic and trusting, like that of the United States of America; the other contemptuous and suspicious, like that of the present French Republic or its younger sister, the new Republic of Portugal.

In the opinion of many modern political writers, the complete scheme of civil tolerance implies—

The dogma of tolerance.

Perfect equality, civil and political, among believers in any religion whatever, and unbelievers.

The free manifestation and diffusion of all opinions and all systems.

The perfect neutrality of the State, and its indifference to religion and irreligion.

This description seems to us to err both by excess and by defect.

On the one hand, as we shall see better by-and-by, it is not necessary for the existence of tolerance that it should be raised to a dogma ; and the most liberal tolerance does not require official indifference in religious matters. Moreover, the State, by dissociating itself from religion and from God, does not remain neutral ; it professes practical atheism, and by its very abstention preaches religious indifference, and so, as Sarcey said, men are accustomed to do without religion, and are slowly and gradually drawn away from the faith.

On the other hand, simple individual liberty does not give liberty to religious bodies ; it gives no security to the social form and organization which are essential to all religions. The programme of tolerance, therefore, is not complete, unless it contains some provision guaranteeing the freedom of religious society.

It may be said that complete civil tolerance does not yet exist except as a dream. In many countries the head of the State must belong to some particular religious body. The rulers abandon the position of unstable equilibrium in which they would be placed by abstract neutrality, in order to show themselves either timidly friendly to religion or, more frequently, boldly hostile to it ; and the Church nowhere enjoys perfect freedom. Even in Belgium, where civil tolerance exists to a greater extent than in any other country in Europe, the priority of civil marriage, which is obligatory under the Constitution, is derogatory to the liberty of worship.

In spite of the variety of opinions and systems, neither complete intolerance nor complete tolerance finds any defenders, as we shall proceed to prove. We cannot allow any class of persons to arrogate to themselves the exclusive right to be called tolerant, and to fix the reproach of intolerance on all their opponents ; and this is the less permissible because the specious banner of tolerance often covers the most insidious designs against religion. M. Briand, addressing the extreme Left in the French Parliament, repeated, almost word for word, the statement of Sieyes in the Constituent Assembly of 1791, when he said : "You have so little idea of liberty that you cannot tolerate it."[1]

[1] Session of October 25, 1910.

II.

Now that we have arrived at civil tolerance, we have reached the heart of our subject, but we are still faced with this difficulty: In the minds of many, if not of most persons, the problem of tolerance is reduced entirely to civil tolerance; and no one can remain indifferent to a matter in which every practice supposes a theory, in which every speculation leads straight to practical conclusions, in which religion and its rights, the State and its mission, the private individual and the guarantees of his liberty, are all vitally concerned. But this universal interest is mixed up with too many different passions to facilitate clearness of views and harmony of conclusions. Philosophers do not agree upon the principles, nor historians upon the facts, nor politicians in their appreciation of the facts or the lessons they teach.

Moreover, the problem of tolerance varies in its aspect with the centuries; its Protean form changes with the various doctrines which bear upon tolerance and its fundamental principles, with the political factions which use it as a weapon of party strife, and with the circumstances which increase or diminish the necessity for it. It originated in the day when, thanks principally to the influence of Christianity, men rose in conscientious resistance to a tyrannical law. It was then harmoniously solved in Europe by universal acceptance of the same faith, and was again raised at the time of the disastrous schism which destroyed the religious unity of the civilized world. It spread till the beginning of the nineteenth century, when it was radically modified, as discussions extended to the existence and personality of God, and soon after to morality and social order. An intolerance of an unforeseen character arose at the same time, so violent in its first outbursts that its very exaggeration put an end to it, apparently for ever. But by degrees it reappears, preparing and already renewing its attacks on religion.

The problem of tolerance does not present itself, either theoretically or practically, in the same form to-day as yesterday; nor was it yesterday the same as it was the day before.

Our task therefore is somewhat complicated, and the order to be followed creates a new difficulty; we have to state and discuss principles, and to come to a conclusion on controverted facts, and therefore cannot adopt a purely logical or a purely historical method. Considering the unequal manner in which the facts agree with the theories, and also the diversity of the principles appealed to, we have thought it best, for the sake of clearness, to divide the subject into three periods, ending respectively with the Reformation of the sixteenth century, the French Revolution, and the present day.

The first period, in which a great Empire fell and gave place first to barbarous kingdoms and then to the Christian republic of the Middle Ages, is more full of events than theoretical discussions. All interest is concentrated on the explanation of facts, and is finally absorbed in a judicial institution—the Inquisition. This is what, in spite of the multitude and diversity of facts, gives to this period a sufficient unity. The principles are, then, in the acts, and we have only to consider the policy followed and form our judgment upon it. In the course of the second period tolerance is discussed among Christians, or at least among theists ; acts are distinguished from opinions, and are influenced by them. We shall principally occupy ourselves with a rapid review of systems, and with criticisms upon them, without refusing to the facts the consideration they demand. In the third period the ground of the discussion is changed ; it is no longer religious, but legal. The adversaries of religion flatter themselves that they have secured a lasting victory for tolerance. We shall have to test the truth of their assertion. Finally, we shall elect for a theory of tolerance which is in accordance with Catholic principles, and is the only one that can be justified by sound reason.

CHAPTER II

CIVIL TOLERANCE DOWN TO THE SIXTEENTH CENTURY

I. SUCCESSIVE POLICIES IN THE MATTER OF HERESY.

SUMMARY: Intolerance of the Christian Emperors.—This is real, as are their encroachments on the domain of religion.—But these Princes are excusable, and their acts must not be exaggerated.—Sketch of the imperial policy in the matter of heresy.—Attitude of the Popes. —Successive phases of under the barbarian Kings, and under Charlemagne.—Intervention of the people.— The principle of repression introduced into legislation in the thirteenth century.—Obstinate and relapsed heretics incur capital punishment, even death by burning.—Organization of the Inquisition.—This law governs Europe until the sixteenth century.

As heirs of an unrestrained despotism, the Roman Emperors did not at their baptism lay aside the traditions of absolutism to which the world had become accustomed. Without a miracle such as God is not in the habit of working, they could not at once solve with any certainty a question which their predecessors had never even put to themselves —that of the limits by which their power was bounded. For the first time two autonomous societies, religious and political society, had to exist on the same territory. Many encroachments on the domain of religion must have been committed unconsciously, and the complete powerlessness of the victim made even the thought of protest impossible. It is true that dogmatic definitions and the sacred functions of the Church were left to the Bishops ; but for everything else, for all that concerns the exterior discipline of the Church, all right was arrogated by the Christian Emperor : the right of banishing Arian or Catholic Bishops according to his own will,[1] the right of assembling Councils, of legislating for priests and monks, of imposing religious uniformity ; and such acts as these surprised no one.

Unless we make allowance for the circumstances and customs of the time, we shall be unjust to the Princes, who thought they were acting within their rights, and also to the Church, which permitted their acts ; and we shall not be able rightly to apportion the responsibility. The objections thus made will have only the value of anachronisms.

But when we deal with excesses and encroachments, we must not exaggerate or darken the reality.

The pagan Emperors had hunted down sorcerers and magicians with the utmost severity.[2] This policy was not inspired by any zeal for orthodoxy, nor can the baptized Emperors who continued it be charged with religious fanaticism. Diocletian

[1] " Naturally," writes Mommsen, " the divergence of religious opinions among the different Sovereigns and the good pleasure of the monarch gave rise to much that was arbitrary, and to numerous variations in fixing the line of demarcation between true and false Catholics " (*Roman Penal Law*, translated by Duquesne, t. 2, p. 312).

[2] This severity had its influence on the argument of the apologetical treatises, and partly explains the silence maintained on the argument of miracles at that time ; it was necessary to guard against any suspicion of magic.

had already condemned the Manichæans to the flames; and if still later they were under various names the objects of special enactments,[1] these exceptional laws were directed less against heresy than against the antisocial tendencies of the sect. And we should be reluctant to transform into martyrs of free thought the Priscillianists and Donatists who fell under the sword of justice.[2] Neither Leo the Great, who mentioned with approval certain condemnations of the Priscillianists, nor those Bishops[3] who, wearied of the Donatist excesses, brought them up before the magistrates, can be charged with intolerance, even in the most modern sense of the word. And Charles Lea is not justified in writing in this connection that the Church by their act was definitely committed to the extirpation of heresy by all means whatsoever.[4] Even at the present day

[1] The legislation seems to have been milder under Arcadius, Honorius, and Theodosius. The law 4 *De Hæreticis* (i. 5) of these Emperors omits the extreme penalty; but the law 2. eodem, thus sums up a Constitution of Justinian: "Ubicumque Manichæi inveniantur, capite damnandi sunt."

[2] These heresies have a clearly marked antisocial character. "Manichæos seu Manichæas vel Donatistas meritissima severitate persequimur" (l. 4, *Princ. De Hæreticis*, i. 5).

[3] The Bishops, indeed, did not desire any sanguinary measures of repression.

[4] *History of the Inquisition in the Middle Ages*, vol. i., p. 215. This book imposes upon many persons by its confused mass of apparent erudition, but it is as deficient in synthesis as in impartiality and accuracy See the criticism of M. Paul Fournier in the *Revue d'Histoire Eccl.*, t. 3 (1901), pp. 708-719. M. Kurth also does not hesitate to condemn it as unfair and prejudiced. For instance, p. 215 and the following pages of the first volume, full of references as they are, so entirely misrepresent the opinions of various Fathers, the action of the Emperors, and the

TREATMENT OF HERESY

it is well to remember this : disturbers of the public peace and common criminals must not be allowed to find an assurance of impunity in heresy or irreligion.

If we compare the texts of laws with what history tells us of their application, we shall draw these conclusions as to the official repression of heresy by the Christian Emperors of Rome and Byzantium : (1) The Christian Emperors like Constantine desired to unite the Empire and religion ; they saw in religious unity a guarantee of political unity ; orthodoxy was expected to strengthen patriotism.[1] (2) Yet they had no desire to obtain conversions to the faith by force.[2] (3) They were more severe against proselytism and outward manifestation than against the heresy itself ;[3] the proscription was specially directed against certain sects which had become a real danger to the public peace.[4] (4) Their laws

---

influence exercised by the Church on the sanguinary repression of heresy, as to render them unrecognizable. See Maillet-Hanquet, *op. cit.*, pp. 20-26, and the authors quoted below.

[1] "Die Grundsätze auf denen sie (die Strafgesetzgebung) beruht, sind klar ; sie sind gegeben . . . durch die herrschende Ueberzeugung dass in der Einheit des Glaubens eine Schutzwehr des Reichs liege" (Loening, *Geschichte des deutschen Kirchenrechts*, i. 96). See also Diehl, *Justinien, L'Œuvre Religieuse*).

[2] "The Roman State constantly refrained from the use of coercion to make converts, on the ground that conversions obtained by such means would be merely superficial" (Mommsen, *Roman Public Law*, translated by Duquesne, vol. ii., pp. 313, 314).

[3] *Cf.* l. 8, § 5, C. i. 5 ; Theodosian Code, xvi. 5, c. 34, 36, 51, 56, 58, 63, 66. *Cf.* Loening, *op. cit.*, t. i., p. 99. The threat against proselytism dates from Theodosius (Theodosian Code, xvi. 5, c. 3). It was afterwards extended to the holding of public assemblies (cc. 51 and 66, *ibid.*).

[4] "Einzelne Sekten waren in der That eine Gefahr für den öffentlichen Frieden geworden" (Loening, t. i., p. 68).

were more terrible in their texts than in their effects.[1] (5) These laws being enacted *motu proprio* by the prince, no responsibility attaches to the Church.

It is true that the Popes, from the beginning, approved of the protection which the Christian Emperors offered to the Church for the maintenance of its unity; the letters which they wrote to obtain the removal of Bishops or Abbots who favoured schism or heresy[2] can neither surprise nor scandalize

---

[1] *Cf.* Loening, i. 99. Mommsen similarly recognizes that Imperial Rome confined itself to restricting the patrimonial rights of the heretic—his free choice of a residence, and his capacity to hold public office. " In general," he says (*op. cit.*, t. 2, p. 315), "legislation took no other measures against heretics, though there have frequently been penalties prescribed against particular sects." He mentions in a note heavy pecuniary fines, confiscations, banishment, and even the penalty of death. But for this last he refers to the Theodosian Code, xvi. 5. 7. 1., in which this penalty is not mentioned. No doubt he meant to quote xvi. 5. 9. 1., in which this penalty is directed, not against heretics in general, but against certain Manichæans who called themselves *Encratitæ* (continent). MM. Maillet-Hanquet are wrong in speaking of this as a general law renewed by Arcadius. He only ratified the previously existing laws, without specifically mentioning any; and, according to the testimony of Sozomenus, Theodosius intended not to punish, but to terrify. So Socrates does not even mention those laws of Theodosius of which Sozomenus says that they contained heavy penalties ($\chi\alpha\lambda\acute{\epsilon}\pi\alpha s\ \tau\iota\mu\omega\rho\acute{\iota}\alpha s$) against heresy. See C. Theod., xvi. 5. 25; Sozomen., *Hist. Eccl.*, 7, 12 (M.P.G., t. 67, cols. 1445, 1446); Socrates, 5, 10 (M.P.G., t. 67, cols. 593, 594). The picture of the Roman legislation against heresy is much less dark in the learned works of Hinschius, Mommsen, Loening, than in certain French authors—*e.g.*, Tanon, *Histoire des Tribunaux de l'Inquisition en France;* Paris, 1893.

[2] *E.g.*, St. Celestine, Ep. 22 (M.P.L., t. 50, cols. 540, 541). He acted in the interest of peace and for the preservation of others. See also Ep. 19 (M., *ibid.*, cols. 511, 512). So also St. Leo the Great, Ep. 84 (M.P.L., t. 54, col. 922). But see Ep. 45 (M., *ibid.*, col. 833) on the violent acts of the heretics.

TREATMENT OF HERESY

anyone; they prove simply the care of the pastor for the peace of the Church and the safety of his flock, but they did not demand the infliction of torture in the name of religion. M. de Cauzons[1] considers it a plausible conjecture that "if the sentence of death was so rarely passed for religious offences, the fact is due to the influence of the ecclesiastical members of the Imperial Council."

MM. Maillet-Hanquet, though they exaggerate to some extent the severity of the Roman laws, describe in these terms the attitude of the religious authorities: "If they thought it necessary to excommunicate heretics and expel them from the pale of the Church, if they called in certain cases for the interference of the civil power, they do not appear to have acted for the purpose of procuring the enactment of laws condemning heretics to death; they seem rather to have been entirely opposed to such legislation. Nevertheless, when the laws had been finally passed against the Manichæans, they did not think it necessary to raise their voices publicly against them. As they considered the Manichæans as constituting a fundamental danger to society, they could not refuse to society the right to protect itself."[2]

If the Roman Empire classified heresy among offences against the State, *inter crimina publica*, as was made clear by Frederic II., the Merovingians cared much less for religious unity,[3] and the Roman law of the Visigoths[4] reproduces only the penalties

---

[1] Alias the Abbé Thomas, *Histoire de l'Inquisition en France*, t. 1, p. 186.
[2] *Op. cit.*, p. 25.
[3] Loening, *op. cit.*, ii., pp. 46, 48, 53.   [4] *Ibid.*, ii. 43.

prescribed against certain sects—the Manichæans, Eunomeans, and Montanists. Charlemagne was actuated by political motives when he promulgated the celebrated capitulary, which, as we have already seen, was condemned by Alcuin, because it required baptism under pain of death.[1] With scarcely any other exception, the Carlovingian legislation was opposed to the penalty of death, which was not even inflicted for murder, " and this was entirely owing to the influence of the Church, thus showing how she preserved to the beginning of the Middle Ages that spirit of clemency by which she was distinguished in the first days of Christianity."[2]

Antisocial sects, which remind us in some respects [3] of the Manichæans [4] and the Donatists,[5] were the scourge of the eleventh and twelfth centuries. That of the Catharists [6] especially astonished men, equally

[1] *Capitul. reg. Franc.*, i., p. 69, *n.* 26, c. 8 (*Mon. Germ. Hist.*, t. 1, pp. 48-50).

[2] Maillet-Hanquet, *op. cit.*, pp. 28, 29. Relying on a text of the celebrated Hincmar of Rheims, these authors remark that there were already declared opponents of capital punishment, who disputed the right even of the Prince to draw the sword.

[3] We do not wish to exaggerate the resemblance, or to settle the delicate question of the relation between the sects, or whether one was the descendant of the other.

[4] By their dualism, their syncretism, and their effort to obtain universal domination.

[5] By their rigorist and revolutionary schismatic fanaticism. They made the efficacy of the sacraments dependent upon the personal holiness of the minister.

[6] Catharists, or pure persons. In the Middle Ages, " heretics " meant the Catharists; and this name, sometimes corrupted into Pathari or Gazari, has produced the Dutch word *Ketter*, and the German *Ketzer*. The Catharist Church, the only pure Church, (as they professed) and the only one opposed to the wicked and decadent Church of Rome, included (1) the *perfect ones*, who practised an anti-

by its absurdity, its zeal, and its success. Lea says :[1] "Had Catharism become dominant, or even had it been allowed to exist on equal terms, its influence could not have failed to become disastrous. . . . The conscientious belief in such a creed could only lead man back in time to his original condition of savagism."[2] A contemporary author compares the number of such sectarians to the number of grains of sand on the seashore.[3] The danger which they caused to society rekindled the fires lighted against the Manichæans and persons who practised witchcraft. Sometimes the repression was regularly

---

social asceticism, which obliged them to break family ties and live a life of rigorous poverty and solitude ; and (2) simple *believers*, who were allowed to marry and possess property. The latter, if they wished to be saved, were bound, at least at the hour of death, to receive from one of the perfect the *consolamentum*, or absolution, which effaced their sins ; but in case of recovery they were constrained to a rigorous observance of the rules. By this ceremony they were admitted into the Church, of which, until that time, they had been merely catechumens.

[1] *Op. cit.*, t. 1 p. 106.

[2] This judgment is independent of any opinion which may be formed on their mode of life, and is justified by their asceticism alone, which M. Charles Molinier admits to have been opposed to the happiness and development of the human race (Ch. Molinier, *L'Église et la Société Cathares*, in the *Revue Historique*, 1907, t. 94 and 95, p. 290).

[3] William of Newburgh, quoted by Maillet-Hanquet, p. 29. Almost all the documents relating to the Catharist heresy come from Catholic sources. M. Jean Guiraud very forcibly rebukes those authors who refuse on this ground to accept the information so given (*Cartulaire de N. D. de Prouille*, Preface, pp. xx-xxii). M. Molinier considers this language exaggerated. However, his own calculations lead him to the conclusion that there were 3,000,000 to 6,000,000 believers, of whom 2,000,000 to 4,000,000 were in Italy, 200,000 to 400,000 in France, 700,000 or 800,000 in the East, and about 3,100 perfect ones (see the articles quoted, t. 95, pp. 278, 279).

ordered by the public authorities; sometimes, and more frequently, it was the act of the enraged populace, who demanded the execution of the disturbers of their peace, and who, afraid of the clemency of the priests, invaded the prisons in the same fashion as a lynching crowd in modern America, and thus drew down upon themselves the thunders of the Church.[1]

Lea himself, whose testimony on this point is very valuable, gives this example: In 1114 the Bishop of Rheims, who had convicted some heretics by the ordeal of water, consulted the Council of Beauvais as to the punishment to be inflicted; in his absence, the people, fearing the lenience of the Bishops, broke open the prison, and burned the prisoners.[2] "These struggles," observes M. Julien Havet, "between an over-zealous people and a more tolerant clergy were not uncommon at that period."[3] It is well known how energetically Wazon, the Bishop of Liège, whose voice was listened to even at Rome, pleaded with the Episcopate the cause of mercy.

This resistance to exterior severity, however, slackened by degrees, and ceased altogether at the

[1] Some inhabitants of Cambrai had burnt a heretic. Gregory VII., by his letter of March 25, 1077, ordered Godefroi, Bishop of Paris, to hold an inquiry, and excommunicate the authors and accomplices of the crime. "Si eos ad tantam impietatem impias manus extendisse agnoveris" (*Mon. Germ. Hist. Script.*, 7, p. 540, *n.* 31).

[2] *Op. cit.*, vol. i., p. 351. For "Rheims" we must read "Soissons." The passage is borrowed from *Guidberti Abbatis de Novigente Monodiarum*, l. 3, c. 17.

[3] *L'hérésie et le Bras Séculier au Moyen Âge jusqu'au XIII*ᵉ *Siècle;* from *Bibliothèque de l'École de Chartes*, 1880, or *Œuvres*, t. 2, 117.

TREATMENT OF HERESY

end of the twelfth century. The Bishops yielded to the current of public opinion, which was that of the people and the Prince, and which was explained by the antisocial character of the prevailing errors. Moreover, the least scrupulous and least pious monarchs, the declared enemies of the Popes, made themselves conspicuous by an animosity which may have been inspired by various motives—by genuine zeal for religion and social order, by political duplicity, or even by cupidity, for certain confiscations came in very conveniently to fill the coffers of the State.

In short, in the thirteenth century the policy of repression prevailed everywhere; but it must be remembered, as we shall have occasion to point out later on, that the heresy so repressed was that of obstinate or relapsed persons.

Princes and people, united in their desire to repress heretical apostasy, agreed in inflicting on obstinate or relapsed heretics the penalty of death; and the Emperor who first made it a rule of common law, Frederic II. (Constitution of 1224), laid down that this should be death by burning.[1] But custom

---

[1] This form of execution had passed from the Roman law into the barbarian codes. In the summary executions of the twelfth century the people more than once had recourse to it. The *Chronicon Universale Anonymi Laudunensis* (edition Cartellieri-Stecheli, p. 29) records that in 1204 several persons, convicted of heresy in presence of the Archbishop of Rheims at Braine-sur-Nesle (Aisne), were condemned to the stake by Count Robert, Countess Yolande, and numerous assessors. The heretics of the twelfth and thirteenth centuries were connected with the Manichæan sects whose leaders had been burnt under Diocletian. Naturally, the punishment of death by burning commended itself to the German Emperor, who professed

permitted a relapsed person who repented to escape this punishment, and in many countries heresiarchs were practically the only persons to be delivered alive to the flames (see Pirhing in l. 5, t. 7, *n.* 92 ; he quotes Farinacius).

Such is the law which governed Europe until the time of the Reformation, and even after that time was retained on the statute books of various countries, either in its original form or as amended by later edicts of partial toleration, and it did not disappear entirely until the end of the eighteenth century. It must not, however, be concluded from this that there was a relentless or uninterrupted persecution of heresy, real or pretended, during six hundred years. Even those books which profess to give a dramatic representation of the war against heresy show us clearly, if we read with attention, that the treatment of heretics varied according to time and place. The severity shown in Spain, especially after the time of Ferdinand and Isabella—that is to say, from the last quarter of the fifteenth century—was never known in Portugal. In France the Inquisition was most energetic in the thirteenth century, and then only for the purpose of getting rid of the Catharists and the Albigenses. Before Charles V. and Philip II. the struggle against

---

to follow the traditions of the great Roman Empire. "Auctoritate nostra," said Frederic II., "ignis judicio condemnandus" (March, 1224, *Mon. Germ. Hist. Legum.*, t. 2, p. 252). The old Canonists, yielding to the necessity of proving everything by Scripture as well as reason, found their warrant in St. John xv. 6 : " If any one abide not in Me, he shall be cast forth as a branch, and shall wither, and they shall gather him up and cast him into the fire, and he shall be burned."

religious error occupies but little place in the national history of Belgium. The repression was more moderate in Italy, principally in Central Italy and the Papal States, and everywhere short outbursts of violence were succeeded by long periods of tranquillity.

The measures adopted against heresy by the Emperors of Rome and Byzantium, and the appeals made by the Church to the secular arm during their time, call for no special remark, and the encroachments of the secular authorities on the spiritual domain are explained by a confusion of powers very natural at that period. The Church asked only for a twofold protection—protection for her ministers and the faithful against those who were criminals under the common law; protection for her doctrine against those who threatened the unity of Christian society. That protection, which the Church desired to have free from bloodshed, cannot in principle be denied her, without refusing to acknowledge her right to teach or her social constitution, without repudiating even the defence of morality. In short, she justifies herself by the reasons which refute the theory of absolute tolerance of which we shall speak in the following chapters. It is unnecessary to say more at present on the subject.

The severe laws enacted in the Middle Ages against heretics, the capital sentences passed upon them, and the procedure by which they were condemned, raise questions which we cannot pass over in silence. It is of special interest to know what heretics were prosecuted to the death, and on what grounds they became liable to the extreme penalty of the law. In spite of all that has been already written on the subject, the reader will still look forward to the explanation we have to offer of the institution whose name is always connected with the sanguinary repression of heresy in the Middle Ages—namely, the Inquisition. We will endeavour to satisfy him, first disposing of the question of form and procedure.

II. THE INQUISITION.

SUMMARY: The Inquisition was not a single institution, and it had no monopoly of the severity exercised against heretics.—Origin and genesis of the Inquisition.—Etymological definition.—Its procedure and methods.—Punishments inflicted by the Inquisitors.—The surrender of criminals to the secular arm.—Intercession of the ecclesiastical judge.—Definition of the Inquisition.—Objections made to its procedure.—These objections critically examined.—Had the accused person anyone to defend him?—The interrogatory.—The torture.—The intervention of the Church, and especially the duty imposed upon the ecclesiastical judge of appealing for mercy.

It is inexact to speak of *an* Inquisition, since the inquisitions in different countries differed in their origin, which was sometimes political or national, as in Spain;[1] in their procedure, which was influenced by the constitution of the States;[2] and in their

[1] We speak of the Inquisition which, at the request of Isabella, was canonically erected by a Bull of Sixtus IV. on November 1, 1478. Without disputing the ecclesiastical character of the institution, we call it *national*, because its establishment was demanded by motives of patriotism; and *political*, because it at once became a State tribunal. See Landrieux, *L'Inquisition*, pp. 111, 130.

[2] Liège offers in this respect a peculiarity probably unique in history. The citizen suspected of heresy had first to be convicted *par loy et franchise*—that is, by the

THE INQUISITION

action. This, again, differed at different periods. Outside Spain the Inquisition was principally employed against the Catharists.

The Inquisition is not responsible for all the severities exercised against heretics. There was no question of it in the fifth century in the proceedings against the Manichæans and the Donatists, nor did it exist when Alphonsus II., King of Aragon, in 1194 began a persecution against the Waldensians, which became sanguinary under his son, Peter II., in 1197. In England the Inquisition, properly so called, exercised its functions only in the case of the Templars; nevertheless, the Statute of 1400, *De hæretico comburendo*, fixed the penalty of death as the normal punishment of heresy.[1] In France the Inquisition was speedily supplanted by the Parliament;[2] in the Low Countries the great severities were the work of an Inquisition irregularly constituted by Charles V.[3]

With these reservations, we proceed to consider the different points which require elucidation.

First as to the *historical origin* of the Inquisition. There is no great difficulty about the date of its

---

Court of Aldermen—and then sent by them, as a heretic, before the ecclesiastical judges (Lonchay, *Les Édits des Princes-Évêques de Liège en Matière d'Hérésie*, p. 34).

[1] Vacandard, *L'Inquisition*, p. 265.

[2] As early as 1331, a Decree of Parliament declared that the tribunal of the Inquisition was a royal jurisdiction: "*Et declaratum quod curia inquisitionis erat curia regalis, non ecclesiastica*" (quoted by Tanon, *op. cit.*, p. 550). He adds that from that time commenced the decadence of that institution, the last tribunal of which—that of Toulouse—was suppressed under Louis XIV.

[3] See Pirenne, *Histoire de Belgique*, t. 3, pp. 335, 336.

first establishment, as most authorities agree in fixing it approximately at A.D. 1231.

There is much more discussion as to the *genesis* of the institution. Mgr. Douais sees in it an episode of the struggle between the clergy and the Empire. To frustrate the usurping designs which Frederic II. concealed under a show of orthodoxy, Gregory IX. imposed upon him a pontifical judge, by whom he preserved to the Church her prerogatives in matters of faith and her spiritual autonomy. As is usual in the case of wisely-established and progressive institutions, the Inquisition survived the occasion which called it into being, and from the countries in which it was first constituted was extended into the greater part of Christendom. M. Jordan, in a series of exhaustive articles published in the *Annales de Philosophie Chrétienne*,[1] vigorously combats the opinions of the learned Bishop of Beauvais, and declares that they are without foundation. The documents exchanged between the Pope and the Emperor make no charge, and express no fears, of usurpation on the Emperor's part in the matter of heresy, it is true; but this fact does not strengthen the argument of M. Jordan, for we can understand the reasons for such reticence in diplomatic correspondence. On the other hand, the explanation of Mgr. Douais fits in very well with the general purpose of the appointment of pontifical delegates— viz., to affirm and maintain the authority of the Pope whom they represented.

[1] June to August, 1907, and following volumes: *La Responsabilité de l'Eglise dans la Répression de l'Hérésie au Moyen Âge.*

It is certain also that the secular Princes more than once claimed exclusive cognizance of the crime of heresy, and M. Lonchay remarks[1] that numerous conflicts arose on this point between the two authorities, and M. Pirenne relates how as late as the sixteenth century Adrian VI. treated Charles V. exactly as, according to Mgr. Douais, Gregory IX. treated Frederic II.[2] The temptation must have been much stronger for the Emperors of Germany, as they claimed to be the successors of the Roman Emperors; and in prescribing punishments for heretics, Frederic II. took care to lay stress on the fact that he acted on his own authority. See the whole of his Constitution *Commissi nobis*, at the commencement of which he asserts that he holds from God the Imperial power and a material sword, the exercise of which is distinct from sacerdotal functions : " *Quo divisim a sacerdotio fungimur.*"[3]

We would not then refuse to the explanation of Mgr. Douais the value that the prelate attaches to it himself—namely, that of a probable and plausible conjecture—but though the fear of Imperial encroachment perhaps served as the proximate

[1] *Les Édits des Princes-Évêques de Liège en Matière d'Hérésie*, p. 34.

[2] *Histoire de Belgique*, t. 3, p. 336. "The Pope did not intend to abdicate in favour of the State, or to give up to the Emperor and his agents the defence of the Faith. On June 1, 1523, to the great disgust of Margaret of Austria and Charles V., a Bull of Adrian VI. nominated Van der Hulst, although a layman, and by special derogation of Canon Law, *universalem et generalem inquisitorem et investigatorem* in the Burgundian provinces. Thenceforward the Commissary of the Emperor became Pontifical Inquisitor, and ceased to be the agent of the Prince."

[3] In the Constitution of 1224, the heretic is burned by his authority (*auctoritate nostra concremandus*).

occasion, there were other reasons for giving to an Inquisitor delegated by the Pope a regular position by the side of the Diocesan Bishop. We may point to that desire for energetic action against heresy which is so clearly manifested in the Pontifical and Conciliar Acts of the twelfth century; to the insufficiency of episcopal action,[1] which was too local and too dissimilar, and sometimes too wanting in independence to carry great weight; and, finally, to the centralizing and organizing spirit of Gregory IX., of which his codification of Canon Law gives sufficient evidence.

Etymologically, the Inquisition denotes not so much a judicial tribunal as a criminal procedure in which the magistrate takes the initiative, and proceeds to hold an inquiry without waiting for a private citizen to take upon himself, as he was formerly entitled to do, the responsibility of the accusation. In criminal matters the procedure followed by the Inquisition now universally prevails.[2]

As an institution, the Inquisition shows us the action taken by the co-operation of the Church and the State against heresy.

The trial proceeded at first before the ecclesiastical magistrate or Inquisitor, permanently delegated as judge by the Pope, and acting as assessor to the Bishop, who still preserved among his other prerogatives that of judging of religious error. After

[1] This reason is expressly alleged by Gregory IX., when, on April 13, 1233, he informs the Bishops of France that he has invested the Dominicans with the functions of Inquisitors in that country and the neighbouring provinces.

[2] We do not understand M. Vacandard's preference (*L'Inquisition*, p. 275) for the *accusatio*, which is now universally given up.

THE INQUISITION

various changes in the law, it was finally settled that in grave cases, unless the Inquisitor concurred with the Bishop or his representative, there could be no conviction.[1] The proceedings were secret. The accused knew the charges that were made against him, but did not know his accusers, and was not, as a rule, confronted with the witnesses.

By way of compensation a custom was established, and even sanctioned by common law, of summoning a number of men called *boni viri*, or *periti*, whose duty it was, after being sworn on the Gospels to secrecy and impartiality, to express an opinion as to the honesty of the witnesses, to check the depositions, and even to advise as to the sentence to be passed—penance at the discretion of the Inquisitor, imprisonment, or delivery to the secular arm. The opinion of these jurors, as they would be called nowadays, was not binding on the Inquisitors, who were, however, in the habit of accepting it, and sometimes of mitigating the sentence suggested.[2]

The Inquisitor, on arriving in a country with his credentials duly verified, commenced by publishing in the Churches a time of *grace* for all voluntary retractions. When this time had elapsed, the denunciations received led to a preliminary judicial information, which resulted in a certain number of accused persons being brought before the Court. Every accused person was at least suspected of heresy, if not a notorious heretic; and some *prima*

[1] See the Constitution of Gregory X. of 1273. Lea deals with these changes in the law (*op. cit.*, t. 1, p. 375).
[2] Tanon, *op. cit.*, pp. 422, 423.

TREATMENT OF HERESY

facie evidence of guilt was required before special proceedings could be instituted against any person.

The first part of the proceedings was naturally directed to establishing the *fact* of heresy.

This point being established, the accused was invited to retract his errors; and if he refused to do so, the second stage commenced,[1] which often lasted a long time, sometimes for months, or even more than a year. During that time the judge endeavoured by exhortation, by advice, or even by detention in custody, to obtain the conversion or abjuration of the accused persons.[2] In most cases he succeeded, and the heretic escaped on the first occasion from all civil punishment. Sometimes, however, in consequence of the gravity of the

---

[1] We cannot refrain from comparing this procedure with that of certain Roman Emperors, like Decius, who issued edicts of persecution against the Christians. There also we find a general invitation to sacrifice to the gods, a convenient time of grace, and subsequently persistent pressure put upon the victims to induce them to apostatize.

[2] "A way of escape is still open to them (heretics), and the judge does his best in all sincerity to induce them to make use of it. He will endeavour to obtain their abjuration, and will sometimes succeed without any difficulty. Sometimes, on the contrary, and especially when the accused person is a highly educated man and capable of carrying on a discussion, a real theological tournament is commenced, which may last a long time. The Inquisitor listens with patience to his arguments, and replies to them; tries to clear up his doubts; contests his authorities, or quotes others; is careful not to press him unduly, and to give him time for reflection. . . . The Bishop, or the Inquisitor, or, failing them, a commission of ten or twelve theologians, endeavour to persuade the heretic. If he resists, he is not at once delivered to the secular arm, even when in his desire for martyrdom he himself demands it. He is kept in prison six months or a year, if necessary, leniency alternating with severity, threats with promises." (Jordan, *Annales de Phil.*, ix., pp. 46, 47).

THE INQUISITION

offence, the delay of the accused person in retracting his error, or the fact that the judge had good reason for not believing in the sincerity of his retraction, it was considered necessary, even after the abjuration, to impose one of the customary penalties, such as wearing a cross marked upon the clothing, a pilgrimage, fine, or imprisonment; the imprisonment might even be perpetual.

The judge in these cases, contrary to the practice in other trials, had the power to commute the sentence. A distinction was, indeed, made between the *simple* and the *qualified* (irremissibiter) condemnation to perpetual imprisonment. If the condemned person gave satisfaction, the simple sentence was remitted after three years, the other after eight years.[1]

For what purpose were these penalties inflicted? Undoubtedly for the good of the soul, which required to be strengthened in its good resolutions and purified by expiatory penance; but also for the good of the Christian community and the removal of all danger of contagion.[2] If the guilty person

[1] *Cf.* Reiffenstuel, in l. 5, t. 7, *n.* 332.

[2] M. Jordan denies to these sentences the character of penalties, properly so called, and sees in them nothing but works of satisfaction. We think it more accurate to refer them to the penal system, which is suitable to religious society. This system has a twofold purpose: the good of the soul that has sinned, by amendment and expiation; and the preservation of innocent persons. The Councils of the twelfth century laid special stress on the twofold character of the penalties they inflicted. Thus, the Council of Rheims, 1157—" Sic et iis non deerit pœnitentiæ locus, et ab eorum imitatione exsecrabili ceteri revocabuntur" (Mansi, 21, col. 843)—and that of Tours: " Ut solatio saltem humanitatis amisso, ab errore viæ suæ resipiscere compellantur " (Harduin, vi. 2, col. 1597). It is enough to read the wording of the sentences in order to be convinced that the condemnation was penal as well as peni-

remained obstinate, or if he relapsed after recantation, the ecclesiastical judge recorded the fact of his obstinacy or relapse, and sentenced him as an obstinate or relapsed heretic to be delivered over to the secular arm to be treated according to the rigour of the law.[1]

---

tential. The following are some of the considerations which precede the condemnation of a recanting heretic : " Sane, cum indignum valde exsistat dominorum temporalium injurias ulcisci Dominique cœlorum et Creatoris omnium injurias æquanimiter tolerare, cum multo gravius sit æternam quam temporalem lœdere majestatem, et ut ipse peccatorum miserator tui misereatur, et ut sis ceteris in exemplum, et ut crimina non maneant impunita, et ut efficiaris cautior in futurum, et ut non reddaris proclivior sed difficilior ad prædicta et quæcumque alia illicita committenda " (Eymeric, *Directorium*, part 3, *n*. 194, p. 544). Corresponding forms are given for other and less grave cases (*n*. 165, p. 523 ; *n*. 170, p. 530 ; *n*. 179, p. 534 ; *n*. 186, p. 539). In absolving the heretic who yielded to threats, the Church did not profess to believe unreservedly in a conversion which was always, to a certain extent doubtful. This is shown by the precautions taken. Pegna, in his notes on the *Directorium* of Eymeric, speaking of heretics whose conversion was wanting in spontaneity, recommends that they should not be allowed to communicate with persons whom they might corrupt (*Direct. cit.*, p. 556, Commentary on *n*. 202). But in the case of a voluntary submission the Church saw a germ of conversion, and watched its development with extreme solicitude. We do not agree with M. Jordan in saying that amendment was supposed to have been obtained ; we should rather say it was supposed to have been begun.

[1] " Damnati vero per Ecclesiam sæculari judicio relinquantur, animadversione debita puniendi, clericis prius a suis ordinibus degradatis " (C. *Excommunicamus*, 15 *De Hæreticis*, v. 7). These expressions are borrowed from the Council of the Lateran (1215) rather than from a Constitution of Frederic II. (1231), which is perhaps two years later than this decretal. Raynald (*Annales Baronii*) quotes it in its entirety in the year 1229 (t. 21, pp. 37-41). Mgr. Douais (*L'Inquisition*, p. 137) relies on a Register of Gregory IX. to bring it to 1231. See Potthast, *Regesta*, *n*. 8445, pp. 9675, 10043.

THE INQUISITION

The ecclesiastical judge, in delivering a condemned person to the civil power, insisted that he should be spared the penalty of death or mutilation. The order was in these terms: "As the Church has exhausted all the means at her disposal ... we cast you out from the dominion of the Church, and deliver you to the secular arm. But we earnestly pray the secular tribunal to inflict upon you a moderate sentence, stopping short of death or the shedding of your blood."[1] Such is the formula of Eymeric, and that of Bernard Gui is similar to it: "We give him up as a heretic to the arm and judgment of the secular court, affectionately praying that court, as the sacred Canons recommend, to moderate its judgment and sentence, and to spare the condemned person from death or mutilation."[2]

In effect, then, the Inquisition may be defined as a mixed tribunal established against heresy, in which the ecclesiastical judges sought out persons guilty or suspected of heresy, demanded their abjuration or retractation, imposed various

[1] "Cum Ecclesia non habeat ultra quid faciat, ... de foro nostro ecclesiastico te projicimus et relinquimus, seu brachio sæculari tradimus. Rogamus tamen et efficaciter dictam curiam sæcularem quod circa te citra sanguinis effusionem et mortis periculum sententiam suam moderetur" (Eymeric, *Directorium*, part 3, p. 550; *cf.* pp. 554, 559). The variations indicate whether there is question of a relapsed but penitent heretic, one impenitent but not relapsed, or one who was both impenitent and relapsed.

[2] "Eundem tamquam hæreticum relinquimus brachio et judici curiæ sæcularis, eandem affectuose rogantes, prout suadent canonicæ sanctiones, quatenus citra mortem et membrorum ejus mutilationem, circa ipsum suum judicium et suam sententiam moderetur" (*Practica Inquisitionis Hæreticæ Pravitatis*, ed. Douais, p. 127).

penances, and handed over to the secular arm those whom they found obstinate or relapsed.

If we add that from the time of Innocent IV.[1] and Alexander IV.[2] it was permitted to use torture in order to obtain confessions, we can easily understand the objections made at the present day against the inquisitorial procedure, and the popular idea of its action, entertained by those who are prejudiced against the institution itself, and those who are opposed to all authority and all judicial tribunals.

We should not be justified in condemning the procedure merely because a public officer acted as accuser, instead of waiting for a private individual to take the responsibilities and consequences of a criminal action; for even at the present day in serious cases a private person is merely a complainant, but the proceedings against the accused are conducted by the public prosecutor. M. Vacandard himself admits that the system of prosecution by a private accuser " was scarcely applicable to trials for heresy."[3]

But the secrecy maintained as to the names of the witnesses and informers, the restrictions as to the choice of an advocate, the traps set in the interrogatories the torture, the frightful torture, are some of the features of the trial which make men look upon a person suspected of heresy as a victim delivered up without defence, to the fanaticism of an ecclesiastical judge.

[1] C. *Ad extirpanda* in Eymeric, Appendix, p. 8.
[2] November 30, 1259 (?), Potthast, *Regesta*, 17714.
[3] *L'Inquisition*, p. 275.

THE INQUISITION

Nevertheless, this is not a correct description. We willingly admit that the procedure of the Inquisition was not perfect; we have improved upon it, no doubt, and still we have not reached perfection. But it satisfied two conditions which should induce us to withhold our condemnation: it was not behind the times, and it was regulated by a sincere desire to do justice.

The accused person did not know who had denounced him, or who had given evidence against him. But why? Because numerous murders had shown the danger of disclosing their names.[1] In theory the interrogatory was meant to give him an opportunity of contradicting the case for the prosecution; but, as Boniface VIII. had decreed, if the judges decided that there would be serious danger in revealing the names of the accusers and witnesses, they might refuse to make them publicly known. Does this mean that no discussion was allowed on the subject of these persons? Not at all. The law considered the interests of the accused, who was able, by naming his enemies, to destroy or weaken[2] the effect of their evidence. The Inquisitors were bound to communicate the names of the witnesses to the Bishop, and the Bishop to the Inquisitors. The jury, moreover, had to decide on the admissibility of the evidence.[3] On the whole, considering the period, were not these provisions perfectly wise?

[1] Lea and Tanon admit this, as well as Mgr. Douais and M. Vacandard, who on p. 52 quotes the two first-mentioned writers.

[2] According to the degree of the enmity. See Eymeric, *Directorium*, p. 479.

[3] Boniface VIII., C. *Statuta*, 20 *De Hæreticis*, in 6° (v. 2).

Even at the present day, considering the difficulty of obtaining true evidence (such is the effect of the fear of consequences in sealing men's lips), and the scandalous impunity given to the worst malefactors by the refusal of witnesses to give evidence, we may reasonably doubt whether complete publicity is in all cases to be recommended.

Had the person accused of heresy no one to defend him? Let Eymeric answer, whose *Directory* has become classic. He says (p. 479): "An advocate must be given him, and must not be refused him." And his commentator, Pegna, says (p. 480): "It is a question of natural justice." The texts, it is true, have left room for misconception. "Neither advocates nor notaries can favour heresy, or a notorious or convicted heretic," is all that we can find in the written law, notably the famous Constitution *Si adversus*, 11 *De Hæreticis*.[1] The chapter may be easily misunderstood, but it would certainly be an exaggeration of its scope to read in it any prohibition against employing the assistance of advocates or notaries in cases of heresy. As long as there was any question of the guilt of an accused person, he was unrestricted in his defence;[2] it was only when the fact of heresy was established that the advocate had done his work. After that it was considered that there was no reason for advocacy, which could only encourage heresy. At that time the punishment to be inflicted was not a subject for argument; it depended on the guilty person himself to show

[1] See Eymeric, p. 104.
[2] Eymeric thought it unnecessary to allow assistance to an accused person who confessed; but Pegna corrects him on this point (p. 480).

the only extenuating circumstance that could help him—namely, his repentance and conversion. Moreover, we must not forget that the law permitted an accused person to object to an Inquisitor for good cause; that it granted a right of appeal from every sentence that was not final; and that even after a final sentence there was always a right of special application to the Sovereign Pontiff.

There was no lack of precaution to secure a fair trial for the accused persons.

But what are we to say of the tricks by which certain Inquisitors endeavoured to embarrass the accused and make him contradict himself? Do not the public prosecutors and examining magistrates of the present day follow the objectionable procedure of their medieval predecessors? Need we be surprised to find in a directory for the use of Inquisitors a warning as to the subtleties of heretics and the best means of defeating them? In dealing with a sect whose members were trained in craft and duplicity a little cunning seems to be logically permissible, and can offend no one except those of the falsely-styled chivalrous school, who would always give an advantage to the criminal in his struggle against authority.

The art of punishing has this in common with the art of healing, that it condemns and rejects as erroneous and pernicious certain practices which have hitherto been considered justifiable. One of these is torture. It is not a clerical invention; it is a relic of Roman law, accepted by lawyers who professed their admiration of that law. The study of the Digest, which was held in great honour in the latter half of the twelfth century, excited an enthusiasm which was followed by that of humanism. The Roman law was looked upon as reason reduced to writing; men swore by its solutions of problems, and its prescriptions were accepted without question. In admitting a moderate amount of torture into the procedure against heretics, Innocent IV.[1] showed himself to be a Pope friendly to progress; he followed the current of opinion. If he had resisted it, he would no doubt have been applauded at the present day, but he would have been condemned by his contemporaries as obscurantist and retrograde. "It is all very well," it would have been said, "to be gentle in purely ecclesiastical trials, but a mixed tribunal, entrusted with a social duty of the first importance, cannot show weakness, or neglect any modern means of obtaining information." Why should we not at once frankly admit that torture is less to be condemned in theory than in practice, which is apt to be abused? Even in our own day, in the more or less important affairs of life, are not threats, promises, and punishments, constantly used for the purpose of arriving at the truth? That was all that was intended. Counting on the impression of pain actually felt, it was thought that a moderate amount of suffering (and the law permitted no more) would leave the innocent person free to assert his innocence, and loose the tongues of the guilty. Torture, moreover, could only be applied to persons already half-convicted, and it was only permissible in such moderation as to do no lasting harm. We

[1] C. *Ad extirpanda*, May 14, 1252, quoted by Eymeric, *Directorium*, Const. *Apostolicæ*, pp. 7 *sqq.*

may add that, under the penal law then in force, judges were anxious not to convict a man except on his own admission. Even then the disadvantages of torture were not disregarded; Eymeric recommends that it should only be employed after careful consideration, describing it as an unsafe and ineffective method of discovering the truth.[1]

The subtleties of interpreters led to a straining of the letter of the law,[2] and such abuses naturally brought the use of torture into disrepute as a means of obtaining evidence, and no one regrets its disappearance. However, if we would judge fairly of the procedure of a past time, we must not omit to take all the circumstances into consideration. Our gentler methods and the efficiency of our police make it easy for us to organize our procedure on the principle first formulated by a Pope, that the greatest possible misfortune is to condemn an innocent person.[3] Formerly the necessity of more energetic social defence made men fear most of all to let a guilty person escape. Finally, we may observe with Mgr. Landrieux,[4] that torture at any rate was an improvement on the system formerly followed—namely, that of trial by ordeal.

We have now to consider the attitude of the Church, and her part in the work of the Inquisition.

[1] *Directorium*, three pars., *n.* 154, p. 517.
[2] The law forbade the repeated use of torture. To escape this prohibition, commentators held that the same torture might be continued through several sittings.
[3] " It is a less evil to acquit the guilty than to sentence an innocent person to death " (Alexander III., Ep. 118 to Henry, Archbishop of Rheims, M.P.L., t. 200, col. 187).
[4] *L'Inquisition : Les Temps, les Causes, les Faits*, pp. 107 *sqq*.

According to the account that has already been given, the Church took part in the judicial proceedings, and, indeed, claimed a principal part, and at first even exclusive jurisdiction; but in the case of an obstinate or relapsed heretic she stayed her hand, and delivered him to the secular authority for punishment, instructing her judge to implore of that authority a leniency which she forbade him to show. Does not this look like a sinister comedy played at the expense of heretics, in order that the Church might glut her appetite for cruelty, and at the same time save her reputation for clemency?

This accusation has often been made; let us look carefully into it. The intervention of the Church and the preponderant part which she claimed are explained at once by her spiritual mission. Before a heretic could be punished it was necessary to establish the fact of his heresy—that is to say, his obstinate sin against faith—a matter entirely ecclesiastical, which the Church was clearly bound to reserve to herself, unless she consented to give up her independence. The teaching authority established by God to define the truths of religion is alone competent to say whether an offence against religion has been committed. "To say with certainty whether there had been heresy, and in what that heresy consisted," Mgr. Douais wisely remarks, "it was necessary first to possess the doctrine which was contradicted, and then to determine with the necessary authority what that doctrine was."[1] In this sense, and in this sense only, the Pope forbade the secular power to take cognizance of

[1] *L'Inquisition*, p. 130.

heresy,[1] and it was all in favour of accused persons that they escaped from the hands of an authority much less scrupulous than the ecclesiastical authority. If, in spite of the intervention of pontifical delegates, the Popes were obliged more than once to repress or prevent the abuses engendered by human passions ; if the pressure exerted by the State brought about strange and regrettable condemnations ; if political animosity led to the burning of Joan of Arc ; if the antireligious fury of Pombal delivered the Jesuit Malagrida to the flames—what abominable crimes would have been committed in the name of religion if secular Princes had been the supreme guardians of orthodoxy !

But why, then, did not the Church deal with the whole case ? Why did she stop in the middle when

[1] Even Catholic authors, such as MM. Vacandard and Jordan (*Annales*, t. 9, p. 23), seem to have exaggerated the scope of this prohibition. The words of the decretal, " Donec eorum negotium per ecclesiasticum judicium terminetur " (Until their cause shall have been decided by an ecclesiastical judgment), do not prove by themselves that the sentence of the Inquisitors put an end to all proceedings. In our own system, on the conclusion of the criminal proceedings, there remains sometimes a civil process to be dealt with by other judges, who at first have no jurisdiction, because the policy of the law requires that before the party injured by any felonious act can seek civil redress for it, the matter shall be heard and disposed of before the proper criminal tribunal. Later on we shall have occasion to return to this point. Commentators have given to the text an extended significance which has been practically accepted. But if we consider well the terms of the law, the only point which the sentence of the Inquisitor finally decided, and which the secular authority had no power to reconsider, was whether the Court found itself dealing with an obstinate or relapsed heretic. M. Vacandard himself quotes these texts of the period of the decretals (1234) : The C. *Excommunicamus*, 15 *De*

dealing with an obstinate or relapsed heretic ? Why give a man over to the secular arm when she was as competent to decide the measure of his punishment as the fact of his guilt ? Was there not some cruel device in this transfer of jurisdiction ? We could understand a claim of exclusive jurisdiction, which gave everything to the Church ; we could understand that the Church should reserve to herself the right to decide the fact of heresy, leaving the question of punishment entirely to the civil magistrate, but it is less easy to understand why this question of punishment should partly remain with the Church, and be partly transferred to the State. The key to the enigma is supplied by the mixed character of heresy, by the common interest of both authorities in its repression, and by historical precedents.

Heresy, primarily a religious matter, though

Hæreticis, v. 7, which delivers to the secular judgment, *sæculari judicio relinquantur*, heretics condemned by the Church ; the Constitution of Frederic II. (March, 1232, *Mon. Germ. Hist.*, t. 4, *Legum* 2, p. 288), in which the Emperor orders the punishment of those whom the Church has condemned and handed over to the secular authority, *sæculari judicio assignati ;* a *processus inquisitionis* of the middle of the thirteenth century, the formula of which gives up the heretic to secular judgment : *per sententiam definitivam hæreticum judicamus, relinquentes ex nunc judicio sæculari*. And in the text itself (1298), which contains the decretal of Boniface VIII., the delivery to the secular authority is mentioned in the C. *Super eo*, 4 *De Hæreticis*, v. 2. The ch. *Præsidentes*, 6 eodem, while permitting excommunicated civil magistrates to exercise their judicial power and office against heretics (*justitiam et suum officium exercere*), evidently contemplated the active exercise of this power, existing concurrently with the decretal. And if the secular authority sometimes consented simply to execute heretics, in France certainly, as M. de Causons admits, the secular magistrates were not long content to accept the part of passive executioners (*op. cit.*, p. 474, *n.*).

THE INQUISITION

having political and social effects, was primarily within the jurisdiction of the Church; therefore the first proceedings were exclusively ecclesiastical, and so would have continued to the end if there had been merely a question of protecting the interests of the two societies. For a first offence, when the heresy was not obstinate, the State had no need to interfere; it left matters to the Church, which lacked neither vigilance nor power to take all precautions necessary for the public good, and, on the other hand, the submission—at least the outward submission—of the heretic who retracted his opinions allowed her to listen to the voice of mercy, and in her zeal for souls to undertake the task of complete conversion, and so to effect two desirable results, the public good and the salvation of a soul.

So far there was no offence cognizable by the civil tribunal, or at all events the offence had not been consummated; that is to say, the fact of heresy had not presented itself with all the characteristics and in all the conditions necessary to bring it under the application—at least the absolute application—of the penal laws of the period.

But if the Church failed in her efforts, the offence assumed such a character as to require punishment both from the religious and from the social point of view. The Church, assured of the support of the secular arm, surrendered to the civil authority the purely vindictive character which was not in keeping with her own merciful nature; seeing that her exhortations and corrective penances were without effect, she declared that she had done all in her power, and then, adopting for the crime of heresy, an offence within her cognizance, the procedure followed when clerics or exempt persons were convicted of forgery, theft, homicide, or other offences against common law, she delivered the incorrigible offender to the secular power. This is the reasoning of the decretals,[1] the Council of Constance,[2] and of St. Thomas.[3]

A relapse into heresy created a legal presumption against the reality of the first repentance. Sincere, perhaps, before God, and therefore admitted to sacramental absolution, the relapsed penitent had not sufficiently gained the confidence of the Church, and had too entirely forfeited her esteem to deserve the benefit of ecclesiastical treatment. In his case, as in the case of an obstinate heretic, the Church declared herself powerless, and placed him at the mercy of the secular arm.[4]

[1] "Cum Ecclesia non habeat ultra quid faciat"—As the Church can do no more (C. *Cum non*, 10 *De Judiciis*, ii. 1.

[2] "Hæc sancta synodus Joannem Hus, attento quod Ecclesia Dei non habeat ultra quid agere valeat, judicio sæculari relinquit et ipsum curiæ sæculari relinquendum fore decernit" (This Sacred Council, considering that the Church can do no more, gives up John Hus to secular judgment, and decides that he shall be handed over to the secular court).

[3] 2, 2, Q. xi., Art. 3. The Church first endeavours to bring about the conversion of heretics. When she despairs of this, she hands them over to the secular arm. The use of this mixed procedure dates from the seventh century for the clergy; for Bishops from a still earlier period. See the monograph quoted by Viollet, p. 271. Even the expression "the Church has done all in her power" is formally used in such trials. See the decretal *Cum non*, 10 *De Judiciis*, which goes back to 1191-1198. There was there a case of a priest who had been guilty of an offence against common law, and proved incorrigible.

[4] St. Thomas justifies the treatment of the relapsed in the same manner as the impenitent by the distrust they

The Church was prompted to deliver none but the impenitent or relapsed, not only by her own natural inclination to mercy, but also by the very nature of heresy. Religious error may be innocent; it becomes heresy only when committed knowingly and deliberately, and to deserve the extreme rigour of the law it must be entirely without excuse. The Church desired to exhaust all her powers of persuasion, all her means of reclamation, before she was convinced of the full culpability of the heretic. What charges of cruelty would she have incurred if she had lightly permitted the sword of secular authority to fall upon the heads of her children without putting forth all her efforts to avoid it!

But when once she had declared that she could do no more, the Church had to consider her own respect for tradition, and the respect due to the temporal Sovereign.

Let us go back to the very origin of the Inquisition. As we have already observed, Frederic II., who was hypocrite enough to urge the Pope to more zeal for the defence of the Faith, and to suggest his own example as one which the Pope would do well to follow,[1] showed in the fight against heresy an eagerness which raised suspicions as to his own ambitions and usurping intentions. By his Constitutions of 1231 and 1232 he endeavoured to secure for himself the leading part in the repression of religious error, but Gregory IX. had the intelli-

---

inspired, and by the social danger caused by their inconstancy. The similarity, as we have seen, was not complete. The relapsed penitent escaped the penalty of fire; his dead body only was burned.

[1] Lea, *op. cit.*, t. 1, p. 233.

gence to foresee and ward off the blow. The appointment of the Inquisitor enabled the Pope to keep in his own hands the whole spiritual part of a trial for heresy; but he had no desire, and perhaps he did not consider himself qualified, to take away from the Prince the secular power claimed by the latter. Frederic II. asserted his claim loudly enough; it was in his own name, and by his own authority, that he took his severe measures against heretics, and condemned them to the stake.[1] Let us go back farther in history. To whom did the Bishops appeal when driven to extremities by the excesses of the Donatists and other sectaries? To the secular Princes. And the Emperors had placed heresy in the list of crimes that were dangerous to the public welfare. The old Roman Empire bequeathed this tradition to the Empire of the West and the Lower Empire; it became the tradition of the Holy Empire and the Kings of France.[2]

[1] See the texts quoted in connection with the origin of the Inquisition. This point, moreover, cannot be disputed. Neither the custom nor the written texts which from the time of Louis VIII. (1226) prescribed the penalty of death were established or published under the influence of the Church.

[2] Speaking of the Manichæans and Donatists, Arcadius and Honorius had declared: "Volumus publicum crimen esse, quia quod in religionem divinam committitur, in omnium fertur injuriam" (Theodosian Code, l. 40, *De Hæreticis*, xvi. 5, or Code of Justinian, *De Hæreticis*, i. 5, l. 4, § 1). Frederic II., in his turn, declared in his Constitution *Inconsutilem:* "Statuimus in primis, ut crimen hæreseos et damnatæ sectæ cujuslibet, quocumque nomine censeantur (prout veteribus legibus est indictum) inter publica crimina numerentur." And independently of the ordinances of Louis VIII. (1226) and St. Louis (1228), an ordinance of Louis X. (December, 1315) confirmed the Constitutions of Frederic II.

THE INQUISITION

We know what respect the Church pays to traditions. In the present case she was bound to pay especial respect, because the tradition was in harmony with true principles on the mixed nature of the crime of heresy and the relations of the two powers. But did not the Church misunderstand the rights of the temporal sovereignty when she promised impunity at the price of a retractation? M. Jordan seems to suggest that she did.[1] But this is through a mistake as to the meaning of the laws.[2] Read the Constitutions of Frederic II. The Emperor does not punish all heretics, but only the obstinate ones handed over to him by the Church, and those who by returning to heresy are convicted of having made a lying abjuration.[3] Before the civil tribunal the offence consisted in obstinacy or relapse, as under our laws certain acts, as, for

---

[1] When he says (*Annales*, t. 9, p. 46) that heretics had incurred the penalty of death.

[2] And also by disregard of the law in force on the relations of the two powers. In mixed causes the secular authority at first left the Church to use its own means of repression and correction. If these means effected the conversion of the guilty person, the Church did not hand him over to the secular arm (see c. *Cum non, De judiciis*, ii. 10). Shall we find fault with a system which was the precursor of our own penal law reforms, especially of the conditional condemnation? It may be interesting to observe that the pagan persecutions similarly offered impunity for religious offences, and even rewards as the price of return to the State religion.

[3] "Ab Ecclesia damnati et sæculari judicio assignati . . . Item mortis sententiæ duximus addicendos si quos hæreticorum, ad judicium tractos, in extremo vitæ periculo hæresim abjurantes, postmodum de falso juramento constiterit et fide mentita convinci ac eos contigerit ejusdem mortis spontaneam incurrere recidivam, ut sibi damnabilius iniquitas sit mentita, et pœnam debitam mendacium non evadat (C. *Commissi*).

instance, usury, or adultery by a husband, are punishable only when accompanied by aggravating circumstances. If any additional offence were committed, the course of civil justice could not be stopped by a canonical absolution. Thus, when Charles V. had issued his rigorous edicts against the preaching of heresy, and the printing, purchase, and sale of heretical books, a distinction was made in the Low Countries between the crime of heresy and the crime of contravention of the decrees so promulgated.[1] The obstinate heretic was handed over to the secular arm, but the fact of his reconciliation with the Church did not prevent the secular tribunals from punishing the repentant sinner for disobeying the published orders.

There remains still the objection, a specious one at first sight, which is suggested by the illusory prayer for mercy which the Church compelled her Inquisitors to make. How shall we excuse the Church for asking mercy for the heretic, and at the same time urging the execution of the law by which he was condemned to death? She causes a prayer to be made, but takes care that it shall not be granted, and this is what the canonical laws, by a masterpiece of irony, call an effective appeal. This little historical problem, as MM. Maillet-Hanquet well call it,[2] can only be solved by going back to

---

[1] See Poullet, *Histoire du Droit Criminel dans l'Ancien Duché de Brabant*, p. 60, and the texts quoted by Lonchay, *loc. cit.*, p. 28. The latter adds: "It is because this distinction has not been understood that the history of the Inquisition has not yet been treated as it should have been." Tanon remarks that by a similar distinction the Parliamentarians in France appropriated, in the matter of the Reformation, all inquisitorial power (*op. cit.*, p. 553).

[2] *Op. cit.*, p. 107.

THE INQUISITION

the beginning, and observing the progressive advancement of ideas.

If this official intercession had been invented expressly for the case of heretics, and if the ideas of the eighteenth century had been those of Innocent III., we readily admit that we should understand the severe criticism that has been passed upon it. But the case is quite different when we observe the dates, and distinguish between the first establishment of a practice and its continuance as an ancient custom.

The Eleventh Council of Toledo (675) had already,[1] under the most severe penalties, prohibited "those whose duty it was to dispense the sacraments of the Lord" from judging a cause which might end in a capital sentence, as also from inflicting or ordering any mutilation whatever. Alexander III. († 1181) renewed this prohibition in a letter to the Archbishop of Canterbury;[2] it is found also in the Acts of the Fourth Council of the Lateran (1215); the clergy were forbidden also to be present at the execution of any sentence attended by bloodshed.[3] A short time before, in 1209, Innocent III., wishing to regulate the manner in which a criminal cleric should be degraded, and then delivered to the secular arm, added this direction: "The Church must intercede effectively that his life may be spared." It was a way for the Church to inculcate

[1] In its Sixth Canon, which became, in the decretal of Gratian, c. 30, C. xxiii., Q. 8. See Harduin's *Concilia*, t. 3, col. 1026.

[2] Which became c. *Clericis*, 5, *Ne clerici vel monachi, etc.* (iii. 50).

[3] This Canon became the c. *Sententiam sanguinis*, 9, *Ne clerici vel monachi* (iii. 50).

more and more on her ministers that spirit of mercy which Jesus Christ had left to them as their inheritance. When introduced into the general law,[1] this procedure was to be observed by the ecclesiastical judge who handed over to the secular arm an obstinate or relapsed heretic. Being unable to interfere reasonably with the course of public justice, but nevertheless desirous of accomplishing her mission of redemption, the Church attempted a benevolent intervention in order to reconcile with her clemency the laws of public vengeance ; she interceded where she had no right to command. " From the first," remarks Hinschius,[2] " the Church, anxious for the reformation of criminals, exerted herself to save the lives of those whom the secular authorities had condemned to death. In declaring it effective, Innocent III. made it sufficiently clear that this prayer was not an unmeaning ceremony, but that he wished a serious step to be taken, which might have a real influence on the fate of the criminal."[3]

Innocent III., moreover, did not desire that heretics should be punished with death.[4] The

---

[1] c. *Novimus*, 27 *De verborum significatione* (v. 40).

[2] *System des Katholischen Kirchenrechts*, t. 5, p. 50, *n*. 5.

[3] According to Trautmansdorff (*De Tolerantia Eccl. et Civili*, French edition, p. 125), it was long disputed whether a Bishop could deliver anyone to the secular arm, foreseeing the uselessness of his appeal for mercy. Boniface VIII. seems to have settled the question, and decided that it sufficed to make the appeal. We have not been able to verify the assertion of this author, but, if he is speaking the truth, nothing could more conclusively prove the sincerity of the Church's intentions.

[4] This must be admitted, since the Pope's biographer, M. Luchaire, who was not a Catholic, has ratified the

THE INQUISITION

efficacy of the request for mercy became more doubtful[1] when Frederic II. issued his merciless edicts against heretics, and when the Popes in the middle of the thirteenth century insisted on their

---

previous judgments of M. Havet (*L'Hérésie et le Bras Séculier*, p. 165, *n*. 3) and M. Ficker. The latter, in M. Havet's opinion, has made this point clear. M. Tanon (*op. cit.*, pp. 449, 450) finds in the letters of Innocent III. sufficiently clear allusions to the possible infliction of capital punishment for heresy, but neither the Pope's conduct nor his most explicit decrees can be reconciled with this opinion. " In the legislation of Innocent III., as in his letters," writes M. Luchaire, " there is no question of death for heretics; he never asks for more than their banishment and the confiscation of their goods. If he speaks of having recourse to the secular sword, he does not mean by this anything more than the use of such force as is necessary for the measures of expulsion and expatriation prescribed by his penal code. This code, which appears to us so unmerciful, constituted in comparison with the customs of the time a real progress in a humanitarian direction. It regulated and mitigated the procedure of repression in the matter of heresy; it forbade summary executions, the victims of which were not only declared heretics, but sometimes also persons simply suspected of heresy" (*Innocent III., La Croisade des Albigeois*, pp. 57, 58).

[1] Mgr. Douais thinks, nevertheless (*L'Inquisition*, pp. 267, 268) that the civil judge could still take this prayer into consideration, and it is true that the general application of a law is compatible with special exemptions. Nor can it be denied that in all periods of history the Inquisition furnishes examples of heretics who, in spite of their obstinacy, escaped with their lives. But we have not sufficient materials to judge of the efficacy of the ecclesiastical intercession. Perhaps it varied with the latitude which the civil law allowed to the judge. Certainly the Sovereign retained the right to commute the punishment. In 1235 Gregory IX., wishing for an exemplary punishment for certain heretics who had killed the Bishop of Padua, solemnly excommunicated them, and demanded their banishment. He himself, in a similar case, commuted this last punishment into another less severe. See *Annales*, Raynald, t. 21, edit. Theiner, pp. 111, 112.

enforcement,[1] and it certainly seems to have been abolished from the fifteenth century. Then a doctrine was formulated which was to find its classic expression later in Bellarmine, Suarez, and the great Canonists of the seventeenth and eighteenth centuries.[2] According to this opinion the Church has the right to condemn to death, and the capital punishment of obstinate or relapsed heretics becomes the common work of the two powers. By not sending to the stake the heretic delivered to him by the Church, the secular magistrate offends against the decretal of Boniface VIII.,[3] and exposes himself

---

[1] Innocent IV., C. *Cum adversus*, October 30, 1243 (B.R., t. 3, part i., pp. 295 *sqq.*). See also his other Constitution, *Ad extirpanda*, May 10, 1252, a sort of collection of decrees against heresy, in ll. 3 and 4 of which he prescribes exile only, while in l. 34 he demands the enforcement of the laws of Frederic II.—Urban IV., C. *Licet ex omnibus*, March 20, 1262 (B.R., t. 3, part i., pp. 437, 439). Not before.

[2] See the references in the chapter on the Right of the Sword.

[3] *Ut Inquisitionis*, 18 *De Hæreticis* in 6° (v. 2). Such is not the original meaning of this decretal; it obliges lay magistrates and officials to obey promptly the orders which the Bishop or Inquisitor may give them in a case of heresy; but the injunctions in the decretal relate to the drawing up of the process and the ecclesiastical punishments, and not to any sentence of death, which neither the Bishop nor the Inquisitor could pass. Look at the gloss; it assigns to this decretal the special object of securing the arrest and imprisonment of heretics whom the Inquisitor or the Ordinary desired to apprehend or detain in custody. Consult the very formula by which, as M. Vacandard says, "they got rid of an impenitent or relapsed heretic." It contained no injunction. M. Vacandard translates: "We remove thee from our ecclesiastical tribunal, and deliver thee to the secular arm. But we pray and that effectively, the secular Court to moderate the sentence in such manner as to avoid all shedding of blood or peril of death" (*L'Inquisition*, p. 214).

THE INQUISITION

to the penalties prescribed against lay officials who refused to carry into effect the sentences of the Inquisitors.

Under such a system the prayer for mercy seems to have been unnecessarily imposed upon the ecclesiastical judge, and it may be asked, What was its object?[1] We answer, No longer to relieve the Church from responsibility, but to save the judge the penalty of irregularity. An authority which believes that it possesses the right of the sword may have excellent reasons for forbidding certain of its ministers to take part in the exercise of that right. The Church has always insisted on expressing her opinion that the shedding of blood was incompatible with the clerical character of her judges; but it was the general opinion at that period that what was inconsistent with the office of a judge was not necessarily so with that of a legislator, and we can understand the distinction. The enactment of a law permitting capital punishment is much farther removed from the actual punishment than a sentence which condemns an accused person by name; we do not feel the same repugnance for the judges as for the executioner who carries their sentences into effect, and the retention of the death penalty on the statute book does not excite the same horror as the sight of an execution.

The Canonist Reiffenstuel is an unimpeachable witness, and he tells us that Bishops and other prelates having temporal jurisdiction would be

[1] Certain ecclesiastical judges neglected to comply with the rule, and a question arose whether their omission did not make them irregular (Suarez, *De Censuris*, d. 47, s. 1, *n.* 12).

irregular if they condemned any person to death or mutilation, or if they recommended such a punishment, or required that it should be inflicted on any particular individual; but they could, without fear of irregularity, appoint judges to try the criminal, and direct them to pass sentence according to law, and to see that the sentence was carried out.[1]

Consequently, after the fifteenth century the ecclesiastical judge, pleading for the life of a guilty person, could not do much to help a heretical client; but he avoided staining his hands with blood, and he fulfilled the conditions which the law required under pain of irregularity.[2]

Certain authors of the eighteenth century went still farther than those whose opinions we have quoted. In the opinion of Cardinal Petra, for example, the laws against heretics derived all their force from pontifical approbation. It is only in the name of the Church that the Sovereign can sentence them to death; the Inquisitor decides everything. The civil magistrate's duty is not to judge, but to obey. Thus, the intercession on behalf of the condemned person is reduced to a mere formality; it is an old custom which has lost all its significance.[3]

Thus, then, from the thirteenth to the nineteenth century the current opinion has varied. Until the fifteenth century the Church, if she does not save

[1] In l. 5, t. 12, *n*. 95.
[2] Irregularity is an impediment under ecclesiastical law to the reception or exercise of sacred Orders.
[3] See Petra's Commentaries on the Constitution *Cum adversus*, (s. 1, *n*. 7 *sqq.*; s. 2, *n*. 24); Constitution of Alexander IV., *Quod super* (*n*. 16); *Ad audientiam* (*n*. 8, t. 3, pp. 4, 5, 7, 133, 147).

the heretic, cannot be said to condemn him to death.
" The Church delivers impenitent heretics to the
secular arm. . . . She does not save relapsed persons
from the danger of death."[1] The thirteenth-century
author quoted by M. Vacandard is not shirking a difficulty, but simply telling the truth, when he says :
" Our Pope does not kill, nor order that anyone shall
be killed ; it is the law which kills those whom the law
permits to be killed ; they kill themselves who do
the things which bring this penalty upon them."[2]
In this first period, the prayer of the judge is the
prayer of the Church herself,[3] and it serves to show
at least by what order the blood was shed. From
the fifteenth to the eighteenth century the sentence
of death is considered also as an ecclesiastical
sentence ; the judge, in praying that the life of the
heretic may be spared, is no longer the organ of the
Church : he only refrains from taking part in passing
the capital sentence in order to avoid irregularity.
Finally, in the opinion of some authors of the
eighteenth century, the prayer on behalf of the
heretic ceased to be anything but an ineffective
and antiquated formality.

But we must remember that at that time the
Inquisition also was in most countries nothing but
a nominal institution. Our rapid review of opinions,
in which we have anticipated the following period
so as not to have to return to this special point of the
procedure against heresy, leads us to this interesting

[1] Such are the expressions of St. Thomas (2, 2, Q. 11,
Art. 4 *c.* et ad 1).

[2] *L'Inquisition*, p. 213.

[3] " Pro quo debet *Ecclesia* efficaciter intercedere " (C.
Novimus, 27 *De verborum significatione*, v. 40).

conclusion : the sentence of death is attributed to the Church in proportion as its application to heresy becomes less frequent. But we may remark that at no time was the plea for mercy a " device," or a " cruel mockery," or an " empty form," as has been suggested.[1]

The plea, which at its inception was seriously put forward and often produced a good effect, reflects the real spirit of the Church—a sincere desire to spare human life, and show respect for the human body. It served also to keep ecclesiastical judges in mind of the nature and the limits of their mandate. Ecclesiastical authorities never used it to save appearances, or to seem mild and gentle while striking with implacable severity. It is true that apologists of the nineteenth century have exercised their ingenuity to lighten the responsibility of the Popes ; but the Popes themselves never attempted to disguise their action,[2] or refused to accept the responsibility.[3]

[1] According to Lea, this prayer of the Church was " merely a device to avoid responsibility for its own acts . . . a hypocritical adjuration " (*op. cit.*, t. 1, p. 224). M. Tanon (*op. cit.*, p. 474), who nevertheless gives a better account of the origin of the custom, considers that " it was merely a cruel mockery in its application to heretics, and the fiction on which it rested could not be disguised by the casuistry of the most subtle doctors." M. Vacandard looks upon it as an unintelligible subtlety, an empty form, a legal fiction (*op. cit.*, pp. 212, 215, 295).

[2] It is sufficient to read the Bulls of Innocent IV., Alexander IV., St. Pius V., etc.

[3] Similarly, the Church has been unjustly accused of reticence because in her laws she says that the heretic is delivered to the secular arm to undergo the punishment he deserves, instead of saying plainly that she gives him up to be put to death. The formula, indeed, is older than the legislation which condemns obstinate heretics to death.

THE INQUISITION

The condemnation is thus shown to be unjustifiable. To make the prayer the sham and subterfuge it is represented to be, the first condition is wanting—namely, that the Church should have thought of using it to lighten her own responsibility.

The continued use of the prayer for mercy after it had become an empty form will surprise no one who knows how tenacious courts and chanceries are of their old procedure, and who will observe how many old customs have outlived the original reason of their institution; there are in England many such survivals in the ceremonial of public life.

Would it be rash to add that, even if without immediate effect, these intercessions, continued for centuries, exercised a good influence on the amelioration of manners, the mitigation of punishments, and an improvement in the whole course of criminal legislation?

III. WHAT HERETICS WERE PERSECUTED.

SUMMARY: Two contradictory exaggerations.—Certain heretics are deserving of pity.—In general, the seduction of the masses is more feared than speculative errors.—Liberty of controversy.—The complaint of Servetus.—The Waldenses.—The heresy persecuted is a reformist revolutionary movement.

An honest and careful examination has convinced us of this, that, considering the manners and customs of the centuries during which the Inquisition

---

And the Church, in her intentional want of precision, showed her respect for the secular authority, with which it rested to decide on the penalty incurred by the criminal handed over. See, for example, the ch. *Ad abolendam*, 9 *De Hæreticis* (v. 7), of Lucius III.

exercised its functions, its procedure has not that odious and retrograde character which its opponents desire to fix upon it; and the irregular and improvised Courts of the people, and the regular Parliaments of Sovereigns, have condemned more heretics to death than the tribunal of the Inquisition.

Having thus disposed of what we may call a question of form and method, we proceed to the substantial issue, What heretics were condemned to death? The prejudices and passions of controversalists represent persons condemned for heresy sometimes as innocent victims of fanaticism, sometimes as criminals and rebels, who for other reasons had already deserved the gallows.

There is exaggeration on both sides. We have no desire to blacken the characters of those unfortunate people, and we should augur ill for a cause which could only be defended by detraction and calumny. We willingly admit that all active suppressions of heresy have been cruel in taking interesting and even inoffensive lives; the Catharists of the thirteenth century, the Anabaptists, the Lutherans, the English Protestants of the sixteenth, included peaceable and conscientious persons, who died with nobility and courage, and who deserve all our pity.

But the interest we feel in individuals must not blind us to the nature of the causes in which they were, knowingly or unknowingly, implicated, and if we only reflect a little we shall find that they resemble those innocent persons who sometimes swell revolutionary movements in spite of themselves, and find themselves involved in the consequences.

WHAT HERETICS WERE PERSECUTED 157

The character of the heresy, as well as time and place, had its influence on the energy employed to root it out, and the seduction of the masses and their mystical and revolutionary ardour often necessitated severe, and in some respects harsh, measures of repression. Lea practically admits this. " The only heresies," he says, " which really troubled the Church were those which obtained currency among the people, unassisted by the ingenious quodlibets of dialecticians."[1] " The schoolmen were allowed to indulge in endless wrangling, for the most part, without censure."[2] Farther on, he expresses his surprise at the impunity allowed to some of the novel ideas : " Averrhoism had thus fairly conquered a position for itself, and it is one of the inscrutable problems why the Inquisition, so unrelenting in its suppression of minor aberrations, should have conceded impunity to speculations which not only sapped the foundations of Christian faith, but by plain implication denied all the doctrines on which were based the wealth and power of the hierarchy."[3] " After this (1443) scholarship, however heretical, had little to fear in Italy."[4] The same Frederic II., who was so jealous for orthodoxy in his Constitutions, introduced Averrhoism into Germany. It would, therefore, be quite incorrect to attribute an effect of universal and perpetual terror to the Inquisition, which, as Lea admits, " had always been weak and unorganized " in Germany,[5] and in Italy had " extended its toleration to the most daring speculations."[6]

[1] *Op. cit.*, t. 3, p. 550.   [2] *Ibid.*, p. 555.   [3] *Ibid.*, p. 565.
[4] *Ibid.*, p. 568.   [5] *Ibid.*, p. 648.   [6] *Ibid.*, p. 565.

Summing up the opinions of the writers of that period, Viollet observes: " All are agreed that the heretics of the twelfth and thirteenth centuries were guilty of offences against the common law."[1] M. de Cauzons (Abbé Thomas) represents the war against heresy as a war to the death between the Church and the revolutionary spirit. In this warfare, he adds, in which names doubtless differ, and perhaps doctrines also, the fundamental idea of the assailants is that the Church, and especially the Papacy, is the enemy. Against the Church pamphlets are circulated, and political passions are aroused; against her defenders all means are considered justifiable, including incendiarism and murder."[2]

The law of the Third Council of the Lateran (1179), which enjoins that an end should be made of certain sects, " alludes," he says again, " not to isolated heretics, but to active partisans, armed, as we know from contemporary chronicles, parties who must be destroyed at any cost, in order to prevent the overthrow of the social edifice."[3]

And, to speak precisely, if we wish for the purpose of this discussion to recall simply the dominant facts of the repression of heresy, we shall see that the three great periods of activity coincide with the ravages of three antisocial and seditious heresies—Manichæism and Donatism (fifth century), Catharism (twelfth and thirteenth centuries), and Anabaptism (sixteenth centuries).[4]

---

[1] *Hist. du Droit Civil Français*, p. 339. He refers to Canon 27 of the Lateran Council of 1127.
[2] *Op. cit.*, p. 259.   [3] *Ibid.*, pp. 275, 276.
[4] The proscription of the Manichæans by Diocletian has been already mentioned, and we have also quoted Lea's

It would be a mistake, then, to look upon every execution of a heretic as an act of good justice in the common acceptation of the word; but it would be equally absurd to weep over heretics as martyrs of free thought; their errors had no scientific or doctrinal value, such as might give them a claim to consideration. Those who confined themselves to speculation, or only expressed their novel opinions within their own schools, escaped the notice of the Inquisitors, or, at all events, were not molested by them, and they had much less to fear from them than from their colleagues in the Universities. In fact, until the great apostasy of the sixteenth century obliged the Church to be more vigilant, theological, philosophical, and scientific speculations might be indulged in without let or hindrance. It is not until the seventeenth century that we meet with a case like that of Galileo. Thus, Michael Servetus, who could not have been ignorant of the laws against heresy and the tribunals established for their administration, expressed, in the cell in which Calvin kept him confined, his astonishment at seeing himself threatened with death for a simple question of dogma.[1] The case of the Waldensians

---

opinion of the antisocial action of the Catharists. He says: "The documents of the Inquisition constantly refer to 'heresy and Waldensianism,' designating Catharism by the former term as the heresy *par excellence*" (*op. cit.*, t. 1, p. 82). M. Lonchay (*op. cit.*, p. 40, *n.* 3) observes that the Anabaptists were treated rather as public enemies than as heretics. The imperial decree of Spires condemns them to death without the intervention of any spiritual judge: "Etiam sine ulla præeunte spiritualium judicum inquisitione."

[1] "It seems to me," he wrote, "that it is a serious thing to put men to death merely because they err on questions

is equally significant. Their leader, starting from an ascetic idea which was perfectly orthodox, was kindly received at the Third Lateran Council. Alexander III. embraced him, approved his vow of poverty,[1] and simply warned him not to preach without being authorized to do so by the priests. The Waldensians soon disregarded this warning, and, when left to themselves, condemned ecclesiastical property, and maintained that every layman in a state of grace had a power over the sacraments which was lost by a priest in a state of sin. This, as M. Jordan remarks,[2] was an idea " fundamentally destructive of all notion of Church and hierarchy." Thus, in 1194, Alphonsus II. of Aragon declared these misguided people to be outlaws; to destroy the Church was to destroy Christianity—that is to say, the social constitution of the Middle Ages. From that time, without taking into account the erroneous teachings on the subject of property in general and the civil power, the germ of which was to be found in the preceding errors,[3] or quoting

---

relating to the interpretation of Holy Scripture." We know that Calvin had recourse to a referendum of the reformed communities, which were not unanimous in his favour, and he felt the need of justifying his conduct by a book: *Defensio orthodoxæ fidei de SS. Trinitate, contra prodigiosos errores Michaelis Serveti, Hispani, ubi ostenditur hæreticos jure gladii coercendos esse*.

[1] See Cartellieri-Stechele, *Chronicon Universale Anonymi Laudunensis*, p. 29.

[2] Art. cit., *Annales de Phil. Chrét*, t. 8, pp. 575, 576.

[3] Thus Wycliffe maintained that mortal sin caused a Sovereign to lose his State: " Nullus est dominus civilis, nullus est prælatus, dum est in peccato mortali" (Proposition 15, condemned by the Council of Constance). See Jordan, art. cit., p. 576.

their directly antisocial tenets[1] we may conclude that their religious anarchy was then publicly combated, as political anarchy was at a later period—with this difference always, that formerly the teaching itself was punished, while nowadays the legislator boasts that the law punishes only the excesses to which the teaching naturally leads.

The repressive measures were much less severe in practice than in theory, and if, instead of searching the laws to find what heresy was punishable, and what heretics might be molested, we look to history for information as to the dogmatic errors which were actually made the subject of prosecution, we shall find that the heresies which were really hunted to death were those which, when spread abroad among the masses, sowed the seed of religious anarchy, and tended to the ruin and overthrow of the Church and society. In other words, the heresy persecuted was a *revolutionary reformist movement*.

[1] For example, the Albigensians and Waldensians contended from the words of Our Lord, "All that take the sword shall perish by the sword" (St. Matt. xxvi. 52), that society was not permitted to shed blood even in self-defence against malefactors and invaders. (Guiraud, quoted by Jordan, p. 576, l.c.)

IV. THE REPRESSION OF HERESY CONSIDERED FROM THE TRUE POINT OF VIEW.

SUMMARY: The true reason for the repressive measures taken against heretics not to be found in law books or speculative works.—Many authors reason from a too individualistic point of view.—The social explanation is the true one.—The repression then seems natural.—The convictions of the heretic could not arrest the severity of this repression.—A word on the number of the victims.

When we inquire who were the heretics against whom orthodoxy was excited, we begin to understand the true spirit of their long-continued pursuit. In the Middle Ages there was no lack of well-educated men and sagacious politicians; the common people, too, had their natural good sense and good feeling. The fact that such a society unanimously agreed to wage a war of extermination against heresy warns us that we must not seek for the real motives of the campaign in the temporary irritation of blind fanaticism, or in *ex post facto* arguments intended, not so much to persuade others as to produce a certain intellectual satisfaction. Nor shall we find in legislative texts, or treatises on procedure, or speculative works, the reasons for the laws which give to a particular epoch its distinctive character. Penal laws, for instance, tell us what acts are prohibited and what penalties are imposed for the commission of them, but they do not tell us why they are punished so severely: they give us a doctrinal principle, but the facts which led to the enactment of the law are taken for granted, or mentioned without any attempt at proof. In the case we are now considering, a heretic is put on his trial alone, separated from the rest of the party

THE REPRESSION OF HERESY 163

to which he belongs, and the judge who convicts and sentences him seems actuated by a desire to bring him by force to that faith which we consider as the gift of God. A duel is then begun in the name of the law between the judge, assisted by the executioners, and the accused, who is called upon to retract errors which he holds as truths. It is an assault upon the conscience, in which the argument of the stronger is enforced by fear; the man who resists the assault has the air of a hero, punished for his courage and sincerity.

Presented in this form, the proceedings against heresy are repugnant to our reason, our hearts, and even our religion. But this point of view is individualistic, and an important social fact like that of the repression of heresy cannot be understood without an explanation bearing upon the interests of the community.

Let us consider the laws in connection with the circumstances in which they were enacted. What do we see? First of all the East sees the rise of heresies on the subject of the person and nature of Christ; these heresies are purely theological, but their supporters are turbulent and factious, and their propaganda is not free from violence. The Christian Emperor desires to protect the unity of the Church, first as a matter of duty, and secondly for political reasons. To arrest the contagion, he banishes the innovators, but without making the crime of heresy punishable by death.

In the twelfth and thirteenth centuries the heretics attack the Church, and the moral order which she establishes and maintains. To attack the Church or the State is to threaten the society which is placed under the Pope and the Sovereign, and therefore the Sovereign punishes obstinate heresy with death, his action being anticipated by the verdict of the people. It is a severe measure, but the foregoing observations show us the true object of it, which is not the oppression of an individual conscience, but the defence of the community. Such a heretic, it is true, may be only a misguided person who leaves the Church, without any intention of plotting against her, but he is in too bad company for the Sovereign to feel secure. Heretical conspiracies and the dangers that follow from them make it unavoidable that all heresy should be looked upon as a first step towards conspiracy, and in those days authorities were not content with punishing the assassin, but searched for the error which had supplied him with his weapons; therefore, as long as Christianity was established by law, the punishment of heresy must have seemed as natural as to-day is the punishment of any attack upon public morality, which was then inseparable from the faith—as natural as will always be the suppression of any attempt to shake the foundations of society. Society in the Middle Ages was founded on religion, as well as on the family and property. We punish the thief because in stealing the goods of another he disturbs the social order and violates a law which exists for the protection of the public. How much more did the fanatical heretic disturb the social peace of our ancestors, and threaten to endanger the welfare of the whole community! At that time every heretic made men fear a fanatic, as the Russian police suspect a dynamitard in every Nihilist; and when the people attacked a heretic,

THE REPRESSION OF HERESY

as a crowd in the United States attacks certain malefactors, they yielded to a natural instinct of self-preservation, even if sometimes they committed acts of regrettable violence.

Will it be said that a heretic was not like a thief, but that he represented a principle or a conscientious conviction ? It would have been hard to make men believe that at that time of religious unity ; moreover, anarchists and conspirators have their convictions, but they are not such as modern judges consider as a reason for acquittal, and the conviction of the heretic was of the same class as these. The agreement of Popes, Princes, and people, to repress heretical apostasy may be explained by motives of social defence, and their action is not difficult to understand. As to the severity of the repression, it must be considered in relation to the manners of the age ; the punishment of death was inflicted for various offences much less dangerous to the society of the Middle Ages than heresy.[1] Lea has the honesty to

---

[1] The Abbé Vacandard seems to us to be mistaken as to the opinion of St. Thomas on the subject of the repression of heresy by capital punishment. On this point we share the opinion of M. Marc Dubruel (*Nouv. Rev. Théol.*, 1908, t. 40, p. 66 *sqq.*). In the passage in which St. Thomas treats formally of capital punishment (2, 2, Q. 64, Arts. 2 and 3), he declares that two conditions are necessary to justify the taking of life—namely, a sufficiently grave offence, and the necessity of punishment for the sake of the community. " If any man be dangerous to the community, and be corrupting it by any sin, the killing of him for the common good is praiseworthy and wholesome." The two conditions are found in the article quoted by M. Vacandard : the comparison between corrupting the faith by heresy and the offence of tampering with the coinage shows the gravity of the crime of heresy ; but the Church excommunicates the heretic, and delivers him to the secular arm, in her anxiety to save the innocent

admit this,[1] and MM. Maillet-Hanquet tell us that " under the criminal code of Charles V. death was the punishment of blasphemy, magic, sodomy, coining, falsification of weights and measures, and theft, and we find to some extent the same severity in the criminal law of the preceding age."[2]

We believe that no impartial judge would have any difficulty in coming to this conclusion. The interests of the Middle Ages necessitated the repression of heresy ; the manners of the age and the scale of punishments in force render a bloody repression inevitable.

(*aliorum saluti providet*), for fear of a general ruin (*Ne tota domus, massa, corpus, et pecora ardeant, corrumpantur, putrescant, intereant*). M. Vacandard passes a severe but unmerited condemnation on the thesis and arguments of St. Thomas for having neglected this second condition. He is similarly wrong when he accuses him of mutilating and distorting a passage of St. Augustine. We willingly admit that the great Bishop of Hippo never claimed for the Church the right to kill her rebellious children. St. Thomas makes no such assertion, but he may claim to have the support of St. Augustine to legalize such repression of heresy as the civil judge may think necessary for the good of society, even if it extends to the shedding of blood. The following is the passage quoted : " The Catholic Church may console herself for the grief caused her by the loss of a few, if this loss brings back the rest and gives security to the multitudes." And St. Augustine goes on to say : " Especially as the heretics in question bring about their own death." But this secondary consideration cannot lessen the force of a general statement. We regret to find the Angelic Doctor the object of such criticism as M. Vacandard has recorded on pp. 205-208, 211, 289, while an author like Lea finds himself rather flattered (pp. vii, viii).

[1] " We have only to look at the atrocities of the criminal law of the Middle Ages to see how pitiless men were in their dealings with one another " (*op. cit.*, t. 1, p. 234).

[2] *Op. cit.*, p. 98.

THE REPRESSION OF HERESY

Were the victims of the judicial repression of heresy numerous? The most absurd figures have everywhere been given, but, on the other hand, general history tells us of rejoicings, feasts, abundance, and general prosperity, during the centuries and in the countries in which the Inquisition exercised its functions. Such statements by themselves contradict the arbitrary estimates that have been made, and in reality, if we take the trouble to draw up an accurate list of the executions and the places where they took place, we shall find that the number is insignificant in comparison with the number of places in which no such repression took place, or little trace is left of it. M. Vacandard says: "The stake had but comparatively few victims."[1] Lea had already said: "I am convinced that the number of victims who actually perished at the stake is considerably less than has been imagined. ... The records of those evil days have mostly disappeared, and there is now no possibility of reconstructing their statistics; but if this could be done, I have no doubt that the actual executions by fire would excite surprise by falling far short of the popular estimate."[2] He goes on to mention a statement quoted by Dom Brial in his preface to vol. xxi. of the *Recueil des Historiens des Gaules*, to the effect that Bernard Gui put to death no less than 637 heretics during his service as Inquisitor of Toulouse, and adds: "Now, that, as we have seen, was the total number of sentences uttered by the tribunal during those years, and of those only forty were capital."[3] M.

[1] *L'Inquisition*, p. 249. [2] *Op. cit.*, t. I, p. 549.
[3] *Op. cit.*, p. 550.

Jordan remarks that this collection of sentences is the most complete that has been preserved.[1]

Bernard Gui completed the suppression of the Catharist heresy. The second Spanish Inquisition sacrificed a larger number of lives, though it is difficult to say how many. Gams,[2] whose estimate is moderate, gives a total of about four thousand.

The French Reign of Terror in less than three years was responsible for a larger number of victims than all the Inquisitions put together in three centuries.

V. WHAT AUTHORITY MADE HERESY PUNISHABLE WITH DEATH?

SUMMARY: The question is not asked to excuse the Church, but it has another practical purpose.—Our explanation is not that accepted by theologians and canonists later than the sixteenth century.—Cause of differences of opinion. Repression of heresy may be ecclesiastical or social and political.—Bloody repression was from the social and political side. It absorbed the ecclesiastical repression.—Proofs.—How the ecclesiastical power, nevertheless, was able to insist on the enforcement of the laws against heresy. — Actual result: to-day heresy is not, even theoretically, punishable with death.

From the thirteenth century obstinate or relapsed heretics incurred the penalty of death, and we know why. We know also the judge who condemned them, and the hand that struck them. It remains to be seen who was the principal author of that severity. Did the secular arm that struck them act in its own name or as the mandatory of the spiritual authority? Did it serve the religious or the civil society?

[1] Art. cit., 1909, p. 47, n.
[2] *Die Kirchengeschichte von Spanien*, t. 3, pp. 68-76.

CAPITAL PUNISHMENT

We look upon this as a serious and practical question. Other persons, under the influence of hatred or prejudice, are disposed to look upon it as a mere quibble. They suspect us of wishing only to invent excuses for the Church, and will tell us that we are wasting our time, that they cannot follow us, that the case has been decided. Let us say at once that our object is not to excuse the Church or relieve it of its responsibility. We do not deny the approval that the Popes bestowed on the laws under which heretics were proscribed and punished with death, nor the exhortations they addressed from time to time to the secular Sovereigns to observe and enforce the laws. Whatever may have been the character of the punishment, whether civil or canonical, that approval and those exhortations are enough to create responsibility.

Does not the discussion then become futile? By no means. To specify the authority for a capital sentence is to discover the law which made it legal, and implicitly to define the cases and circumstances in which it may be, or may have been, legitimate. A full explanation of the past throws light upon the future.

A second observation seems necessary. We have seen, in treating of the right of the sword, how theologians and canonists since the Reformation, impressed by events and influenced by the current of opinions, appear to have exaggerated the repressive jurisdiction of the Church, and especially her original jurisdiction. Our explanation therefore shall not be taken from their works, nor echo their opinions. We doubt also whether the authors of certain pontifical letters[1] have always grasped the real nature of the penalties which they considered justifiable. It often happens that the true explanation of facts and usages is only discovered after the occurrence of the facts to be explained. Moreover, the close union between the two powers lessened the importance of rigorous exactitude, and sometimes led to mistakes. " Undoubtedly, from an abstract and speculative point of view," justly remarks Father Choupin,[2] " we may consider heresy under a twofold aspect—as a religious offence or a civil crime. But at that time in practice, in the real concrete order, these two points of view were identical." It is with the distinctions between the two powers as it is with the very nature of their jurisdiction : they are gradually made clear by discussions and facts. In our own time, also, writers of repute have fallen into opposite errors on this subject. But the canonists and theologians of one period and one country are not

[1] It is important to remember that the promise of infallibility covers all acts of teaching by the Pope, where he teaches the whole Church on a point of faith or morals in the exercise of his supreme Apostolic authority, but not the arguments used, still less the motives or subjective reasons which have led to the definitions. That is why a cautious interpreter of such acts attaches much more importance to the exact wording of the definition than he would in the case of civil enactments. The context, though it cannot be put aside altogether, furnishes much less conclusive argument in the former case than in the latter. The Bulls, in which we find the assertion of an indirect temporal power only, may have been issued by Popes who were convinced of their direct temporal power, and, similarly, the idea that certain Popes have formed of the penalties enacted against heretics does not fix the meaning of those penalties if that meaning is not taught in the authoritative decree.   [2] *L'Inquisition*, p. 52.

CAPITAL PUNISHMENT

the whole Church; their mistakes do not take away from the significance which the documents possess by themselves, and which has been made clear for us by so many declarations of past ages.[1]

Still less need we trouble ourselves about the manner in which a directory for the use of Inquisitors, composed by a fiery Inquisitor of Aragon and much criticized in his lifetime, understands the prosecution of heresy.[2] Even if such a work contains no mention of social considerations, and if it enters into minute details on the signs of heresy, what is there to wonder at, and how does it affect our argument? The Inquisitor was not a secular magistrate, and his duty was essentially to decide on the existence of heresy, and to endeavour to bring convicted heretics back to the Church.

After these preliminary observations we may now confidently invite our readers to examine calmly and deliberately the question before us—namely, whether heresy was punished by death as a civil or a religious offence.

Certainly the proscription was directed against the religious error itself, and not only against the criminal excesses which followed it. In this respect, as we willingly admit, and have already remarked, there is a difference between the laws of former ages

---

[1] In some respects those earlier ages resembled our own much more than did the Middle Ages and the commencement of the modern age.

[2] "Acer hæreticæ pravitatis in regnis regis Aragonum inquisitor" is the description of Eymeric in Pegna's preface. "Multos habuit vir ille dum viveret adversarios," adds the biographical notice by the same Pegna. In our opinion, M. Jordan gives far too much attention to manuals of procedure.

and those of our own time: the former struck at opinions professed or published,[1] the latter only at offences committed. Yet our question is not answered, for the war against religious error may, as Father Choupin admits, proceed either from the strictly or formally religious or the social and political point of view. Religious error stains the soul, and takes away from it the principle of supernatural life. If it spreads, there is danger of it contaminating other souls; this is the formally religious point of view, and the penalty imposed for voluntary error tends towards the double object contemplated by the Councils—the reformation of the guilty and the preservation of the innocent.

---

[1] Mgr. Douais is right in saying (p. 160) that "exteriority or publicity was an essential condition of the offence," and (p. 149) that "the acts liable to punishment were distinctly outward acts, and it is their publicity which gives them the character of offences." We cannot deny this without forgetting the old maxim, "Cogitationis pœnam nemo patitur" (C. *Cogitationis*, 14 *De Pœnitentia*, d. 1), and contradicting a universally accepted principle of jurisprudence (see Reiffenstuel, *De Hæreticis*, in l. 5, t. 7, *n.* 235; and Schmalzgrueber, *eodem*, *n.* 87). And the axiom is not explained by simple want of proof, for ecclesiastical censures which strike the guilty person without the intervention of the judge do not extend to interior acts. Even in the tribunal of sacramental confession the interior act confessed is judged simply as being contrary to the law of God, and does not form the object of reservation or ecclesiastical censure. We cannot agree with the criticism of M. Jordan (*loc cit*., t. 9, p. 35). No doubt the Church requires of her children an outward profession of faith, and therefore the Inquisition was entitled to ask for such a profession from persons suspected of heresy; but suppose the case of a person who simply admits that he has given an interior consent to a heretical proposition: he is not within the cognizance of the ecclesiastical judge, as a person would be who admitted a public discourse or an outward act of heresy.

CAPITAL PUNISHMENT

From the other point of view, the influence which religious truth exercises on the private relations of citizens among themselves, and the public relations between the Government and its subjects; the assistance it gives in the performance of all the duties of justice and charity; the happiness it gives to men at peace with themselves;[1] the consolidation of public peace, the tightening of social bonds, and all the other blessings which come from unity in religious truth, require that such doctrines as threaten the loss of these blessings should be effectively proscribed. Moreover, these doctrines, by weakening religious authority, endanger that alliance of the two powers on which was based the public order of Christendom. The Church, in fighting against heresy, seeks to provide men with the most abundant means of sanctification. Civil society desires to place at their disposal more elements of order, of social peace, and temporal welfare; therefore, instead of ordering its repression of false doctrine on the evil effects produced, it punishes the error which contains the germ of those effects.[2]

[1] Experience teaches us how true are the words of Jesus Christ that there is a peace which He alone can give, and the world cannot give. Irreligious socialism excites envy, but can never give contentment; it may raise wages, but it can never remove hatred and malice and all those sentiments which embitter misfortune and alienate sympathy. The Christian in poverty and misfortune has more real peace than the wicked man in the midst of affluence and success.

[2] M. Jordan seems to have lost sight of this distinction. In the *Annales* (t. 9, p. 22) he says: "At the present day certain doctrines are prosecuted because they are dangerous; formerly they were prosecuted because they were false." Even if this assertion were literally true, it would not be conclusive for the present question. If the falseness of a

CIVIL TOLERANCE

The two possible points of view being thus clearly distinguished, is it difficult to see which of the two dominates the whole history of the bloody repression of heresy? Under the Roman Empire itself, and under all the systems of government which followed, the heresies treated with the greatest severity were those which were antisocial in character, or those whose extirpation was demanded by political considerations. The Roman law formally declares that it is severe in the public interest, " because whatever is committed against Divine religion is committed against the right of all."[1] " Law and reason command that all wicked men should die, such as those who habitually do evil and consent to evil, such as sodomites and thieves, heretics and traitors, and all wicked men and women." Thus, the Assizes of Jerusalem[2] (1170-1180) placed heretics among thieves and traitors, and by a common reason justified the punishment prescribed against all. Frederic II., in issuing his famous Constitutions, especially declares that he confirms the principle of the Roman law, and ranks heresy amongst the offences against the State.[3]

---

doctrine is decided to be dangerous, if " the Inquisition never admitted that error could be inoffensive " (Jordan, p. 32), the repression of former times might be social as well as that of to-day. Whether the public danger of errors is in their falseness or in the acts to which they lead, the formal principle of repression is not changed: they are prosecuted because they are dangerous; the prosecution is dictated by considerations of public order; the motive of the repression is social.

[1] C. *De Hæreticis*, i. 5, l. 4.
[2] The code of laws framed for the kingdom of Jerusalem at the instance of Godfrey of Bouillon, the Crusader.
[3] C. *Inconsutilem*.

CAPITAL PUNISHMENT

The political and social motives of the repression of heretics are affirmed, for the Roman Empire by Loening,[1] Hinschius,[2] and Mommsen;[3] for Castile by Lea;[4] for the lower Middle Ages and the beginning of the sixteenth century by M. Lonchay;[5] and it would not be difficult to multiply such proofs.

Let us consider the reasons given to justify capital punishment for heresy. The greatest canonists appealed to considerations of public order. " Obstinate heretics in their impenitence are punished with death, because they disturb the peace and tranquillity of the Republic."[6] " The reason of the great severity (death and imprisonment for life) shown to heretics is found in the gravity of this crime, and the immense harm it causes, not only to the Church and religion, but also to the common welfare and the peace of the Republic."[7] " The reason for punishing heretics with death is that heresy is so great a crime, not only against religion, but also against the public peace and tranquillity."[8] Finally, Pichler, who considers that the penalty of death is justified both by canon law and civil law, alleges " the enormity of the crime of heresy, which destroys the faith, the foundation not only of the Christian

---

[1] *Op. cit.*, t. 1, p. 96. [2] *Op. cit.*, t. 4, p. 791.
[3] *Roman Penal Law*, Duquesne's translation, t. 2, p. 206.
[4] *Op. cit.*, t. 2, p. 184. " All this shows that Alfonso and his advisers recognized the duty of the State to preserve the purity of the faith, but that they considered it wholly an affair of the State, in which the Church had no voice beyond ascertaining the guilt of the accused."
[5] *Les Édits des Princes-évêques, etc.*, p. 25.
[6] Pirhing, *Jus Canon.*, Comment. in l. 5, t. 7, *n.* 92.
[7] Reiffenstuel, *Jus Canon. Universum*, Comment. in l. 5, t. 7, *n.* 323.
[8] Schmalzgrueber, *Jus Eccl. Universum*, in *eundem locum*, *n.* 165.

State, but of eternal salvation. It ruins an incalculable number of souls, and does more than any other crime to disturb the public tranquillity."[1]

It might be said that these canonists unconsciously feel the insufficiency of purely religious reasons to justify capital punishment, so careful are they to seek the complement of their proof in reasons of social mischief.

It was in its own name and on its own initiative, as history tells us, that the Roman Empire took its strong measures against the Manichæans, and later against the Donatists; it was on his own authority—he expressly declares it—that Frederic II. prescribed sentence of death by burning against obstinate or relapsed heretics; and that Raymond of Toulouse introduced the same punishment against the Catharists and the Albigenses of the South. The Anabaptists, as we have seen from the testimony of M. Lonchay, were hunted down as public enemies rather than as heretics.

These positive reasons, which seem to us conclusive in themselves, are corroborated by these additional considerations: If heresy was prosecuted to the death as a religious offence, how is it that the magistrate appointed to decide the case from this point of view—that is, the ecclesiastical magistrate —was forbidden to pronounce sentence?[2] How is it

[1] Pichler, in *eundem locum*, *n.* 5.
[2] The doctrine which would recognize in the Church the full power of insisting on a sentence of death, and at the same time would oblige the Prince to pass the sentence, at first sight presents an artificial and factitious character which does not belong to the simple truth.

According to Gonzales (*Comment.*, l. 5, t. 7, c. 9, *ad*

CAPITAL PUNISHMENT

that the Popes who approved the Constitutions of Frederic II., and pressed for their enforcement, abstained from incorporating them in their canonical collections ? The frankness of the declarations contained in Papal Bulls proves conclusively that they were not really influenced by a desire to save their own reputation for clemency, and, as we have seen, such an attempt would have been ineffective.

Everything is made clear if capital punishment was legalized and inflicted only from the civil point of view. There was nothing to prevent the Church from recognizing that the same criminal act, as a civil offence, deserved the punishment which she had never prescribed against a religious offence.

Moreover, in our theory, there is another explanation of the plea for mercy which the ecclesiastical judge was directed to make ; even if the condemned person hoped for no good result, the plea served at least to mark the secular character of the punishment. The ecclesiastical judge, in pleading for mitigation, not only showed that he remembered the personal clemency which was suitable to him as the minister of Christ, but he took away from the punishment the strictly ecclesiastical motive.

But what are we to say of the pontifical Constitutions which enjoined upon the secular powers to enforce the rigorous laws enacted against heretics ? Can such an admonition be conceived if the punish-

---

abolendam), the Spanish Inquisitor himself passed sentence of death. But the Spanish Inquisitor had a royal commission, and was thus invested with a double jurisdiction. Moreover, Paul IV. and St. Pius V. had, by a special privilege, exempted the Spanish Inquisitors from the penalty of irregularity.

ment was not meant to satisfy the Church as well as the State ? We must first inquire whether the Popes promulgated these Constitutions as spiritual heads of the Church, or whether they did not rather make use of the political prerogatives which they possessed as Christian Princes, as Sovereigns of certain States, or as collators of the imperial dignity. Not one of the Constitutions quoted was of universal application ; all were limited to Italy and had their origin in the special solicitude which the Popes owed to that country. But even when we consider pontifical Acts properly so called, they create no difficulty to the acceptance of our theory. The Pope may properly declare to Princes what duties are imposed on them by a due regard for the welfare of their subjects or their States ; the pontifical injunction that Princes should keep in force the most rigorous laws enacted against heretics did but declare how far the right of the civil power extended,[1] and what, in the existing condition of legislation and according to the customs of the age, was the proper manner for them to fulfil their duty to the

---

[1] The condemnation by Leo X. (May 16, 1520) of the thirty-third proposition of Luther goes no farther than this. The proposition was : " It is contrary to the will of the Holy Ghost to burn heretics "; and, in condemning it, simply affirms that certain heretics in certain circumstances may legitimately be condemned to death by burning. He does not specify the circumstances or the grounds which may justify the sentence, nor the heretics who may deserve it, nor the authority which may pass the sentence. From this condemnation, " we may conclude with certainty that the sentence of death for heresy is not always necessarily unjustifiable." See Yves de la Brière, *L'Emploi de la Force au Service de la Vraie Religion*. Études, October 5, 1911.

CAPITAL PUNISHMENT

Church and to the communities over which they ruled.

All this brings us to the conclusion that in proscribing heresy the Princes acted in the interests of the Church and the Faith ; but in going so far as to pass sentences of death, they protected the social order, of which they had the direct and immediate charge. The same civil repression of obstinate heretics—such, at least, is our opinion—served at the same time the defence of the Church and the defence of the State, just as the ecclesiastical punishments inflicted on penitent heretics safeguarded the interests of spiritual society and civil society. But inasmuch as the secular power legalized and inflicted an irreparable corporal punishment (death or mutilation), it acted in its own name and for the maintenance of public order.

Our reasoning and its conclusion lead to one remarkable result. The religious offence of heresy exists to-day as it did in the past. If you consider it, as such, worthy of capital punishment, you authorize the enemies of the Church to maintain that she holds the sword always suspended over the head of the apostate, and that only her want of power prevents her from striking ; and the clamour of disapproval which you will arouse will produce the melancholy result of keeping outside the Church many worn and weary souls that long to live in Catholic unity and truth.

But heresy is no longer the social offence that it once was, because agreement on the subject of religion is no longer at the base of our societies. If, then, the social conditions of a certain period were necessary to explain the severity of the time, the Catholic may say, as well as the unbeliever, that nowadays heresy is not punishable with death. Looking at the change that has taken place in manners and ideas, we may even anticipate that it never will be so again, and may bid a final farewell to punishments which will be henceforth unjust and undeserved.

CHAPTER III

CIVIL TOLERANCE FROM THE REFORMATION TO THE FRENCH REVOLUTION

ARTICLE I. REVIEW OF THE FACTS OF THIS PERIOD.

SUMMARY: At the Reformation the principle of civil tolerance has no advocate.—Proof of this.—Political character of intolerance emphasized.—Universal decadence of the Inquisition as a mixed tribunal of repression.—Collective wars and repressions.—Protestant intolerance.—Its long-continued severity against Catholics in various countries of Europe and even in America.—Truces in religious wars.—Edicts and treaties of tolerance either on a social basis or on a geographical basis.

WHEN the Reformation appeared, the principle of civil tolerance was nowhere advocated or practised. "The unity of religion," says M. Pirenne, "was a guarantee of political unity in the view of the Princes of his [Charles V.'s] time. . . . Everyone, even Thomas More and Erasmus, proclaimed the necessity of a State religion."[1] M. de Bélesbat, in the plea for clemency which he addressed to Louis XIV., said: "It is stated as an incontrovertible axiom that for a State to maintain itself

[1] *Histoire de Belgique*, t. 3, p. 332.

in peace there must be one King, one law, one faith."[1]

The conviction which is the basis of civil intolerance imprints its own character upon it. "What is the nature," asks M. Jules Lemaître, "of the intolerance of the old régime?" and he answers: "Even under the appearance of religion it is always essentially political."[2] "In France," says M. Tanon, "the Reformers were considered as criminals who disturbed the State by their rebellion against religion and their overt or secret conspiracies. In so far as they were heretics, they belonged, of course, to the Church; but, in addition, they were seditious, and rebels against the King, because they violated his ordinances; and disturbers of the public peace, since the welfare of the kingdom and the tranquillity of the State depended principally on the preservation of the Faith. Thus considered, heresy, which was a crime ordinarily within the cognizance of the ecclesiastical judge, was absorbed in the crime against the State, which was exclusively within the cognizance of the secular courts: the ecclesiastical judge was concerned only with simple heresies, which in themselves did not amount to disobedience to the King, or sedition, or public scandal."[3] We have already seen that, according to an order of May 17, 1331, the tribunal

[1] Quoted by M. Dedieu, *La Question Protestante d'après des Documents Inédits*, in the *Revue Pratique d'Apologétique*, t. 10, p. 407.

[2] Second Conference of 1910 on the relations of Bossuet and Fénelon with Protestants.

[3] *Histoire des Tribunaux de l'Inquisition en France*, etc., p. 353.

of the Inquisition itself was regarded, not as an ecclesiastical tribunal, but one of royal institution.[1] According to the testimony of M. Pirenne, " it was not only the Catholic convictions of Charles V., however firm and sincere they may have been, that dictated his conduct ; it was principally political reasons, universally accepted, and professed alike by his enemies and his partisans."[2] " The repression of heresy, as he looked at it, was a public service, a police regulation, directed in the name of the Sovereign against a new species of crime."[3]

The centralizing and jealous absolutism of the Sovereigns of the sixteenth and seventeenth centuries, in bringing cases of heresy under their own jurisdiction, destroyed the Inquisition, which, moreover, was too slow and too old to cope with the religious movement whose audacious and turbulent youth was intoxicated with its rapid success. The words of M. Lonchay, " The history of the Inquisition has not yet been treated as it ought to be,"[4] remain as true as ever, especially for this period. It is certain, nevertheless, that from the sixteenth century the Inquisition declined as a mixed court of criminal jurisdiction. In France, under Francis I., the Parliaments, with their *chambres ardentes*, had already supplanted it, and its existence was only nominal when the last tribunal—that of Toulouse— was abolished under Louis XIV.[5] The fact that it

[1] *Histoire des Tribunaux de l'Inquisition en France*, etc., p. 550.
[2] *Histoire de Belgique*, t. 3, p. 332.   [3] *Ibid*, t. 3, p. 336.
[4] *Les Édits des Princes-évêques*, etc., p. 28.
[5] Tanon, *op. cit.*, p. 554. It had already presented the extraordinary spectacle of a Grand Inquisitor declaring himself a Calvinist, and going bravely to the stake (1538).

disappeared more slowly elsewhere was not a sign of its greater vitality.[1] Even in Spain, in which it killed some germs of Protestantism, *autos-da-fé* became less and less frequent; freemasons, blasphemers, and sorcerers sometimes settled their accounts with the Spanish Inquisition.[2] It was always languishing in Bohemia; and, as we already know, it made only a short appearance in Germany in the thirteenth century. It disappeared early in South Germany and in Poland. England had never known the Inquisition properly so called, except for the suppression of the Templars. In 1414, Henry V. established a sort of half-secular Inquisition, which was abolished by Parliament under Elizabeth, but without any mitigation of the severity of the laws; in England death was the normal punishment for heresy. Rome and the pontifical States possess an Inquisition which is more truly ecclesiastical. Its secrets have not been revealed, but its moderation is well known; not a single capital sentence for simple heresy can be laid to its charge. Under Sixtus I.[3] the Roman Inquisition finally became the Holy Office, the jurisdiction of which over faith and morals extends to the whole world.

[1] In Spain, after being suppressed by Napoleon in 1808, and re-established in 1814, it was finally abolished in 1820. Pius VII. had confirmed it in 1816, only on condition that torture and capital punishment were completely given up. Portugal preserved its tribunal of the Inquisition until 1821, while Goa had none after 1815.

[2] Under Ferdinand VI. See Llorente, *Histoire crit. de l'Inquisition d'Espagne*, t. 4, chap. 41, art. 2, p. 53 sqq.

[3] C. *Immensa æterni Dei.*

SINCE THE REFORMATION

The period we are considering is thus not so much one of judicial repression as one of violent struggles and commotions, in which wars, massacres, and collective repressions, play a more important part than individual trials before courts and tribunals.

The revolutionary Reformation, not content with destroying religious unity in Europe, made rapid progress over the Continent; and how cruel and pitiless it was when it was in power! The tribunals set up by the Calvinists and English Protestants employed all manner of ingenious and brutal tortures, and the list of their victims included those for whom their intrepid courage, their brilliant services to the State, the nobility of their birth, their sacred character, even their youth and gentle sex, might well have excited the pity of their judges. The leaders of the Reformation and their disciples called for the massacre and extermination of those who professed any belief but their own; their fury, always excited against the Papists, extended sometimes to dissenters of other sects. Protestant St. Bartholomews, especially in the South, preceded and followed the Catholic[1] St. Bartholomew. England is not alone in presenting the spectacle of a people subjected to three successive conversions—first to schism, then to the Catholic Church, and again to schism and heresy. In the Palatinate, Frederic III. passed in 1563 from Lutheranism to Calvinism, and all his subjects were compelled to follow him or go into exile. His son Louis in 1576—that is, only

[1] Or, rather, political. The remark is M. Jules Lemaître's. Scholastic manuals, in spite of their boasted impartiality, do not present the facts in the true light.

thirteen years later—compelled them to return to Lutheranism ; and in 1583 Casimir forced them a second time into Calvinism, and its preachers pointed out his duty in the following lines :

> *O Casimire potens, servos expelle Lutheri ;*
> *Ense, rota, ponto, funibus, igne, neca.*[1]

Thus, in modern times two kinds of civil intolerance have come into conflict, one of which displayed the ancient Catholic standard, while the other waved the flag of some new sect—Lutheran, Calvinist, Anglican, or what not. But what a difference there was between them ! The former, at least, was legal and regular, while in Germany, France, and the Netherlands, the latter was often the work of fanatic rebels and grasping usurpers. Protestant intolerance, even when, like the other, it carries out the designs of constituted powers—designs generally framed for political purposes—is distinguished from the other by its arbitrary procedure, its principle, and the field of its application. Catholic Princes may be severe and tyrannical, but the respect which they profess for spiritual authority always places some restraint on their excesses, which more than once have been checked and rebuked by the Popes. They protect a religion whose creed they have accepted as subjects ; they protect it in favour of a Church which presents its credentials, and claims to be regarded as the authoritative organ of a religion necessary to salvation. Their intolerance is comprehensible, and does not degenerate into arbitrary despotism.

[1] Oh, mighty Casimir ! expel the servants of Luther :
Slay them by the sword, the wheel, the water, the rope, the fire.

But the Protestant Sovereign is not bound to follow any counsel but his own. If he does not himself compose the articles of an unstable creed, he listens to the teacher who pleases him best ; and he practises his intolerance, which knows no fixed rule or limit, in the name of a Protestantism which prides itself on introducing liberty of private judgment. Thus the intolerance of the theologians of the Reformation is a mystery which excites the curiosity and puzzles the ingenuity of historians to the present day.[1]

Catholic intolerance acts on the defensive; Protestant intolerance is aggressive. The Church desires to remain in countries from which the Reformation insists on excluding her, and to maintain her ground where Protestantism is determined to overthrow her ; she seeks to preserve the faithful whom Protestantism seeks to snatch from her, and to prevent apostasies which Protestantism would enforce, even by violent means.

Of the two kinds of intolerance we shall see that the Protestant is always the most arrogant, the most severe,[2] the most opinionative, and the most persistent.

For more than two centuries a fierce Protestant intolerance raged in England ; it was unremitting against Catholics, but sometimes harassed the Nonconformist sects also. When Cromwell glorified

---

[1] See the different attempts at explanation in Ruffini, *La Libertà Religiosa*, p. 59 *sqq*. We shall have occasion to return to this subject in Part III.

[2] The severe edicts of Charles V. were, in a great measure, simply threats ; the English persecutions were, in both England and Ireland, a long and painful reality.

188   CIVIL TOLERANCE

liberty of conscience as one of the most precious gifts of God, he had just sworn to maintain the Constitution which refused to grant liberty to Catholics. The Mass appeared to him a symbol of political hostility. Popery was a crime. Charles II. tried in vain, on December 26, 1662, and March 15, 1672, to include Catholics in a Declaration of Indulgence; and in the very year (1689) in which James II. proclaimed complete liberty of conscience in Dublin, the English Parliament, rallying round William of Orange, expressly excluded Catholics from the benefits of the Toleration Act.[1] The Catholic Emancipation Act was not passed until 1829, and even now Catholics are ineligible for certain high offices of State.

In the time of Christian III., Denmark, which was closed to priests under pain of death, deprived Catholics of their political rights and all rights of succession. The code of Christian V., published in 1663, was equally severe against them, and it was only commercial and diplomatic reasons that moderated the severity of the rule, which lasted until the middle of the nineteenth century.

The most enlightened Sovereigns of Sweden—even Gustavus Adolphus, who was praised for having declared himself the enemy of religious intolerance—did not know how to be equitable towards Catholics; and Görtz, the Minister of Charles XII., was accused of permitting the violation of the fundamental laws of the kingdom by tolerating to some extent the liberty of Catholic worship. The Patent of Tolerance of 1783 gave them some measure of

[1] Macaulay, *History of England*, t. 3, pp. 84, 208 (ed. 1855).

SINCE THE REFORMATION

liberty, but reserved to Lutherans the monopoly of all public offices, and punished conversions to the Faith.

It is unnecessary to speak at length of the Calvinistic intolerance of Switzerland, which was shown in the middle of the nineteenth century in the war on the Catholic Sonderbund, with the support of Palmerston, and in the framing of the federal Constitution. An article of this charter makes the banishment of Jesuits one of the enactments of Modern Helvetia.

At the end of the seventeenth century the French Protestant pastor Jurieu maintained that Papists had no right to interfere with Protestants, but that the latter had the right to coerce and punish those who differed from them, and to have recourse to the secular arm for that purpose.[1] Similarly, at the Diet of Augsburg (1555) the Lutheran Princes claimed to regulate the religion of their own States, but refused to grant the same authority to Catholic Princes. Neither Henry IV. nor Richelieu succeeded in obtaining for the Catholic subjects of the German Princes the toleration which they granted to the Protestants of France.

Is it necessary to mention the Catholic martyrs of the Netherlands ? In spite of all the edicts of tolerance which appeared in that country, the laws imposing restrictions on Catholic worship were not abolished at the French Revolution.

[1] *Des Droits de Deux Souverains en Matière de Religion, la Conscience et le Prince;* Rotterdam, 1687, p. 284 *sqq*. Without imposing religion by force, this Calvinist advised the State to forbid Catholic worship and to take away their churches from Catholics. In short, he elaborated a plan of persecution for the use of contemporary Masonic Lodges.

In America, the Puritans displayed an intolerant fanaticism in Massachussets. Maryland, on April 25, 1649, under a Catholic majority, adopted the Act of Tolerance, the first decree of complete liberty for all Christians, voted by a legislative assembly. As soon as the Protestants obtained a majority, the Act was abolished; restored later by Catholics, liberty perished again after 1676, when the country came under the rule of William of Orange. In the eighteenth century Catholics were not tolerated in Virginia nor the Carolinas, New England, the philanthropic colony of Georgia, New York, or New Jersey;[1] and when the American Constitution was debated, an article forbidding that any profession of faith should be a condition of holding any public office was rejected for fear lest power should pass into the hands of Catholics.

Maria Theresa, reproaching Joseph II. for showing too little interest in the progress of Catholic truth, said with justice: " I do not see this indifference in all Protestants; on the contrary, I should wish that everyone could imitate them, and that no State permitted this indifference."[2]

However, conflicts wore themselves out, and commercial relations led to treaties of peace; and the impossibility of agreement made men resigned to separation. Sovereigns granted edicts of tolerance to Dissenters, the most celebrated being that which Henry IV. signed at Nantes in 1598, to give relief to the French Huguenots; others in Germany and Switzerland were in favour of the Lutherans and

[1] See Ruffini, *op cit.*, pp. 315, 316.
[2] Letter of July 5, 1777; edit. Von Arneth, l. 262, t. 2, p. 146.

other Protestants. Or, again, rulers of States made compromises either on a geographical basis or a social basis, either by division of territory or on the broad foundation of mutual understanding. The Sovereign decides on the religion of his subjects—"*cujus regio, illius et religio*"—or he engages not to molest the professors of another faith. The territorial solution is intolerant in principle, as it gives the Government the right to make a particular religion compulsory. The toleration of different religions in the same State may be dictated by practical considerations, but it does not require new theories or any sacrifice of principles. We have considered the facts, and now proceed to examine the doctrines of the same period.

ARTICLE II. THE DOCTRINES OF THE SAME PERIOD.

1. *Doctrines of Intolerance criticized.*

SUMMARY: Principles of intolerance.—The political absorption of religion.—Religious unity regarded as indispensable to the State.—Territorialism.—Refutation of these doctrines.

Christianity has rendered impossible for ever in our countries that political absorption of religious life which was the foundation of the intolerance of former times. Only the fierce enthusiasm of Zwingli and Calvin would have thought of ever again identifying the Church and the State. But though the distinction between the two is strictly observed, civil intolerance may be defended on this other principle, "Religious unity makes the unity of the State." When such unity really exists—above all, when it is the result of voluntary adherence to a religion which has been proved to be true—the proposition, though exaggerated in its expression, is not altogether unreasonable. But, taken literally as always true, it leads to an absolute intolerance, which imposes religious unity as essential to the State—nay, more, as the State's necessary work: without being identified with religion, the State goes so far as to define what it is.

This absolutist idea, which was given up for centuries, reappeared in its old form towards the end of the Middle Ages. In the middle of the sixteenth century it took concrete form in *Territorialism*, whose classical axiom was *Cujus regio, illius et religio*. The State, as an exclusive association, assumed the exclusive right to define, as well as to protect, the interests of its members. To the pact which united them (*pactum unionis*) was added another, which made them subject to political direction in all things, even including religion (*pactum subjectionis*). The citizen, being controlled in all outward acts, was free only in his inward thoughts.

A similar doctrine, embellished with ancient quotations, is found in Grotius[1] and J. J. Rousseau,[2] those modern politicians who assert the universal supremacy of the State; and, in fact, many collectivists have not yet discarded it.

And yet it is radically false: the State, not having religion for its object, does not find in religion the principle of its unity. It is therefore not true to say that "religious unity makes the unity of the State."

[1] *De imperio summarum potestatum circa sacra*, t. 2, c. 8.
[2] *Du Contrat Social*, l. 4, c. 8.

DOCTRINES OF INTOLERANCE

But, since it strengthens the bonds of union between citizens, this unity is a great benefit to the State, provided always that it is unity in the truth. Religion, in fact, is so far-reaching in its influence on the life of every individual, and on men's relations with one another, that common error on the subject of religion cannot fail to be prejudicial to the community. Such outward tranquillity as would be produced by agreement in common error would be more fitly called atrophy than real peace. In proportion as it is false,[1] a common religion gives tranquillity only in lessening vitality; religious lethargy is an essential condition of its continuance. Agreement in common error, which is by nature precarious, is only lasting in the paralyzing effect it produces on men's minds.

Religious unity does not make the unity of the State; and the contemporary States in which this unity does not exist are not necessarily the worse for its absence: such is the position we take up towards the intolerance which makes a dogma of the necessity of unity to the State.

Still more absurd than the theory which makes the unity of the State depend on religious unity is the territorial theory which places the principle of this unity in the will of the Sovereign. The principle *Cujus regio illius et religio*, Protestant in its origin,[2] makes the citizens mere slaves of the

[1] Religions, in fact, are never wholly false; some retain more truth, and some less. In proportion as they agree with the true religion, they may, by that part of the truth that they contain, become socially beneficial; but always less so than the true religion.

[2] "It was, alas! the Reformation which had the sad courage to adopt for its own profit the ancient axiom *Cujus*

Sovereign. The advocates of this principle, in their desire for unity at any price, do not hesitate to purchase unity by the oppression of all consciences, except that of the tyrant to whom they allow absolute despotism.

2. *The Doctrines of Tolerance.*

SUMMARY : Different schools of tolerance, according to the motives and the form of tolerance.

When the disruption of Christendom appeared irremediable, there were not wanting clear-sighted men[1] who insisted on the necessity of mitigating the severity of laws and decrees. The rigorous measures taken against the French Calvinists were disapproved by many Bishops,[2] who declared that it was more important to convert than to punish, and that force was a poor means of conversion.

There is no longer need to discuss such counsels; but alongside the Catholic doctrine appeared a new doctrine of civil tolerance, which its advocates presented as if it were a dogma. It is, perhaps, too

---

regio illius et religio." Thus speaks Georges Frommel in the Protestant collection, *Foi et Vie, les Destinées de l'Individualité à travers le Develcppement du Christianisme Catholique ;* Paris-Geneva, 1903, p. 16. The author gives the axiom in this form, *Hujus regio cujus religio.*

[1] Such as Justus Lipsius, *Civilis Doctrinæ,* l. 4, cc. 2 and 3.
[2] See Dargaud, *Histoire de la Liberté en France et de ses Fondateurs,* t. 1, p. 370. In spite of his distinctly anti-Roman bias, this author, in describing the Assembly of Notables held in 1560, mentions as advocates of tolerance Marillac, Archbishop of Vienne in Dauphiné, and Jean de Montluc, Bishop of Valence. The latter declared that " bloody executions on account of religion were barbarities as contrary to the Gospel as to the great Councils of the primitive Church."

DOCTRINES OF TOLERANCE

much to speak of a *dogma*, for unity was wanting. The advocates of the civil tolerance which was made a dogma did not agree on the motives that prompted it, or the practical conclusions to be arrived at. In giving their names, we must not confuse their ideas; they pleaded different causes, and it would be wholly incorrect to suppose that for or against the same kind of tolerance a battle was fought, lasting for centuries, and ending to-day in a triumph of the modern idea over the religious idea, and especially over the Christian and Catholic idea.

Let us see, then, what arguments were successively adduced in favour of civil tolerance, and within what limits tolerance successively found champions and defenders.

1. *The Motives appealed to in Favour of the Dogma of Tolerance.*

SUMMARY : Weakness of the arguments of the opponents of tolerance.—Reasons adduced by the supporters of the dogma of civil tolerance.—The syncretist idea.—The obscurity which covers the true religion.—The voluntary character of the religious society, and its spirit.—The respective position of religions and the State.—The incompetence of the State.—The designs of Providence.—Liberty of conscience.—The abuses of intolerance, and its evil results.—The advantages of tolerance.—The benefit of religion.

The reasoning of the opponents of the dogma of tolerance, Catholic as well as Protestant, has not always been very logical; and the weakness of their arguments has facilitated the task of a party which could not fail to become popular, as giving the advantage to man and liberty, as more favourable to interests of the economic order, and later, also, as being more in accordance with the inexorable necessities of fact.

In the sixteenth century the misuse of Scripture was frequent : men did violence to texts in order to justify their violence to persons. One would hardly believe that the parable of the Wedding Guests could ever be quoted in favour of intolerance ; but it was, nevertheless. Did not our Lord say, *Compelle intrare*—compel them to come into the hall of feasting, that is, into the Church ? And, in spite of the context, in which no violence is done to those who were first invited, but made various frivolous excuses for their refusal, the words, which were intended to show the generous hospitality of the giver of the feast, and to inculcate zeal in the preaching of the Gospel, were quoted as justifying the use of the sword. This was what was argued, and the discussion filled volumes. Bayle took the text as the title of a voluminous apology for excessive tolerance.

Similarly, Kings were invested with a sort of Divine authority, which gave them the right not only to promote religion, but also to regulate its outward observance ; and the writers of the period, forgetting the solemn warning of St. Paul as to the new spirit inculcated by Christ, justified the severity of the Christian code by the obsolete severity of the Jewish law.

But we need not dwell on these arguments : time has done justice to them, and our work is devoted to tolerance.

Great is the variety of reasons by which men have

sought, and still seek, to establish tolerance on absolute principles. These reasons are either religious or philosophical: they have their origin in God, His power, and His providence; or in man, his rights, his interests, and his weakness; they are suggested by abstract considerations of theory, or by the concrete counsels of experience, which men describe as universal. We shall consider these various reasons under several principal heads, which the reader will have no difficulty in grouping for himself into these two classes: the one which refutes intolerance, and the other which more directly seeks positive support for the dogma of tolerance.

Many persons find a reason for tolerance in the concept they form for themselves of the *Christian* religion, or of *religion* in general.

The *syncretist* idea has always been accepted by some persons, and has again come into favour. Manès long ago sought to exploit it for his own advantage.[1] It reappeared later with the Socinians and Anabaptists; and it has again become popular together with the Modernist heresy. Some persons, possessed by this idea, reduce the essentials of faith to a certain number of fundamental points, and maintain that on all other points opinion and discussion should be free, as in the Church contradictory opinions are permitted on questions not yet defined.[2]

[1] St. Epiphanius said of Manichæism that it was a πολυκέφαλος αἵρεσις (a many-headed heresy), and compared it to the hydra. See *Hæreses*, lxvi. 87 (M.P.G., t. 42, cols. 171, 172. *Cf.* De Stoop, *Essai sur la Diffusion du Manichéisme dans l'Empire Romain*, p. vii).

[2] This idea finds favour with many Protestants. It is that of the *Arminians* of Holland, the disciples of Arminius, who was Professor of Theology at Leyden in 1602,

198   CIVIL TOLERANCE

The *obscurity*, or lack of evidence, of the true religion serves to others as an argument for not granting privileges or favours to any of the existing religions.[1] What competence, they ask, does the

---

and was engaged in an interminable quarrel with his colleague, Francis Gomarus. The *Gomarists*, more purely Calvinist, and more intolerant, reserved to the ecclesiastical synods a religious jurisdiction which the *Arminians*, who were more inclined to tolerance, but accused of semi-Pelagianism, attributed to the States of Holland.—The English *Latitudinarians*, who came into existence in the reign of Charles I. (1625-1649), owe their name to their tendency to regard as important only certain fundamental points, outside of which the fullest latitude of opinion was allowed to everyone.—Jeremy Taylor, in his Θεολογία ἐκλεκτική, *A Discussion of the Liberty of Prophesying* (1647), secs. 1 and 16, regards as necessary only the articles of the Creed, and denies that the Christian sects are different religions.—John Milton, in his tract of sixteen pages, *Of True Religion, Heresy, Schisme, Toleration* (1673), desires to unite all Protestants against their common enemy, Popery, and limits the fundamental points to the acceptance of Holy Scripture as the only rule of faith, and the rejection of implicit faith as understood by Catholics (I believe what the Church believes).—Chr. Thomasius, a Sophist, who took pleasure in drawing from the principles of the Reformation corollaries which were embarrassing to the leading Reformers, taught also that fundamental rules were sufficient. *Cf. Das Recht evangelischer Fürsten in theologischen Streitigkeiten* (1713), Second Proposition.—The fundamental articles are even indicated by the Catholic priest Bartolotti, in his *Exercitatio politico-theologica* (1782), p. 17, a work more interesting than original, in which he has borrowed largely from Protestant authors, and does not spare his praise of Joseph II.—In Germany a man who admitted the fundamental articles was, in the eyes of Protestants, less a heretic than a schismatic. *Cf.* Thomasius, *Problema juridicum, an hæresis sit crimen* (1697), a dialogue between an orthodox believer and himself (*n.* iii.).

[1] J. Bodin, *Colloquium Heptaplomeres* (1597), p. 129. Jules Simon, *La Liberté de Conscience*, fourth lesson (1857). Jeremy Taylor (*op. cit.*, secs. 1, 3-11) argues thus from the obscurity of the true religion to plead the cause of tolerance. Basnage, *Tolérance des Religions*, pp. 44, 94-96.

DOGMA OF TOLERANCE

Sovereign possess to discern the ways of salvation, even with the aid of an official clergy?[1] Or, rather, others maintain, the truth is not identified with any religion. Every religion possesses some portion of the truth, which renders them all worthy of the same respect.[2] Much more, the different religions form a harmonious concert which proclaims the infinite majesty of the Supreme Being.[3] Many

---

[1] We know the argument of Lessing. Positive religions, founded on belief in contradictory evidence, give to their adherents a justifiable subjective conviction, which does not destroy the conviction of the adherents of another religion. In a certain family, authority depended on the possession of a wonderful ring. One possessor, who was equally fond of all his three sons, had two rings made, exactly similar to the original, and each son had a ring which his father left to him as the real one. After the death of their father, how were they to be undeceived? All three held to their subjective belief in the words of their father. The judge was obliged to decide in this way: "Prove the virtue of your ring. Increase it by gentleness, forbearance, benevolence, and complete submission to the will of God.... Then in a thousand years or so you will appear at the judgment-seat, and a wiser judge than I will decide between you" (*Nathan der Weise*, Act iii., Scene 7).

This apologue, specious as it seems at first sight, will not bear examination. Religions, with the exception of the true one, are not the daughters of God: why should they share the affections of God, as three sons share the affection of their father? To suppose the three rings identical is to suppose that all religions are equally good, which is not true. And how can we imagine that God would tell his children such a lie as the father in the story deliberately told to two of his sons? Does God approve all religions equally?

[2] *Cf.* Ruffini, *La Libertà Religiosa*, pp. 284-286. This idea is found in the philosophy which led the way to Modernism.

[3] Bayle, *Commentary*, etc. "Tolerance is the one thing in the world most likely to bring back the golden age, and to produce a harmonious concert of many voices and instruments of every kind—a harmony at least as agreeable as the uniformity of a single voice" (Second Part, c. 6, p. 415). Nearer our own time, Dargaud wrote (*Histoire*

others, less enthusiastic by nature, profess with regard to dogmas[1] a scepticism which leads them to an indifference[2] incompatible with any kind of zeal for orthodoxy : morality with them is the only thing of any importance.

Others ask, What is the Church ? A society of men, voluntarily banded together to offer public worship to God.[3] What spirit does it inherit ? The spirit of meekness, which is inconsistent with violence and coercion.[4] From these premises they

---

de la Liberté Religieuse en France et dans ses Fondateurs, t. 4, p. 430) : " Let all the different religions offer the incense of their prayers side by side ; these manifold prayers will be pleasing to God, and where we see only dissension, God will see harmony. The expressions of adoration are different, but the meaning is the same." Celsus had long before used similar language.

[1] Glanvill, *The Vanity of Dogmatizing*. The author repels the accusation of scepticism, but objects to the positive affirmations of a dogmatism that admits no doubt. He preaches a modest philosophy, which contents itself with saying : *I think so* (p. 223).

[2] Frederic the Great of Prussia: " There is no one religion which differs very much from the others on the subject of morals ; thus they may be all equal in the sight of Government, which consequently leaves every man free to go to heaven by any road that suits him. Let him be a good citizen, and that is all we require of him" (Works, t. 1, *De la Superstition et de la Religion*, Art. 3, p. 241, 242). Carlantonio Pilati, *Di una Riforma d'Italia*, the work of a very anticlerical Catholic, who goes so far as to say : " Equal tolerance of all religions produces indifference in men's minds, and indifference produces peace and tranquillity and mutual love."

[3] Locke, *A Letter concerning Toleration*, etc., pp. 321, 331.

[4] Roger Williams, an American author, who during his travels in England addressed to Parliament his famous dialogue between Truth and Peace, entitled *The Bloody Tenent of Persecution* (1644). His book was burned by order of the Presbyterians. The author wrote an answer to

DOGMA OF TOLERANCE

argue that there is an essential opposition between Christianity and intolerance.

Similarly, we are asked to consider the respective position of religions and the State. Being fully autonomous in the opinion of some writers, they are by the very fact exempt from all legal prohibition.[1] Many modern writers attribute to the State a supremacy over all religions; but this supremacy does not authorize the State to interfere—at least, in private worship.[2] Being without light of its own, the State would be compelled to listen to the voice of a Church, and consequently to change its sovereignty into vassalage.

But has the State the right to exercise any constraint whatever in religious matters? Neither God nor the people have given it any authority to direct souls.[3] Famous Sovereigns have spoken clearly on

---

objections, the title of which begins with the words, *The Bloody Tenent yet more Bloody*. The preface to his first work contains his principal assertions on tolerance.—Bayle, *Commentary*, part 1, c. 3, p. 372. *Supplement*, c. 7, p. 506.— Jules Simon, *La Liberté de Conscience*, p. 278.

[1] The *Congregationalists* or *Independents*, founded by Robert Browne, 1581.—Busher, *Religious Peace*, p. 18.— Roger Williams, *op. cit.*, preface and p. 96. G. Noodt, *De Religione ab Imperio jure gentium Libera*, pp. 7, 20, 25.

[2] The Arminians were called *Remonstrants*, from a defence or *Remonstrance* which they presented to the States of Holland in 1610; while a reply or *Counter-Remonstrance* of the Gomarists gave them the name of *Counter-Remonstrants*. The Remonstrants gave to the State jurisdiction over public worship. Similar principles are found in Puffendorf, *De habitu religionis christianæ ad vitam civilem*, 1687, nn. 6 and 43. As to insufficiency of means for settling controversies, see also Jeremy Taylor's *Discourse of the Liberty of Prophesying* (1647), secs. 3-11.

[3] Roger Williams, *The Bloody Tenent*, preface.—Thomasius, *op. cit.*, Prop. 7.—E. Saurin, *Réflexions sur les*

this subject. " I am King of peoples," said Stephen Báthori, " but I am not King of consciences."[1] And Maximilian II : " To interfere with consciences is to force the citadel of heaven."[2] The State, in its attempts at usurpation, is powerless ; for how will it undertake to convince ? and is there any religion without real conviction ?[3] To convert by force is to people the State with hypocrites ;[4] to gain souls by the promise of rewards is to degrade men, and to be guilty of simony.[5] Will it be said that it is for the good of the community ? But unity of

---

Droits de la Conscience, p. 488.—Boehmer, *Jus Ecclesiasticum Protestantium*, l. 3, *Dissertatio Præliminaris de Jure Circa Libertatem Conscientiæ*, sec. 20.—Anonymous, *Jefferson's Notes on the State of Virginia*, c. 2, p. 37.—Bartolotti, *Exercitatio Politico-Theologica*, c. 2, p. 37.—Basnage, *op. cit.*, p. 41.

[1] " God," he said in his edict of religious pacification (*De pace Religionis Servanda*), " has reserved to Himself three things—the power to create out of nothing, to know the future, and to rule men's consciences."

[2] *Dominari conscientiis est cœli arcem invadere*. In his correspondence with Maria Theresa, Joseph II. similarly admitted his incompetence : " What power do men arrogate to themselves ? Can it extend to passing judgment on the Divine mercy, to saving men in spite of themselves, to assuming dominion over men's consciences ?" (Von Arneth, *Maria Theresia und Joseph II.*, *Ihre Correspondenz*, t. 2, l. 260, June, 1777).

[3] All the advocates of the dogma of tolerance use this argument. Especially Busher, *op. cit.*, p. 17 ; G. Noodt, *op. cit.*, p. 38 ; Jefferson in the work quoted above, on the seventeenth question ; Thomasius, *Problema Juridicum, an Hæresis sit Crimen*, c. 11 ; Trautmansdorff, *op. cit.*, p. 120.

[4] Almost all use this argument. See Busher, *op. cit.*, p. 17 ; *Jefferson's Notes*, Appendix, pp. 26-28 ; Trautmansdorff, *op. cit.*, p. 134 ; Philipot, *op. cit.*, p. 33 ; Puffendorf, *De Habitu Religionis ad Imperium*, n. 48 ; Basnage, *op. cit.*, p. 58.

[5] Thomasius, *Das Recht Evangelischer Fürsten in Theologischen Streitigkeiten* (1696), Prop. 1 ;—Bayle, *Commentary*, etc.

DOGMA OF TOLERANCE

worship is not necessary for the good of the community;[1] for virtue has nothing to do with any particular form of religion.[2] The State has the right to interfere with religion only so far as to prevent the formation of associations opposed to public order and good morals.[3]

Some authors, taking higher ground, appeal to God Himself, His example, His Divine plan, His power: shall we punish, they ask, what He tolerates?[4] Shall we go against the dispositions of Providence, which has allowed men to arrive at different religions by the natural use of their reason?[5] And what have we to do with upholding a Divine religion? Cannot God's omnipotence do without our help?[6]

From the seventeenth century we note the first appearance of those arguments which are in favour to-day; they tend to base tolerance on the inviolability of conscience.[7] It is impossible to force men's inward judgment, or compel them to see what they do not perceive; we might just as well (to use the expression of De Bonald) "command the circulation of the blood."[8] One man calls heresy that

---

[1] Reinhard, *Meditationes de jure Principum Germaniæ cum primis Saxoniæ, circa Sacra* (1714), p. 70; Boehmer, *Jus Ecclesiasticum Protestantium*, l. 3, *Dissertatio Prælim.*; R. Williams; and many others.

[2] Thomasius, *op. cit.*, Prop. 1; Lessing, *Nathan der Weise*.

[3] Noodt, *op. cit.*, p. 24, and many others.

[4] Reinhard, *Meditationes*, p. 70.

[5] Noodt, *op. cit.*, p. 12; Basnage, *op. cit.*, pp. 47, 54.

[6] Jules Simon, *op. cit.*, p. 228.

[7] Hence arose those discussions on what was called the rights of the two Sovereigns—*the Conscience and the Prince.*

[8] *Réflexions Philosophiques sur la Tolérance des Opinions.* *Œuvres*, t. 7, p. 159.

which is only another man's error; and error is not a crime. The crime is committed by the will; it cannot reside in the intellect.[1]

There still remain numerous *practical considerations*, which the doctors call to the rescue of their reasons, and which carry conviction to the crowd better than the reasons themselves.

History shows us how many crimes and excesses may be laid to the charge of intolerance: coercion disturbs the public peace,[2] and makes a sincere search after truth impossible; it puts a premium on cowardice and hypocrisy;[3] it makes religion the sport of ignorance or the caprice of Sovereigns,[4] and brings about a fatal reaction which drives men to atheism and infidelity; and society rushes towards the abyss in which morals are lost.[5]

On the other hand, it is not difficult to see that coercion will do as much service to error as to truth; the rights of the conscience which is in possession of the truth are also the rights of the conscience which errs in good faith.[6] Therefore, if you wish

[1] G. Noodt, *op. cit.*, p. 33; Thomasius, *Disputatio an Hæresis sit Crimen*, viii.

[2] J. Bodin, *Heptaplomeres*, p. 357; R. Williams, *The Bloody Tenent yet more Bloody*, pp. 111, 112; Fuhrmann, *De Tolerantiæ Religiosæ effectibus Civilibus*, sec. 5, p. 35; Bayle, *Commentary*, etc., p. 375, and *passim;* J. Simon, *op. cit.*, l. 4, p. 254.

[3] See the authors quoted in *n.* 4, p. 202.

[4] Barbeyrac, *Traité de la Morale des Pères de l'Église* (1728), p. 180.

[5] Bayle, *Commentary*, etc., part 2, c. 2, p. 399 *sqq.;* Boehmer, *De jure circa Libertatem Conscientiæ*, sec. 19.

[6] Bayle, *op. cit.*, part 2, c. 8, p. 422, *sqq;* Noodt, *De Religione*, etc., p. 33; Thomasius, *Problema Juridicum*, etc., ix. This theory is opposed by Saurin in the very title of his book, *Réflexions sur les Droits de la Conscience, où l'on fait voir la Différence entre les Droits de la Conscience*

DOGMA OF TOLERANCE

to avoid all risk of oppression of the truth, you must make it a universal principle that no one shall be molested on account of his religion.[1]

And why these useless persecutions,[2] when the light of truth is sufficient to dissipate the mists of error?[3] Catholics, in their peaceful relations with non-Catholics, have abundant opportunities of making conversions by teaching and example;[4] and the advantages to liberty and peace[5] are crowned by that given to religion itself.

Can we, then, doubt the providential usefulness of heresy? It purifies the Church, and gives her better-instructed and more zealous ministers, forced by their contact with heresy to develop their intellectual activity and the ardour of their devotion. How much scientific progress is due to heresy![6]

In short, there is no good that tolerance does not encourage us to wait and hope for. With peace and improved manners, it brings also progress in arts and sciences; it opens an era of abundance and prosperity.[7] "Misdirected zeal," wrote Frederic II.

éclairée et ceux de la Conscience Errante, on réfute le " Commentaire Philosophique " et le livre intitulé " Droit des Deux Souverains."

[1] Bayle, *Commentary*, etc., pp. 444, 523, and *passim;* Boehmer, *op. cit.*, sec. 20.

[2] Michel de l'Hôpital, *Harangues*, e.g., that of 1561, t. 1, p. 469.

[3] Williams, *The Bloody Tenent.*—Milton, *Areopagitica*, 65, 67.—*Jefferson's Notes*, and Appendix, III., pp. 26, 28.

[4] Joseph II., Letter of July 20, 1777 (edit. Von Arneth, l. 264, t. 2, pp. 151, 152).

[5] Williams, *op. cit.*, preface, ii.; Fuhrmann, *op. cit.*, sec. 34; Bayle, *Commentary*, l. 2, c. 6, p. 415.

[6] Bartolotti, *Exercitatio*, etc. (1782), c. 4, pp. 155, 156; Basnage, *op. cit.*, pp. 72, 89.

[7] Bartolotti, *ibid.*, c. 4, pp. 154, 159.

of Prussia, " is a tyrant that depopulates provinces ; tolerance is a tender mother that cares for them and makes them flourish."[1] " Let there be liberty of belief," said Joseph II., " and there will no longer be but one religion, which will be that of directing all the inhabitants for the good of the State."[2]

If a solemn treaty of tolerance were concluded among all the rulers of the world, it would insure " a rich harvest of conversions, and victories and triumphs for the true Church."[3]

Let us conclude, then, with Voltaire[4] that intolerance can only be justified when it is necessary to put down fanaticism and its excesses.[5]

[1] *De la Superstition et de la Religion*, Works, t. 1, pp. 241, 242.
[2] Letter of June, 1777 (edit. Von Arneth, t. 2, p. 160).
[3] Saurin mentions this theory, but without admitting it (*op. cit.*, p. 693).
[4] " In order to deserve tolerance, men must begin by not being fanatics " (*Traité de la Tolérance*, c. 18).
[5] The law of religious liberty which Jefferson caused to be passed in Virginia in the beginning of 1786 is very interesting reading. In its preamble it enumerates, so to speak, all the reasons for tolerance. " God has created free thought ; attempts at coercion only tend to make cowards and hypocrites, and are contrary to the Divine plan laid down by the Author of our religion. Our Saviour, who is Lord of the body as well as of the soul, condemned the use of force in teaching religion ; the wicked acts of public authorities have resulted only in establishing false religion, in the greater part of the world ; our rights do not depend on our religious convictions ; privileges are fatal to religion ; the magistrates have nothing to do with our opinions." See also *Questions sur la Tolérance* (Abbés Trailhé and Maultroit ?) ; Geneva, 1758.

2. *Practical Conclusions of Systems of Tolerance.*

SUMMARY : Systems of Saurin, Joseph II., Philipot, and Puffendorf.—Covenants or decrees of tolerance, especially the treaty of Westphalia.—To what acts or opinions their tolerance extended.—What part was left to a dominant religion.—Many excluded Catholics from the benefit of tolerance.

The manner of understanding tolerance has varied as much as the motives for introducing it. Thus, in 1697 the Calvinist minister Saurin summed up his opinions in these terms : " The Magistrate should do all he can for the propagation of true doctrine and the extinction of error, without doing violence to consciences or depriving subjects of their natural or civil rights."[1] Joseph II. similarly declared in 1777 that he did not intend to treat the religion of his subjects as a matter of indifference; but he refused to consider that religion in purely civil or temporal relations.[2] The Protestant pastor Philipot refused to allow Dissenters to have temples or schools or the right of meeting.[3] Puffendorf did not recognize in those who differed from him the right to propagate their religion; he wished to have a sort of fundamental religion made obligatory on all persons, according to a *publica formula fidei*.[4]

In his Edict of Wöllmer (July 9, 1788), Frederic

[1] *Op. cit.*, sec. 5, p. 684.
[2] Letter of July 20, 1777, to his mother : " I would give all I possess to see all the Protestants of the States [of Maria Theresa] become Catholics " (edit. Von Arneth, l. 264, t. 2, pp. 151, 152).
[3] *Les Justes Bornes de la Tolérance*, pp. 30-32.
[4] *De Habitu Religionis ad Vitam Civilem*, sec. 49.

William II. forbade proselytism by non-recognized bodies. The Peace of Westphalia (1648) guaranteed liberty to three Christian bodies only—Catholics, Lutherans, and the Reformed Church. But, according to the maxim *Cujus regio illius et religio*, the Prince was at liberty to adopt any one of these as the religion of the State, and order the banishment of the other two, provided he adopted all the formalities necessary to take away the ignominious or penal character of the measure. The jurisconsults of Germany thus came to distinguish between a *qualified tolerance*—a tolerance by right, which the Princes could not refuse to religions protected by international agreement—and a *simple* or precarious tolerance, which depended on their good pleasure.[1] The edict of tolerance granted by Henry IV. similarly limited its operation to the Huguenots and to certain parts of France.

So much for *official acts*.

Nor are the authors who emblazon on their banner the dogma of tolerance any more agreed either on the sects to be protected by that banner, or on the place to be reserved for the true or privileged religion.

In the course of the centuries of which we are treating, few writers, philosophical or political, preach tolerance of all religions ; many confine their attention to Christian bodies, and require an agreement on fundamental points, or, at least, on those articles which are necessary for the good of the State.[2]

[1] *E.g.*, Fuhrmann, *De Tolerantiæ Religiosæ effectibus Civilibus*, sec. 4, p. 19.

[2] Jeremy Taylor, *op. cit.*, sec. 19.—Trautmansdorff, *De Tolerantia Ecclesiastica et Civili*, pp. 146-149.

SYSTEMS OF TOLERANCE

The tolerance shown to the Socinians and Anabaptists was much opposed from this point of view,[1] and the exclusion of atheists was generally insisted on.[2] Some writers even threatened them with most severe penalties,[3] and no one thought of allowing the preaching of revolutionary or immoral doctrines.[4]

According to some, tolerance should be restricted to the private exercise of the religion, or be extended only to outward acts commanded by religious sentiment.[5] Philipot distinguished three things in religion, and his distinction was generally accepted—the three things being " the soul, the body, and the habit. The soul of religion is the faith of the heart; the body is the confession by the lips; the habit is the public profession of such a religion."[6] The magistrate has no power over the soul or the body—he would be usurping a prerogative of God—but he

---

[1] Philipot, *op. cit.*, p. 26; Taylor, *op. cit.*, sec. 18.

[2] Fuhrmann, *op. cit.*, p. 38; Pufendorf, *De Habitu Religionis Christianæ ad Vitam Civilem*, sec. 7; Philipot, *op. cit.*, p. 52; Joseph II., who thus laid down the conditions of his tolerance: " Provided that the service of the State is properly performed . . . that your Supreme Being is not dishonoured, but reverenced and worshipped " (edit. Von Arneth, t. 2, letter 260, of June, 1777); Bartolotti, *op. cit.*, c. 4, p. 194.

[3] Saurin would have legalized capital punishment to exclude irreligion and atheism (*Réflexions*, etc., pp. 510-514).

[4] *E.g.*, Noodt, *De Religione ab Imperio*, etc., pp. 40, 41; Taylor, *op. cit.*, secs. 15, 16; Thomasius, *Problema Juridicum*, etc., n. 12; Milton, *Areopagitica*, p. 68.

[5] Saurin, *op. cit.*, p. 495, pp. 502 *sqq.*

[6] *Les Justes Bornes de Tolérance*, pp. 30-32. Bayle himself excluded the diffusion of atheism. The atheist, he reasoned, has no positive conviction; he cannot, then, say that he is entitled to spread his errors, and his atheist propaganda attacks the fundamental principles of the State (*Commentary*, p. 431).

has power over the habit. Others were inclined to grant a wider liberty, not excluding public preaching and proselytism; some were willing to permit changes of religion.[1]

Most authors defend themselves against the charge of professing or favouring religious indifference. Blasphemy continues to be forbidden.[2] Their system of tolerance may be reconciled with a privileged religion, which obliges the Prince to be just towards all, but permits him to reserve his favours and all public offices to the members of his own communion;[3] or an official religion, alone subsidized and encouraged.[4] Others, however, granted to the religion they considered the best nothing but the example of the Prince and his private encouragement.[5]

Many jurists are at the same time tolerantists and upholders of the supremacy of the State.[6]

One point strikes us as worthy of notice—namely, the almost unanimous agreement of Protestant and rationalist professors of tolerance in refusing liberty to Catholics. Thus, Locke, Milton, the later English thinkers, the German Thomasius, and even Bayle

[1] Fuhrmann, *op. cit.*, p. 53, sec. 15.
[2] Pufendorf, *op. cit.*, n. 48. Thomasius is more liberal (*Problema*, etc., n. 12).
[3] Fuhrmann, *op. cit.*, p. 83, sec. 31; Saurin, *op. cit.*, pp. 506 *sqq.*
[4] Pufendorf, *op. cit.*, n. 41; Philipot, *op. cit.*, c. 3, p. 127.
[5] Williams, *The Bloody Tenent*.
[6] Pufendorf, *op. cit.*, nn. 44-48; Grotius, *op. cit.*, t. 2, c. 8. Joseph II.'s edicts of tolerance gave rise to a whole Court literature. See *Vollständige Sammlung aller Schriften die durch Veranlassung der Allerhöchsten Kaiserl. Toleranz und Reformations-Edikten ... grössten theils zu Wien erschienen*, 5 vols., Vienna, 1782-1783; vol. vi., Strasbourg, 1786.

himself, showed themselves in their theory opposed to the emancipation of " Papists." The charge against the latter was sometimes that they considered an excommunicated Sovereign as deposed, sometimes that they professed intolerance.[1] Milton and many Germans repudiated the Catholic religion as infected with idolatry,[2] and Saurin described Catholics as enemies of the human race.[3]

3. *Criticism of Doctrines of Tolerance.*

SUMMARY: The incomplete tolerance favoured by these systems varies in its claims: great confusion caused by this.—Their advocates are mistaken as to the intolerance they attack and its principles, as to our convictions (false intellectualism), and as to the practical advantages of their own system.—The question of the reprisals to be dreaded.—Whatever practical wisdom there is in their conclusions does not infer the dogma of tolerance.

We have now fairly stated the arguments adduced during more than three centuries in favour of the dogma of tolerance ; a detailed criticism of them all would be long and tedious, and considering our purpose, our readers will easily dispense with it ; a few remarks will suffice.

One illusion disappears as soon as we glance at the opinions expressed. There is not one theory of

[1] Bayle, *Commentary, Supplement,* c. 31, pp. 559, 560.
[2] Milton, *Of True Religion,* etc., and many others, both in Germany and in England. Taylor, in England, is more moderate, and Williams in America much more liberal.
[3] Therefore, he says, " we have full right to banish them from the world, and cut them off from the land of the living " (*op. cit.,* p. 661). Charity alone counsels greater moderation.

tolerance only; the multitude of such theories would make it difficult to choose between them, and in the period under consideration no theory is absolute, either in its principles or in its conclusion.

This tolerance, limited to certain forms of positive religion, professes to preserve to the community a small inheritance of moral and religious truths, and it does not always grant to the religion which is simply tolerated the right to propagate its doctrines.

The arguments are directed against one form of intolerance only — the aggressive or violent form, which claims to make conversions by force, and to extirpate by violent means heresies already widely diffused. They therefore do not touch the Catholic doctrine, or attack the preventive action taken for prudential reasons, which, without bloodshed or persecution, secures to a kingdom or a republic the great blessing of unity in the possession of religious truth.

Many systems refuse to sanction official indifference, and discuss only the lawfulness or expediency of a certain amount of civil constraint.

While we cannot approve of all the forms of civil intolerance which have appeared in modern times, and are entirely opposed to such intolerance as has for its direct design the eradication of a conscientious conviction, or the imposition of a Credo by force, we admit the justice of more than one criticism directed against the system formerly prevailing, or to the treatises written to defend it. Moreover, tolerance, as we shall define it, comprehends a wider liberty than that advocated by many of the tolerationists whose names and doctrines we have mentioned.

But, on the other hand, the religious error of syncretism or scepticism, and the social and political error of the omnipotence of the State, and of the social uselessness of true religion, vitiate many of the systems enumerated.

The champions of the dogma of tolerance misunderstand equally the nature of our convictions. They consider them as purely intellectual; but is it not the fact that man is influenced by his passions and his pride, as well as by his virtuous inclinations, in forming the opinions that will henceforth remain fixed in his mind? A purely intellectual affair, they argued: they should rather have said a human affair, and therefore in great measure a question of good or evil will.

What are we to think of the practical considerations? They are more specious than real.

Social trouble and disturbance does not arise always from coercion, but much more frequently from heresy, which is far from being the gentle, patient creature that the advocates of tolerance are so fond of describing. Thus, that good simple man, Jules Simon, showed that he had misunderstood the teachings of history when he wrote in these terms of the conduct of the Christian Empire: " The same judges, who had just condemned the Christians in the name of the gods of the Empire, now condemned the Donatists in the name of the Councils and the orthodox faith. It was the same intolerance in the service of another dogma."[1] Not at all; a glance at the picture of the crimes and excesses of the Donatists, which at last wore out

[1] *La Liberté de Conscience*, p. 73.

the patience of the magistrates, is enough to prove conclusively that it was not the same intolerance. Moreover, as we shall have occasion to see again, pagan intolerance was not in the service of any dogma.

The other arguments of expediency are no more conclusive: stress is everywhere laid on the reprisals which intolerant truth would logically have to expect from error, when error got the upper hand.

We do not deny that in a particular case toleration might be promised on condition of reciprocity;[1] but are heterodox or infidel Princes in the habit of regulating their consciences or their policies according to our arguments or our opinions?

Has the idea of retaliation often had anything to do with the persecutions from which Catholics have suffered? On the contrary, that Protestant was perfectly right who declared that for the dominant religion to admit another religion to share its rights would be a very bad bargain, so little could it count on reciprocity.[2] We cannot talk of retaliation as *logical*, for error and doubt are logically tolerant while a reasonable intolerance is the logical consequence of true and assured faith. The only religion that has the right to be intolerant is that which is revealed by God, and is binding on all. Inasmuch as it is revealed by God, it places God alone, and not

---

[1] Thus, in 1751, Maria Theresa obtained the construction of a Catholic church at Copenhagen, in exchange for a Danish Lutheran church, which she allowed to be opened at Vienna.

[2] *Die Toleranz, in ihre rechtmässigen Grenzen zurückgewiesen*, p. 21; Leipzig, 1887. See also Saurin, *op. cit.*, p. 693, and Jurieu, *op. cit.*, pp. 284 *sqq*.

DOCTRINES OF TOLERANCE

the teaching of any fallible teacher, above all human opinions, on which it imposes silence; as binding upon all, it finds in its necessity a motive of charity for all its demands. No form of unbelief or free thought has, even logically, the right to be intolerant; moreover, certitude is the natural accompaniment of truth, not of error; the opinion of a man who is in error is accidental and changeable, and the grace of God is always present to help sincere and honest souls to discover the true religion. No thought of possible consequences then requires the truth to give up its privileges, for its adversaries are not people who fight with moderation or courtesy: a certain intolerance may give them a pretext or an occasion for war, but it does not give them any real justification.

Heresy, it may be objected, has its providential purpose. Who doubts it? Every evil has its purpose, but heresy does not expect truth to call it in to fulfil its purpose. It waits for the opportunity to insinuate itself into the favour of careless or negligent persons, just as diseases attack an enfeebled body, or as in fine weather the growing heaviness of the air announces the approach of a thunderstorm. Why, then, should we open the door to heresy, and so take away from men the happiness or the hope of passing their days in peace?

Has civil tolerance kept the promises which its sponsors made in its name? Has it brought back the golden age? The fight has changed its ground; unbelief has taken the place of misbelief, and sectarian animosity turns with greater violence and insolence against a religion that has laid down its arms.

What, then, does the apology for tolerance, the apology which preceded the French Revolution, really prove? It proves that ill-timed and tyrannical intolerance may do more harm than good; but it proves also that the object of legitimate intolerance is not so much forced conversions as the repression of a crime and the preservation of social peace—it proves, in short, that every practical Government must take times and circumstances into consideration.

But we need no sophistical reasoning to bring us to this conclusion, and the dogma of tolerance finds in it no corroboration.

What, then, are the sources from which the arguments offered for the dogma of tolerance are derived? With the more moderate and more honest men, the dominant consideration is that of practical necessity; they seek to justify existing facts. With the rest it is a mere question of religious indifference. But these are discreditable sources, and we cannot pay much respect to *ex post facto* arguments, or those which are prompted by indifferent and contemptuous scepticism.

CHAPTER IV

CIVIL TOLERANCE OF THE PRESENT DAY

SUMMARY : The policy of abstract principles inaugurated by the French Revolution compels us to change the order of our argument.

No man can escape from his surroundings : the French leaders of the end of the eighteenth century could neither overrule the circumstances nor escape from their influence : though they submitted to that influence unconsciously and perhaps in spite of themselves. Imbued as they were with abstract ideas, they despised the warnings of history ; revolutionary in their ideas, they did not care to progress according to traditional methods, but to break with the past entirely, and clear the ground for the erection of a new social edifice, first for France, and then for the whole world.

Up to this time doctrines have been deduced from the facts, and have been a sort of logical repetition of the facts ; but now the doctrines are to be established first, and the facts to follow them.

It seems, therefore, more convenient this time to reverse our usual order, and give to theories precedence of facts ; instead of finding the doctrine in the facts, we shall find the facts in the doctrines.

Article I. Civil Tolerance of the French Revolution: Doctrine and Facts.

Summary: New principle of tolerance inscribed in the declaration of the rights of man.—Real intolerance.—Its victims.

In proportion as religious discord was accentuated, and the discussion was transferred from Catholicism to Christianity, and then to all positive religions, the doctors of modern tolerance widened their conclusions, in order to give free passage to the ever-growing flood of novelties. But as they thought some kind of understanding on the subject of religion an essential condition of social cohesion, they did not relieve the governing authorities from the necessity of considering their duties towards God. They remained uncompromising Deists.

The Revolution bases its tolerance on what was not an additional concession, but a new principle, derived from the nature of man alone. The Declaration of the Rights of Man, voted on August 23, 1789, and left as a last legacy by the National Assembly in its Constitution of September 14, 1791, contains these conditions: Article 4. " Liberty is the power of doing what we will, so long as it does not injure another; the only limits of each man's natural right are such as secure the same rights to others; these limits are determinable only by the law." Article 5. " The law can forbid only such actions as are mischievous to society—*Quod lex non vetat, permittit.*" Article 10. " No one can be molested for his religious opinions, provided they are not subversive of public order." Article 11. "The free communication of thoughts and opinions is one of the most precious of the rights of man; therefore every citizen is allowed freedom of speech, of writing, and printing, but he will have to answer for any abuse of that liberty in cases determined by the law."

Here, then, we have free opinion, and even its public expression, always authorized in principle. Founded on human liberty,[1] on an individual liberty considered without reference to its social effects, the idea of right implies, not a man's power to do what he will, but to think and say what he will. The vigilance of authority is restricted to the effectual preservation of exterior order; the crime of opinion is erased from the penal code.

But the spirit of intransigentism and persecution took back with usury from the Church and from Catholics all that it conceded to the individual and to heterodoxy. The National Assembly, filled with the idea of its own omnipotence, even going so far as to claim the right to change the religion of the country,[2] created a schism by the civil constitution of the clergy; and in less than a year, from November 10, 1793, to May 7, 1794, they abolished Catholicism, set up a goddess of Reason, and suppressed public worship; then there was another change, and the worship of the Supreme Being was made obligatory in France.

And who can count the victims of this persecution? Taine's figures are sufficiently elo-

[1] Fouillée, *L'Idée Moderne du Droit en France* (*Revue des Deux Mondes*, February 15 and April 1, 1878).
[2] A principle affirmed by the Convention.

quent.[1] He tells us that at the end of the Terror the list of exiles and fugitives for political or religious reasons included more than 150,000 names.[2] "Without counting more than 40,000 temporary gaols, there were 1,200 prisons full to overflowing, with more than 200 prisoners in each."[3] "A hundred and seventy-eight tribunals, forty of them moving from department to department, were busy in all parts of the country, passing sentences of death, which were executed at once, on the spot. Children of seven years, five years, four years old, were condemned: the father was condemned for the son, and the son for the father."[4] Besides the 17,000 persons who died on the scaffold, there were more than 2,000 shot at Toulon. There were the drownings; more than 4,800 (men, women, and children) perished at Nantes. There were the murders by the mob; about 10,000 were killed without trial in the province of Anjou alone. Add to these details the unspeakable horrors of captivity. "We may reasonably estimate that the number of the dead of all ages and both sexes comes very nearly to half a million."[5]

This was the baptism which Liberty received from the French Revolution!

[1] Taine, *Révolution Française*, t. 2. His figures have been disputed by M. Aulard in his work, *Taine: Historien de la Révolution Française*, but he gives us no estimate of his own that we can compare with Taine's. As to M. Aulard himself, see the *Correspondant* of March 25 and April 10, 1909; the articles of M. Cochin, *La Crise de l'Histoire Révolutionnaire*; the *Revue Pratique d'Apologétique* of November 15, 1909; and the bibliography of *Questions Actuelles*, January 15, 1910. M. Cochin declares that "Taine's work will remain as a model of impartial history." [2] *Ibid.*, p. 383.
[3] *Ibid.* [4] *Ibid.*, pp. 388-393. [5] *Ibid.*, p. 392.

Article II. Doctrines since the French Revolution.

1. *Doctrines of Tolerance.*

SUMMARY: On the rights of man an attempt has been made to found an absolute tolerance, which abolishes the crime of opinion.—This theory attracts certain founders of Belgian independence and optimist Liberals like Jules Simon.—How religious liberty is understood.—Catholic Liberalism.

The French Revolution, with its contradictory theories of the individual independence of man and the universal supremacy of the State, was a school of licence and oppression. Its tolerance and its sectarianism have both found admirers and followers. Let us speak first of its tolerance.

There have been men who believed, in good faith, that the Declaration of the Rights of Man was the absolute embodiment of complete and universal tolerance. The true formula which man had vainly sought in God, society, the Church, and the State, he had found at once when he consulted his natural rights and liberty. He had within himself what he had hitherto searched for too high or too far off.

This is what men thought and wrote, and in their joy at the discovery they added: " Henceforth there is no need to discuss the limits of tolerance or extend its boundaries; it has no limits, its empire is infinite; it promises liberty to every opinion, with the serene assurance of a Sovereign who has no fear of being dethroned. The community will be content with regulating outward acts, and will respect the autonomy of opinions; it will even encourage their development in the interests of intellectual progress.

This distinction between acts and opinions[1] was specially attractive to some of the founders of Belgian independence. In a pamphlet which M. Damoiseaux[2] calls the charter of unionist theories, De Potter declares that the intellect is essentially free, and concludes: "Everything may be thought, or spoken, or published, or taught; but nothing may be done that the law forbids."[3]

Such was also the language of optimist Liberalism; these are the words of Jules Simon, who was one of its most distinguished representatives: "To compel the acceptance of a doctrine by violence or undue influence is to degrade man and to disobey the will of God, who has created us intelligent and free."[4] "But what I think, I have the right to say and to teach. God has given me the power of speech to express my thoughts, and has put into my mind the righteous desire to share with others the treasure of truth."[5]

In asserting their right to think and say and write whatever they chose, even in religious matters, the tolerationists tended to substitute liberty for tolerance; they declared themselves in favour of *religious*

---

[1] M. Jordan, in his articles already quoted insists on the opposition between this modern idea and the old; and he therefore rejects the explanation which Mgr. Douais offers of the criminal procedure in the matter of heresy (*Annales de Phil. Chrét.*, t. 159, 1909-1910, pp. 22 sqq.).
[2] *La Formation de la Société Politique Belge*, p. 20.
[3] *L'Union des Catholiques et des Libéraux dans les Pays-Bas*, June, 1829.
[4] *La Liberté de Conscience*, Fourth Lesson, p. 254.
[5] *Ibid.*

DOCTRINES OF TOLERANCE

liberty without any restriction. But it must be remarked that their idea of liberty was not the liberty of a religion, but the liberty of individuals to profess any religion or none at all; to practise the religion they professed, or practically to deny the articles of its creed; to speak and work for religion, or to attack and destroy it.

Thus all alike, orthodox and heterodox, believers and unbelievers, were invited to enter into a friendly rivalry, in which truth and merit would have the opportunity to show their pre-eminence.

Dazzled by this unreal vision, struck by the force of the current which had swept away privileges, and disgusted by the annoyances to which the Church had been subjected under the old régime, Catholics also raised with confidence the standard of modern liberties. The Church was to give up her privileges in return for the liberty which was to be secured to her by the common law. This was the plan formulated by Catholic Liberalism, not as being expedient in certain countries, which would have been reasonable, but as generally good—at least, in our own time;[1] and there was its exaggeration and its mistake. One of its favourite maxims was the one which Cavour repeated as he lay dying—*A free Church in a free State*. We need not give here the whole gamut of its various tones from that of Lamennais, Montalembert, and Lacordaire, which was Catholic first and Liberal afterwards, to that which has so little religion left in it as to be hardly distinguishable from sceptical unbelief.

[1] See Propositions 55, 77, and 80, condemned by the Syllabus.

2. *Doctrines of Intolerance.*

SUMMARY : Principle of intolerance contained in the French Revolution, and affirmed by Defacqz.—Moderate men are divided between two systems : the separatist system, favourable to the liberty of the Church ; and the jurisdictional or State system, which favours religious indifference rather than liberty of religion.—Opinions of Ruffini and Friedberg.—The sectarians take their motto from Gambetta, *Le cléricalisme, voilà l'ennemi*.—Meaning of this expression.—War on the Church in the name of tolerance, patriotism, and intellectual liberty.—Troops enrolled for this war.—The religion of unbelief.—Evidence of the persecuting irreligious spirit.

The very tolerance inspired by the French Revolution led to intolerance and persecution. No doubt it gave to the individual full liberty to think and say what he pleased, but that was all : beyond that it recognized nothing as sacred ; it gave up everything else to the civil law, the supreme judge of all that was demanded by the welfare of the community and the coexistence of liberties.

Defacqz said this in so many words in the National Congress of 1830 : " It is necessary that all forms of worship should be independent, but it is necessary also that the civil law should preserve all its force—nay, more, that the temporal authority should take precedence of the spiritual authority, and to some extent absorb it, because the civil law, being made in the interests of all, must prevail over that which is for the interest of a limited number. . . . Religious liberty is the first necessity of man, but it must be restrained, like all other liberties, for the good of the community."[1]

[1] See Huyttens, *Discussions du Congrès*, t. 1, pp. 587 and 608.

DOCTRINES OF INTOLERANCE

Since religious worship is organized and practised by the community, since by universal consent the Catholic Church possesses the most admirable and most complete of all social structures, the question at once arises, What attitude will the temporal authority adopt towards religious associations, and especially towards the Church? Will it be friendly, neutral, or hostile?

The upholders of the dogma of tolerance are divided into two camps—that of the *separatists* and that of the *jurisdictionals*.

The separatist system, which prevails in the United States of North America, insists on separation and self-government. Leaving all religions to themselves, it gives them complete liberty of organization and expansion. As different States rule different territories, while each preserves its own independence, it permits alongside the State the independent existence of a spiritual power, which is called upon to rule in the domain of conscience, into which the secular authority has no right of entrance; and an agreement that mixed questions shall be decided by amicable arrangement appears as equitable and normal as the conclusion of international treaties to settle questions of territory or frontiers.

But the heirs of the French Revolution do not approve of this method of government, which leaves to the Church a position of independence and honour, and permits her to hope for progress, and perhaps even for the peaceful union of all classes of society at the foot of the Cross of Christ. The State, as they understand it, by an insolent assertion of its supremacy, by the arbitrary rupture of concordats, by vexatious legislation which shows contempt for Christian traditions in the matter of education and the religious life, will provoke and multiply conflicts which it will settle at its own good pleasure, always complaining that it is maligned or misunderstood. Even the protection of individual liberty which they entrust to the State leads to persecution. The State, maintaining its attitude of official indifference, will begin by refusing the least sign of sympathy or encouragement to a positive religion. " From the cradle to the grave," writes Friedberg, " the private individual should be able to pass his life without any obstacle or any encouragement of a religious character coming from the State."[1] Later on, a constant care will be exercised that there shall be no interference with the liberty of irreligion ; and among the things that are considered as interfering with it will be the success of any religious body.

Let us listen to the criticisms of M. Ruffini, whom we have often quoted, on the American separatist system. He is an Italian professor, an opponent of revolutionary violence, and a great preacher of tolerance, and he says : " In these last years the separatist system has turned to the advantage of those Churches whose organization is the strongest, and whose propaganda is the most active ; but it has not been of so much service to the religious liberty of the individual, especially to that liberty which takes the form of unbelief. Rationalism in

[1] See *Die Grenzen zwischen Staat und Kirche, und die Garantien gegen deren Verletzung*, l. 3 ; Tübingen, 1872. According to Friedberg, the words express not so much a wish as a fact. Ruffini, his translator, goes farther.

DOCTRINES OF INTOLERANCE

general, and scientific free thought in particular, are wanting in organization; and for that very reason the separatist system is not advantageous to them, and it leaves them isolated and defenceless against the different organized religious communities, which, under the protection of the separatist system, are too well off to display their spirit of intolerance."[1]

So, then, according to these professors of tolerance, the victory of religion over unbelief, even if won by peaceful means, is an interference with the free choice to believe or not to believe, and the State is bound to maintain in its society a well-balanced mixture of believers and unbelievers.

The view of an advocate of the jurisdictional system, Dr. Emile Friedberg, who died in December, 1910,[2] will give us still further information on this system of tolerance. After definitely refusing to allow the liberty of the Church, as guaranteed by the Belgian Constitution, and recognizing in the law alone the right of regulating the position of the Church, he formulates the following propositions: It is the duty of the State to banish the Jesuits; the law of marriage, the cemeteries, and the relief of the poor, should all be secularized; foreign members of religious Orders should be expelled from the country; others should be forbidden to teach; no convent should be allowed to be opened without previous authorization; the nomination of Bishops and beneficed clergy should be subject to the "exsequatur" of the State; the State will punish

---

[1] *La Libertà Religiosa*, pp. 17, 18.
[2] *Op. cit.*, book 3. He was professor at Tübingen when he wrote.

any violent language used in preaching; it will forbid the Church to excommunicate any person;[1] and it may require a certain standard of education among the clergy. A special organization will watch over the rights of the State, with power to inflict punishments on the clergy and withdraw their civil mission.

At this rate, the pretended liberty given by common law costs the Church as much or more than her ancient privileges, and the State does not even hold an equal balance between religion and unbelief; it must take care to prevent the disappearance of the latter, but not of the former.

If the Revolution which professes tolerance does not secure to Catholics the liberty of the Church, nor, consequently, of their religion, of which the Church is an essential form, what are we to expect of a Revolution which declares its hostility to the Church?

Since 1789 there has been a constant movement of opinion in the direction of a sectarian negation of religion; it is made manifest in facts which leave no doubt as to its purpose.

The motto of the sect is contained in the famous declaration of Gambetta, "*Le cléricalisme, voilà l'ennemi*"; and, be it understood, this clericalism which he describes as "the enemy" does not mean the conduct of fanatical or encroaching clergy: it means nothing less than the Catholic Church. It is she who is to be attacked. But the name of the

[1] This prohibition will appear strange. Friedberg justifies it by a reminder of the civil effects formerly attached to this ecclesiastical penalty. This aversion to ecclesiastical censures is traditional among the State jurists of Germany.

DOCTRINES OF INTOLERANCE

Church is held in affection by the people, and therefore a word is chosen which excites their aversion: the mention of the clergy serves to remind them of three unpopular things—aristocracy, privileges, and authority; and clericalism means the immoderate influence and the tyrannical rule of the clergy. Once more we realize how the art of deceiving people by a war-cry has always been familiar to the enemies of the Church.

Moreover, irreligion does not come into the lists openly and under its own name. At one time war is declared in the name of the rights of the State: the supremacy of the State must be defended against Catholics who dispute it; its independence must be protected against the threats and intrigues of the clergy. Under some such pretext as this Waldeck Rousseau attacked the religious congregations. At another time the impulse is given to the attack in the name of tolerance, which, like all idols, protects only those who worship it. "Many have said, Tolerance is due only to the tolerant: or, Only the liberty of those is to be respected who proclaim their respect for liberty."[1] At another time we are told that patriotism revolts against the obedience which religious promise to foreign superiors; at another the reproach is levelled against all Catholics who acknowledge the authority of the Pope. It has even been said that national unity is alarmed by the antagonistic education given to two classes of youth.

[1] Fonsegrive, *Bulletin de la Semaine*, December 21, 1910. Fuhrmann (*De Tolerantiæ Religiosæ Effectibus Civilibus*, c. 1 fine) had already repeated a phrase of Larræus (*Hist. d'Angleterre*, t. 4, p. 53): "The Roman religion becomes intolerable by its own intolerance."

CIVIL TOLERANCE

Sometimes the campaign takes the form of a war against slavery; men's intellects must be freed from the oppressive and ill-omened yoke of clerical servitude.

"And what," say the enemies of the Church, "may we hope to gain by our action?" The triumph of the secular spirit, the consolidation of the victories of Modernism, the destruction of antiquated ideas, progress, civilization, the Republic. They have a string of high-sounding words to flatter the vanity of people who think themselves learned because they swear by science; or smart politicians because they read a newspaper; or men of good taste because they follow the fashion; or artisans of progress because they have helped to demolish some institution of the past. In the van of the army marches a small band of noisy fanatics, followed by a crowd of weak, credulous people, easily gulled by their leaders, and allured by the hope of something new, some advantage to themselves. They have no thought but of their own interests; many of them cynically admit it, or, at least, confess it to themselves secretly; others put forward loftier motives, which sometimes deceive even themselves; and thus it is that men foment tyranny, while they preach universal liberty.

But how can a thing which is entirely negative, like theistic[1] or atheistic unbelief, become a principle of intolerance? It takes that form when it no longer denotes a state of mind, the situation of a

---

[1] The Proceedings of the Constituent Assembly record that the Declaration of the Rights of Man is made "in the presence and under the auspices of the Supreme Being."

DOCTRINES OF INTOLERANCE

person who has ceased to believe, but when it becomes itself a faith, the Jacobin faith, as Taine said,[1]—when it excites a domineering ambition,[2] or when silly vanity is made the foundation of obstinate dogmatism. "There are nowadays," arrogantly exclaimed Auguste Comte, "but two camps—the one retrograde and anarchist, which still retains a confused idea of the supremacy of God; the other organic and progressive, systematically devoted to the service of Humanity."[3] In whom or in what do these people place their confidence? Not in God, the Author of revelation, but in humanity, groping its way in the dark; not in the Master, who communicates what He sees, but in ignorant man, seeking to discover something new; a general and indefinite confidence in movement and progress, in scientific inquiry—in short (to use a fashionable word), in evolution. For authority is substituted an arbitrary theory, which is not proved, and never can be proved: man is sufficient for himself; there is nothing above him; all things converge towards the great notion of humanity.[4] This creed has but

[1] *La Révolution*, l. 4, c. 2, i.; t. 3, p. 393.

[2] M. Et. Lamy thus sums up the career of one of the revolutionaries: "To proscribe God, because the existence of God would imply the existence of duty: that was the essential work of André Dumont" ("*La Psychologie d'un Révolutionnaire: Le Conventionnel André Dumont,*" *Correspondant*, April 25, 1910, p. 377).

[3] *Système de Politique Positive*, t. 1, p. 398. Far from showing us progress in order and devotion, experience rather confirms the *Mémoires* of Barruel, who saw in Jacobinism, execrable as it was, the product of three successive sects—*Les sophistes de l'incrédulité et de l'impiété*, who formed *les sophistes de la rébellion*, to whom succeeded *les sophistes de l'impiété et de l'anarchie*.

[4] Comte, *Cours de Philosophie Positive*, t. 6, p. 880.

one dogma—the relativity of our knowledge and the perpetual "*fieri*" of truth. It is called *humanism*, inasmuch as it declares itself all for man, without leaving anything to God; it is called *laicism*, inasmuch as it is at war against the Church. There is only one name to describe the party that professes this faith—the anti-Church.

This religion, which is built on very weak foundations, bolsters up its pretensions by the very audacity of its contempt for others. "To believe in an absolute truth," says M. Payot,[1] "denotes an unhealthy state of mind." The Grand Orient of France declares that "all our religious practices are the most serious obstacle to the intellectual and moral development and perfection of humanity."[2] As the Christians of the fourth and fifth centuries ridiculed pagan superstitions, so do the adherents of anti-Church turn our Christian faith to derision; they think themselves superior in wisdom, and declare that they are certain to conquer and to accomplish the great work of society, "the elimination of Catholicism."[3]

[1] *Le Volume*, December 3, 1910.
[2] *Bulletin du Grand Orient*, Fifty-fifth Year, pp. 308, 309.
[3] The President of the French Academy, M. Et. Lamy, in the discourse at the reception of Mgr. Duchesne (1911), expressed in these words the predominant idea of the present Government of France.

Article III. Facts since the French Revolution.

SUMMARY : The jurisdictional system prevails throughout the whole of Europe, except in Belgium.—Decrease of intolerance among different religious bodies.—The anti-Church party wages war against the Christian religion.—This war stealthy and often disguised, but implacable, as honest unbelievers themselves admit.

At the end of the bloody tragedy of the Terror, French Catholics at first enjoyed a certain amount of religious liberty, on which a hostile power looked with a jealous eye. Napoleon gave back to religion its churches, its ministers, and its public honours, but without recognizing the rights of the Church or giving her full liberty. Instead of this, he inaugurated the jurisdictional system, which continued to prevail in Germany, Austria, and the Latin countries. This system gives the Church some dark days and some days of comparative peace, according to the countries and the men who govern them. The civil power may be friendly and just, or it may be vexatious and unsympathetic; it may even descend to persecution, as in the German Kulturkampf and the last years of the French Concordat. The weapon of oppression remains in the hands of the State, which makes use of it according to the necessities of politics, sometimes to divert attention from questions which might be inconvenient to the men in power.

There is one country in Europe which forms an exception to this rule. The Belgian Constitution, while freely granting to its citizens all modern liberties, gives liberty also to the Church, and does not exact any servitude in return for its good-will towards religion.

During the whole of the nineteenth century the conflicts between the different Christian bodies became less bitter, and gave place to a decisive struggle between religion and unbelief. We have seen that at the close of the preceding period Protestant bigotry relaxed its severity to some extent, and Catholics were treated more equitably in non-Catholic countries. A fact unprecedented in history was the publication by Pope Leo XIII. of an Apostolic letter addressed to the Princes and people of the whole world,[1] even to non-Catholics. Catholics live in perfect content in the great North American Republic, where the separation of Church and State coexists with friendly relations and real sympathy.

But in France the anti-Church party establishes a system of persecution worthy of the days of Julian the Apostate, and employs all the resources of the State for the purposes of its campaign. Practising Catholics are systematically excluded from all employment and offices of profit; official education inculcates, if not hatred, at least indifference, or we might even say contempt, for religion. Liberty of association is legalised, and at the same time the religious congregations are dissolved: their goods are confiscated, and the sale produces less than half of the milliard promised to the working classes; their schools are closed, and Frenchmen do not know whether to-morrow liberty of instruction will not be entirely destroyed.

[1] Letter *Præclara Gratulationis*, June 20, 1894. *Epistola Apostolica principibus populisque universis*.

The young Portuguese Republic follows the French one, or, rather, endeavours to outstrip it, in the haste with which it multiplies its laws and decrees of persecution and plunder against the Church.

In Belgium anticlericals do not hesitate to enter into alliance with republicans in their impatience to return to power ; and henceforth they claim a privileged position in the State : they are to define the schools with which Catholics must be satisfied, and they resent the idea of equality as an insult.

When the Bloc was in power in France, it could not restrain a *væ victis ;* the new Government of Portugal flatters itself that under its system of laws it will have made an end of Christianity within two hundred years. This is frank ; but the leaders of the anti-Church party generally endeavour to disguise their intentions, and even when attacking the Church, they pretend to be acting on the defensive.[1] Read their newspapers, listen to their speeches ; they are continually obliged, they say, to resist the monstrous demands of Catholics,[2] to answer their provocations,[3] to put down their treasonable campaigns ;[4] above all, they never forget the advice of

[1] Notice the artful language of M. Ed. Petit (*Moïse Klein*), Inspector-General of Public Instruction, in his Annual Report for 1910 : " Popular education, which ought to be a matter outside and above the strife of parties, is obliged to live in a state of armed defence, and resist the offensive war that is made upon it without any provocation, and though it maintains the neutrality which, both in the school and after the school, is imposed as a law of conscience " (*Questiones Actuelles*, t. 3, pp. 18, 19).

[2] Like that of not paying twice over for the schools : once for schools which Catholics cannot accept, and once for their own.

[3] Every Catholic manifestation is a provocation.

[4] Like the so-called campaign of the scholastic manuals.

Voltaire : " Lie always." Excelling in the art of falsifying figures and distorting facts when they are in power, they pose as models of forbearance ; when they are not in power, as victims, weary of injustice, " fighting against a Government of oppression in order to obtain liberty of conscience."[1] It is painful to have to record these petty vexations, but, alas ! the mask of liberty deceives so many credulous people ; and we cannot help remembering the words of Madame Roland as she went to the guillotine : " O Liberty ! how many crimes are committed in thy name !"

Nevertheless, even among non-Catholics there are many honest and intelligent observers who see and declare plainly on which side are the victims and on which side the persecutors.

" For thirty years," says a syndicalist Socialist, M. G. Sorel, " the Republican Government has been dominated by an anti-Church party, which follows a policy generally cunning,[2] sometimes brutal, and always fanatical in its desire to destroy Christianity in France. This anti-Church party, victorious to-day, hopes to profit by the unexpected success it has obtained since the Dreyfus campaign ; it considers that the system of indifference will be a failure so long as the Church retains any influence

[1] Declaration of the Liberal Left in 1911, when making an alliance with the Socialists.

[2] " For instance, the famous scholastic neutrality was only a trick to lull Catholic vigilance to sleep ; to-day the official representatives of the Government declare that the great end to be pursued in the primary schools is the suppression of religious faith " (see the discourse delivered by Aristide Briand at Angers in 1906, before the League of Education).

worth mentioning : its great desire is to abolish the regular clergy, as its leaders have reason to believe that the secular clergy will not be sufficient to maintain the Catholic religion."[1]

Article IV. Doctrines and Facts examined.

Summary: Examination of the principle of absolute tolerance, founded on man.—This principle is false.—Refutation of objections.—It does not give liberty to religion.—It protects only unbelief.—The suppression of the crime of opinion is more apparent than real.—It does not seem to be final.—Testimony of V. Jacobs.—The French Revolution, fruitless for good, has seen its principle of State intolerance much more applied than its principle of individual tolerance.

The Revolution sought in the rights of the human individual the support, the chief and only foundation, of the liberties that it proclaimed. It promised on that ground absolute, universal, perpetual tolerance, and this tolerance was in practice expressed by the suppression of the crime of opinion.

These few lines sum up the philosophy and the political principles of the French Revolution—the principles, be it understood, of all its liberties ; for there remains still the principle of all its servitudes, the omnipotence of the State, the result of universal suffrage.

These principles may be examined in themselves, in their abstract truth, and then in their application and working.

" Man has the right to think what he pleases and say what he pleases ; but he has not the right to do

[1] *Réflexions sur la Violence*, p. 398.

what he pleases." Is this proposition true? On what evidence is it founded? On the physical liberty of man? Jules Simon suggests this in the passage we have quoted above (p. 222). But man is as free to act as he is to speak and publish. Why should physical liberty give me the right to say anything I choose, while the physical liberty of my actions does not give me the right to do anything I choose? Is it because my actions may do harm, but my words cannot? Is this distinction sustainable? May I not, by speaking and persuading, pervert a man's mind, and incite him to do criminal acts? Or even without directly inciting him to them, may I not sow the fatal seed of evil in his heart and his intellect?[1] Is not that doing harm to a man, perhaps ruining his whole life? Is not that an injury to society?

Is it because, in preventing what is evil, we attack the liberty of what is good, the principle of free judgment? This fear of Fouillée[2] is unfounded. Since when does a good action cease to be free because a bad one is legally forbidden? Since when does the law which punishes the thief lessen the merit of the honest man? And once more, why should restraints on speech and the diffusion of ideas alone have inconvenient results? Whatever

[1] The annals of the Courts of Justice give many examples of this.

[2] "The liberty of evil, misguided liberty, looked at in its results, would not deserve much attention; but the principle of free judgment is so noble, the object it may and should attain is so sublime, that such a faculty cannot be restrained except so far as is strictly necessary to social life" ("*L'Idée Moderne du Droit en France,*" *Revue des Deux Mondes,* August 1, 1878; Summary of V. Jacobs's article).

DOCTRINES AND FACTS

any authority may say, my inward opinion remains always free, and this opinion influences my actions as well as my words. Such is the reality.

Can the prohibition of acts alone be justified by this other reason, that acts alone interfere with the liberty of another person? Even this statement is incorrect, for a man may be coerced by language of ridicule or temptation, by threats and misrepresentation, as well as by physical constraint.

Can it be said that the liberty to say and teach anything whatever compensates by its social advantages for its very real disadvantages—that, like the spear of Achilles, "liberty of opinion heals the wounds it causes"?[1] There is nothing to prove that it possesses this remarkable virtue; and if such is the reason, we are no longer concerned to appeal to an undeniable right of man, but to discuss the social use of a liberty. That is an old way of looking at the question, and if we take that point of view, we take away from the Revolution all credit for invention.

To come back to the question. Either the will of man and the liberty of man have some law, or they have none: if they have none, neither a man's speech nor his actions can be contrary to law; if they have a law, a man may offend against it by the manner in which he forms and expresses his opinion, as well as by the manner in which he acts. The right to think and say what is forbidden by law does not exist, any more than the right to do illegal acts.

[1] Frère Orban, in the discussion of the law on the conferring of academical degrees (*Annales Parlementaires*, Chambre, 1875-1876, p. 546).

The public authority has the power to control the expression of thoughts, like every other outward act. We shall therefore seek in vain in the human individual for any reason why speech should be free and actions restrained.

Fouillée himself has told us : " True liberty consists, not in being able to do evil, but in being able to do good. It is not the power to fall, but the power to rise."[1]

Now how far does this pretended right of man, which does not exist in reality, operate as a safeguard of religious liberty ?

Suppose it to be unassailable in law and respected in fact. In any case, it gives liberty to the individual opinion only. Now, religions do not exist as opinions, but as Churches. The religious liberty which the Catholic claims is that of the Church, and this Catholic religion is the dominant religion of the countries which the French Revolution professed to regenerate. Then, for millions and millions of men this maxim of the Declaration of Rights of Man, already null and void as a truth, is proved to be also null and void as a guarantee of liberty.

What has it given in fact ? Some sincere Liberals attribute to it their generous optimism, and one party of the framers of the Belgian Constitution believed and professed it.[2] So it has not been abso-

---

[1] *L'Idée Moderne du Droit en France* (*Revue des Deux Mondes*, April 1, 1878).

[2] De Potter, for instance. But not all. The Catholics did not base on any abstract right or natural law the religious liberty they granted. " To grant liberty of worship is not to admit that there can be more than one true religion ; and to grant liberty of opinion is not to admit that all opinions are equally good. I will have general liberty, not

DOCTRINES AND FACTS

lutely inoperative. But we cannot forget that the application of this maxim has been the cause of irritating laws, oppressions of every kind, proscriptions, confiscation of goods, and judicial condemnations without number.

In reality, the maxim effectively protected the liberty of unbelief, but it did not give such religious liberty as is demanded by the conscience of believers. Before the French Revolution, favour was shown to faith and religion; now it has passed to irreligion and unbelief.

Indifference tends to become a sort of official religion, which has inherited the privileges and advantages formerly attached to the Christian religion. In the hospitals, the priest formerly offered his services to all sick persons who did not refuse to accept them; he is now not allowed to present himself unless he is actually sent for, and the sick man who is unable to express his wishes must die without sacramental absolution and extreme unction. No religious assistance is officially given to the sailor who goes on a long voyage or the soldier who risks his life on the field of battle. The politicians who adopt the principles of the French Revolution, not content with laicizing the public services of charity and education, insist that all persons who are employed in them shall set an example of the denial of all religion. Everything in the present state of society is intended to accustom men's minds to

---

as an absolute good, but as a lesser evil." Did not these lines from the *Catholique des Pays-Bas* (1828), quoted by M. Damoiseaux (*La Formation de la Société Belge*, p. 16), foreshadow a distinction between the thesis and the hypothesis?

religious scepticism. Little by little the position of Catholics becomes worse, and greater privileges are conferred on unbelievers. The fullest measure of liberty and official patronage is given to irreligious negation, while the Church obtains only a precarious tolerance, grudgingly conceded.

May we at least believe that the crime of opinion has been struck out of our penal code ? There is nothing to guarantee this. What is meant when an opinion is made a crime ? Is it not the State's way of showing that it is interested in the diffusion of the contrary opinion ? Has the State, then, no interest in opinions ? Is the French State indifferent to opinions when it prohibits the teaching Congregations ; when it confiscates the printing-presses of the Augustinian Fathers ; when it closes 20,000 Catholic schools, attended by 1,600,000 children ;[1] when it takes upon itself to maintain the triumph of secularism, and when, in the official Gazette of Madagascar,[2] it describes belief in God as one of " the beliefs of idiots, unworthy of intelligent beings "?

Do the acts of the Belgian Liberal party show that they do not concern themselves with opinion ? Do they not show that the party has lost all claim to be called Liberal ? Victor Jacobs wrote in 1880 : " Fifty years' experience has taught us that whenever the Constitution is silent, or its language is obscure or ambiguous—or, rather, whenever the text leaves an opening for evasion or equivocation—the Liberal party claims to enforce its own opinions. The spirit of the constitution may be opposed to their

[1] Piou, in the French Chamber, June 27, 1910.
[2] The *Vaovao* of December 6, 1907.

proceedings, yet nothing but a formal prohibition will stop them."[1] What would this great parliamentarian have said of the thirty years that followed?

But it is only a short step from taking a lively interest in certain opinions to giving them prevalence and proscribing the opposite opinions, and that step is soon taken by a State which has fallen into the hands of the enemies of religion. Propositions of this kind are already put forward; threats are heard on all sides. M. Piou recently quoted the expression of M. Madier de Monjau:[2] " There is no justice in politics; you get rid of what you do not like. We are the Republic, and we alone." Moreover, to revive the crime of opinion, an anticlerical Administration does not wait for it to be inserted in the penal code. This crime existed in Belgium when, under the two last Liberal Ministries, Catholics were practically excluded from the magistracy; it exists now in France, where there are 800,000 public offices which are normally inaccessible to Catholics—that is to say, to those who practise their religion.

The maxim of the rights of man is not regarded when antireligious passions or personal interests are involved. When an opinion offends the citizen or affects his interests, however closely he may be attached to the principles of '89, he endeavours to stifle that opinion, and, if he is strong enough, to proscribe it. A strike of workmen or the threat of

[1] *Les Droits Naturels de l'Homme* (*Revue Générale*, 1880, p. 682).
[2] French Chamber, June 27, 1910.

some economic conflict, is enough to make the Liberal newspapers forget their Liberalism, and condemn not only criminal acts, but the unhealthy ideas from which they spring.

Opinion, then, has not yet acquired such an inviolable sanctity that the legislator is restrained by any respect for it. Victor Jacobs sums up his impressions in these terms : " Real life has been a constant negation of the maxim of the French Revolution." No security is given to anything by this theory of the rights of man, " which no one has ever applied, which its authors were the first to contravene, and which on the least pretext is put aside altogether."[1]

The French Revolution, which was so very chary of granting real liberty, showed itself much more faithful in practice to the principles of the omnipotence of the State. From the first, and whenever they could, the sons of the Revolution invoked that omnipotence in order to make war on the Church, and to violate those rights of man which they so proudly proclaimed. " The intellectual and moral sense of this country," wrote Leplay, " has been perverted, in being made to believe that liberty with us dates from 1789. The more I think of it, the more firmly I am convinced that that date should rather be considered the date of the gradual disappearance of liberty."

The absolutist principle is no more true, though it has been more enforced. The State is not all-powerful, and its rights do not result from an individual abdication sanctioned by the

[1] *Op. cit.*, pp. 666, 681.

suffrage. We wait in vain for proof of these postulates.

There is certainly a great difference of opinion between the anticlericals and ourselves, but until they have converted us, they will be once more false to their principles if they consider them to be absolutely true, or if they try to compel us to accept them.

CHAPTER V

THE THEORY OF RIGHT CIVIL TOLERANCE

SUMMARY : Two false doctrines opposed : absolute tolerance and absolute intolerance.—Principles and facts to be considered to arrive at a just solution.—The right, of God, the revealer of truth, and the right of universal revealed religion.—Essential freedom of the act of faith. —The intolerance which would convert by force is bad. —The right and duty of every man and of mankind in general towards religious truth.—Office and competence of the civil power.—Positive duties which flow from it.—Practical rules.—Reasonable causes of exception.—Another explanation suggested by the present form of societies : is the State still competent ? —The thesis and the hypothesis.—Why speak of a thesis ?—The Encyclical *Immortale Dei*.—Proofs and advantages of the theory suggested.—It professes a principle of less intolerance than the ideal of Montesquieu and Bara.—No fear of a return to the severity of former times.—Paradox of M. Bouché-Leclercq.—The real fact : constant tolerance of Catholics and frequent intolerance of their adversaries.

THE good government of a nation, which is an art rather than a science, is not regulated by abstract ideas. It has to reckon both with rights, the violation of which is always productive of evil effects, and with existing circumstances, which indicate what is possible and expedient, and its conduct must be regulated by principles and facts. The dogma of absolute tolerance or intolerance does not fulfil either condition. By what primary right of man, by what commandment of God, by what permanent necessity, can absolute tolerance justify its unchanging neutrality or its cold indifference? And what right does the State possess in itself or derive from God to proscribe always and *a priori* persons holding different opinions? The two dogmas, which are equally unmindful of concrete realities, are socially demoralizing—the former by a scandalous indifference or a disastrous weakness, the latter by an inflexibility which is sometimes unjust and often tyrannical. Dogmatic intolerance, caring more for unity than truth, results only too easily in the forcible imposition of false doctrines. On the other hand, absolute tolerance leads to disorder and confusion, and the dogma of this tolerance is not only fatal to social peace, but fails to keep its promises of liberty.

It is not by denying the rights of God, or exaggerating the independence of man, or misrepresenting the functions of the State, that we arrive at the right formula of civil tolerance. The true solution is in a harmonious combination of rights, duties, and facts; and in order to combine them, we must first see clearly what they are.

We first see that above man there is God, with His imprescriptible right to enrich created intelligence with useful or necessary truths, and to institute a religion which shall be obligatory on the whole human race. Next, we remark the fact of a religion which calls itself Catholic—that is to say, intended for the whole world—and which produces its credentials, not to put in evidence truths which we cannot know by intuition, but to make them acceptable to our reason; not to force them on our intelligence, but to obtain a free interior act of faith in those truths. And this religion tells us that God must give the assistance of His grace to the will and intelligence of man in order that man may arrive at that absolute conviction which is expressed by the act of faith.[1] It is impossible for man to force an entry into a soul in order to implant the faith in it, and religion tells us that it would be criminal also, for God desires that His Church shall be composed of willing believers.

It is an entire misunderstanding of Catholic intolerance to suppose that it desires to obtain conversions by force; and when the partisans of the dogma of tolerance appeal to the inviolability of the conscience and the impossibility of producing faith by threats, they attack another kind of intolerance, which is not Catholic at all. Nay, more, they reason as Catholics do, and repeat the arguments which Catholic tradition always used against forced conversions.

The number of the faithful on whom the gift of faith has been bestowed varies with time and place. In some places there are only isolated Catholics or Christians, and there are—or, at least, there have been—communities entirely Catholic or Christian without exception.

Man has a corresponding duty and right to seek the true faith, to embrace it and keep it. He owes this duty to God, out of submission and gratitude; he owes it to himself, for to him it is the principle of all good; he owes it to his fellow-men, for his profession of faith is helpful to others. But for this per-

---

[1] See Rousselot, *Les Yeux de la Foi* (*Recherches de Science Religieuse*, 1910, i., pp. 241 *sqq.*).

JUST TOLERANCE

sonal duty he is not responsible to any human or social authority, since God does not desire that men should be forced to the faith, and the mysterious difficulties which keep men from the faith or lead them astray from it are not under the control of men.

Men who are united in possession of the faith, are bound by the same obligations; religious truth is a gift which they may not cast away, a common inheritance which it is their duty to preserve, a principle of excellent charity which they must practise towards all men. But as all men do not receive the faith, so also all men do not keep it. Apostasies may be individual or collective. Men may simply lose their faith or profess new doctrines. Sometimes it is done quietly, and sometimes it causes scandal and commotion; but we generally find that these defections are contagious, and that a reformer, even when he starts independently and without any mission, may seduce the masses, especially if the relaxation of discipline or the appearance of abuses in the Church furnishes a specious pretext for his denunciations.

The civil power, in its turn, represents the community for the fulfilment of its duties and the promotion of its interests. It cannot enforce intellectual and moral unity, for the only unity that is a blessing is unity in the truth;[1] nor religious truth, for God has made that a matter of free acceptance. But it is the duty, as it is the interest, of the community

---

[1] Unity always brings a certain peace; but unity in error deprives society of all the blessings which result from truth, and is by nature as precarious as error itself. As we have already said, a long and peaceful reign of error may be explained by accidental causes, such as the lethargy of the people, or the truth mixed with the error.

to protect religious truth and to encourage its diffusion. For this twofold reason, and in the measure of its competence, the civil power ought, as the organ of society, to give to the true religion all the help and support possible. As the natural protector of the weak, it is bound to save them from being led away by want of thought.

And the interest due to religious truth attaches, in fact, to the Church, the spiritual society divinely established to teach and spread that truth, and to gather the faithful together. In giving this assistance to the Church, the State can neither absorb the Church nor be absorbed by it.

From these preliminary considerations there flows a moderate doctrine—tolerant or intolerant, as may be. This doctrine may be called Catholic, because it is based on the principles of true religion, and it may also be called practical, not in the sense in which we speak of a practical man, as distinguished from an imaginative man, but because, without neglecting any right or duty, it satisfies real practical necessities, making man as free as is expedient, and society as united, prosperous, and happy, as can be hoped for in the circumstances.

The rules of application of this doctrine may be formulated as follows :

The Sovereign who has the faith will encourage religion, without going beyond his powers or failing in justice, and will keep all the promises by which he is bound.

In a Catholic society the true religion will be publicly honoured and protected. The precautions which justice permits, which are expedient in con-

JUST TOLERANCE

sideration of times and places and persons, will be taken to preserve to the community the blessing of unity in the true faith. For this purpose, the civil power may declare that any public contradiction of the faith or the propagation of heterodox doctrines is an offence, and may inflict reasonable punishment for it.

But no violence may be used, and no acquired right may be interfered with, to impose religious unity on a society which does not possess it, or which, having possessed it, has lost it.

The favour which it owes to the true religion is a positive duty of the State, and requires action on its part. Grave and adequate reasons may dispense from positive duties, and sometimes circumstances render the protection of religion morally impossible. Even the interests of true religion itself may suggest a prudent forbearance. It may be that the liberty granted to error may give greater freedom to truth, or that in the divided state of public opinion on religious subjects it is better for true religion to enter into competition with error on common ground, rather than shelter itself behind privileges.

Such reasons justify the neutrality of the civil power, and it may also be explained by the provision in the positive constitution of many contemporary States which forbids any other attitude. The system of political organizations tends more and more to insist on express stipulations inserted in what is called the fundamental pact of the country. When a charter of this kind, peacefully accepted by the nation, has laid down that the Government shall not interfere in religious questions, are we not justified in holding that differences of opinion, regrettable though they may be, have led the citizens to a tacit understanding not to put their religious interests in common ? Agreeing to be left to themselves and their own devices, they adopt towards religion an attitude which shows they are no longer one body. Their social union has ceased to be complete, and the representatives of the State have no official obligation to protect or defend religion, but also they have no right to oppress it.

This abnormal situation, in which the State to a greater or less extent gives up one part of its functions, is called the *hypothesis*. The *thesis*, then, is verified in a society that is wholly Christian. Does this mean that it takes place oftener than the hypothesis ? By no means ; it does not necessarily follow. We may compare the thesis to an ideal, the perfect realization of which is not possible in this world. Why, then, speak of thesis and hypothesis, and not say simply that we must leave it to circumstances to decide on the attitude to be adopted towards religion ? That would not express our meaning, because we cannot accept with equal satisfaction unity in religious truth, and a division which puts so many of our brethren out of the way of salvation ; because no compromise can have the value or advantages of peace based on true concord ; because communion in the truth is an object for which we must always strive, prudently, no doubt, and without violence, but constantly. And even where complete realization cannot be obtained, it is a great blessing to come near it, and to possess in the ideal that we cherish and the reality that we

JUST TOLERANCE

accept with resignation an end of our efforts, and a rule by which we may measure our social progress. We cannot regard with indifference the two situations or the two official attitudes which may be adopted without falling into a listless and enervating scepticism.

The sight of a Protestant steeple rising alongside a Catholic bell-tower in one of the smiling landscapes on the banks of the Rhine awakens the thought of a sad and painful division; the insolent emblems displayed on a Masonic temple, with all they suggest of human pride, disturb the peace and serenity produced by the contemplation of a majestic cathedral. A religious procession is soothing and edifying, while an atheistic demonstration is irritating and offensive; and this pain, this annoyance, this irritation, show that man, when he follows his natural inclination, does not look on all things as indifferent in religious matters. They tell us where is the order we long for and the necessity to which we must submit. But, however acutely he may feel these things, the sincere Christian does not harbour any thought of violence or persecution; his suffering only produces a desire to spread the knowledge of the truth.

Leo XIII. wrote on the Christian constitution of States a memorable Encyclical—*Immortale Dei* (November 1, 1885)—and a careful perusal of that document will reveal therein the principles from which we started, and the practical rules we have here formulated. The following short extract sums up the most important of our assertions: " The Church, indeed, deems it unlawful to place the different forms of worship on the same footing as the true religion. But it does not on that account condemn those rulers who, for the sake of securing some great good, and hindering some great evil, patiently allow custom or usage to be a kind of sanction for each religion having its place in the State. And the Church is wont to take great care that no person shall be forced to embrace the Catholic faith against his will. For Augustine wisely reminds us, ' Man cannot believe otherwise than of his own free will.' "[1]

This doctrine, derived from the true mission and duties of man, sacrifices no duty, human or Divine; it conceals no truth, either of principle or of fact. It takes man as he is, with his present life and his future destiny; it does not isolate him from the community, or allow him to be oppressed by it; it takes account of the body, without forgetting the soul

True theoretically by all that it asserts of God, religion, civil society, authority, and liberty, it shows itself practically true by its consideration of existing circumstances. It recognizes and deplores the seductions and perversions that result from certain liberties, but it knows that if we try to remove all the ills that trouble us, we run a risk of falling into worse misfortune.

Nevertheless, it does not forget that man and society are capable of being made perfect, in order to preserve its ideal without seeking to enforce it inopportunely.

This doctrine, which is thus in harmony with the personal dignity of man, his social nature, and his desire for improvement, and which takes proper

[1] *Tract* 26 in *Joann.*, n. 2.

JUST TOLERANCE

account of existing circumstances and the possibilities of the future, possesses in the very clearness of its rules, and the simplicity of the reasons which support it, a new confirmation of its truth.[1]

Victor Jacobs, in his remarkable article in the *Revue Générale*,[2] wrote thus: " These rules of the government of the world must not make us forget the ideal for which some Liberal writers showed a preference "; and he went on to quote Montesquieu and Bara : " It would be a very good law, when the State is satisfied with the religion already established, not to permit the establishment of another. . . . This, then, is the fundamental principle of political laws in matters of religion : when there is a choice of admitting or not admitting a new religion into the State, it should not be established ; but when it is established, it should be tolerated."[3] This is the opinion of Montesquieu, and Bara declares that " in theory, the theocratic form of government is the true one. . . . The ideal is the supremacy of one single religion, and its identification with the governing power. . . . The system of the complete separation of the State and religions is only a last resource."[4]

In Montesquieu we find the thesis and the hypothesis. Bara declares for the hypothesis ; but both exaggerate it, and give it a scope which we consider inadmissible and dangerous to liberty. The former, an advocate of one single religion approved by the State, would logically justify all the old persecu-

[1] See Laurentius, S.J., in *Stimmen*, t. 68, p. 27.
[2] *Les Droits Naturels de l'Homme*, 1880.
[3] *Esprit des Lois*, lxxv., chap. x.
[4] *Essai sur les Rapports entre l'État et les Religions au Point de Vue Constitutionnel*, pp. 9, 12.

tions without regard for the truth; the latter similarly cares too little for the true religion, and he has nothing to substitute for the radical separation, which we agree with him in describing as a last resource, but theocracy, an identification of religion with government, in which we denounce the principle of absolute and unrestrained despotism.

Everywhere and always we insist on the distinction between the domain of religion and the domain of civil authority. We maintain that above each of these there is an independent and sovereign authority, in order by this very distinction and this balance of power to set up a bulwark against tyranny and provide a refuge for liberty.

Will anyone venture, in spite of all that has been said, to evoke the punishments and tortures of former times, to dissuade men from accepting our theory and our ideal? We answer with Victor Jacobs: " If ever religious unity comes back to life, it will be reflected in the laws, but the spirit of the age will be reflected in them no less."[1]

What is called civil intolerance has many shades, and does not necessarily mean persecution. The intolerance which the thesis demands is not aggressive. It does not impose a faith or a conviction, but it defends the weak and the welfare of the community.

What is there to be afraid of? Is it not a fact that our formula, derived from the duties of men and society, more modest and much less dogmatic, has given much more real liberty than the pompous but profitless Declaration of the Rights of Man? In the beginning, in the first years of schism and

[1] Art. cit., p. 672.

JUST TOLERANCE

separation, the necessity of accommodating the political system to a situation so new and strange was lost sight of by Catholics and their theologians —they erred by an excess of conservatism; but since the necessity became evident, these same Catholics have been, and always will be, themselves most scrupulous in their observance of the treaties concluded and the liberties granted. This fact is self-evident. Our adversaries themselves, however difficult they find it to get rid of their prejudices, bear witness to our moderation. During the eighty years of its freedom and independence, Belgium has presented this remarkable contrast in the conduct of political parties: When the Catholics have been in power, even with an enormous majority, they have left all constitutional liberties intact, and maintained them with scrupulous loyalty to their promises; whereas the Liberals or Anticlericals, even when in a minority, have attacked these liberties, treated the Constitution as a fraud, and contemplated measures of persecution and confiscation. The paradox of M. Bouché-Leclercq[1] might be expressed in this form: The champions of what are called intolerant doctrines guard and defend liberty; their adversaries deny and attack it—nay, more, they violate it already by the intolerant conception of their tolerance itself.

[1] " The champions of intolerant doctrines declaring for liberty, and their adversaries seeking to impose tolerance upon them by force " (*L'Intolérance Réligieuse et la Politique*, p. 362).

THIRD PART

COROLLARIES AND QUESTIONS

INTRODUCTION

SUMMARY : Purpose and plan of this part.

AFTER the lengthy investigation of the subject that we have now brought to a close, it will be convenient to sum up our impressions and classify the information we have acquired, in order to obtain a permanent benefit from our labours. A general view of the whole subject after the examination of details should not only fix in our minds the most salient facts, the principal things to be remembered, but should enable us to understand better the theories and events, and the consequences that flow from them. We draw our own conclusions, and questions which we have had to leave unanswered easily receive a satisfactory solution.

The third part of this work is intended to give us an opportunity of taking this general view, and disposing of these questions. It is a necessary complement of the two preceding parts, and therefore deserves as much, or more, the kindly attention of the reader.

The title of this part does not bind us to observe any particular order, and we shall make full use of our liberty; but, as our study has been directed to principles and actions or facts, we have thought it advisable to divide our matter into two sections—the first more strictly doctrinal, the second historical. In the latter, after summing up the past, we shall give our impressions of the present, and form some conjecture of the future.

FIRST SECTION: DOCTRINAL QUESTIONS

I. Different Kinds of Tolerance and Intolerance.

SUMMARY: The idea of intolerance cannot be associated with that of the Catholic Church.—That Church put an end to the most formidable intolerance—viz., that which was based on political considerations.—If we divide tolerance into its three kinds, the Church is a great school of private tolerance; its ecclesiastical intolerance is free from reproach; and in the civil order it condemns the intolerance of many Protestants and jurists, and contents itself with claiming a reasonable protection of the truth, inspired by the general principles of good government.—This civil intolerance, as contained in the Catholic doctrine, is different in character from pagan intolerance, the intolerance of Islam, and revolutionary intolerance. — Misuse of the word "tolerance."

THE sons of the Revolution and the various anti-Catholic sects boast that they are the authors—or, at least, the official representatives—of tolerance, and maintain that intolerance is the peculiar symbol of Catholic principles.

It is simply juggling with words to make such statements. In reality, no one professes an absolute intolerance, but every man regulates his conduct more or less according to circumstances; and if no party can claim a monopoly of tolerance, it is still more unjust to associate the idea of intolerance with that of the Catholic Church. Was not the first act of Christianity to abolish an intolerance—viz., that of a religion instituted for the use of a political community?

If we take tolerance in its generic sense, in which it is divided into *private, ecclesiastical,* and *civil,* the Church is a great school of *private* tolerance, for it forbids hatred and pride, and teaches mutual forbearance and inviolable respect for the person of man. The angry impatience of the fanatic contradicts the principles of the Church, whose noblest sons have carried their patience and endurance to the point of heroism. What a distance there is between the declamatory generosity of Victor Hugo[1] and the all-embracing benevolence of men like St. Francis of Sales, St. Vincent de Paul, and so many missionaries and Sisters of Charity! The reader will appreciate in this connection the sublime language in which Cardinal Diepenbrock, Catholic Prince-Bishop of Breslau in the nineteenth century, professed this tolerance: " In spite of the division of religious bodies, which is always lamentable, though permitted by the will of God, and which we must therefore endure with patience and in a spirit of penitence for faults committed, all right-minded men may, and should, profess a mutual esteem, a generous tolerance, and a Christian charity,

[1] It cost him nothing to write a blasphemous line like this: " I would have saved Judas, if I had been Jesus Christ "; but it would have cost him something to forget the criticisms of Louis Veuillot. His bitter and insatiable animosity is well known.

founded on the presumption that both sides are in good faith."[1]

Faithfulness to God and charity to men undoubtedly compel the Church to maintain her *ecclesiastical* intolerance. But this intolerance does not imply any outward constraint. It specifies the conditions on which a man may or may not remain a Catholic; it defines the points to be believed, the duties to be fulfilled, under pain of breaking with the Church or leaving her pale. If some rebellious children, trying to reconcile opposite propositions, have complained of the intolerance of the Church, sensible persons, even non-Catholics, have always admitted its lawfulness and even its necessity. Without this intolerance the Church can neither teach nor guide. She ceases to unite men's hearts and minds, or to form a communion of souls; she loses the very reason of her existence.[2]

Finally, in the *civil* order, the Catholic doctrine, in distinguishing the Church from the State, began by creating the possibility of tolerance. It absolutely rejects the intolerance supported by Protestants, and again recently contemplated by Liberal Rationalists. The latter, returning to old ideas, see no ideal but that of the State and unity, while the Church hopes for everything from the truth. It is religious truth that the Church wishes to see free and safe in society, that she wishes to preserve safe to the multitude of simple and ignorant persons whom she desires to protect from seduction.

[1] Charge quoted by G. Goyau in *L'Allemagne Réligieuse, Le Catholicisme*, t. 3, p. 200.
[2] See the testimonies quoted in the section on Ecclesiastical Tolerance, p. 42.

Loving men and truth as she does, she would have the public authorities take up arms in this twofold cause, as a father for love of his children protects religion in his home. Uniting religion and morality, she would have the protection that is given to morality logically extended to the true religion. Such is the civil intolerance which the Church preaches. This intolerance is measured by times and circumstances, and always stops short of injustice, for fear of causing some greater evil. Anyone who admits that the State is bound to promote the welfare of the community and to defend the weak must see that this intolerance is only a particular application of the principles of good government; and it finds its limit in those very principles, for the same common good which, in theory, calls for the prudent interference of the State in favour of religion may in particular circumstances recommend the State to abstain from interference. And then civil tolerance is a direct result of the Catholic doctrine. As we have said, theologians may have erred in their appreciation of those circumstances; but, whenever the question has arisen, Catholics have shown themselves the most sincere and consistent advocates of civil tolerance.

On the other hand, the deistic systems of tolerance, in the confusion of their multiplicity, have seldom been just or tolerant to Catholics. As to the principles of the French Revolution, we have seen that they have never prevented any sort of tyranny.

It will be worth our while to examine a little more closely this civil intolerance of Catholics, and to compare it with other kinds of intolerance.

One point is worthy of remark—namely, that the civil intolerance of Catholics does not follow, as an immediate and necessary consequence, from the political principles of Catholicism. Catholic policy is always mindful of vested rights, and is only inspired by motives of public good when it devises measures to protect those rights. When these measures of protection suggest what is called intolerance, the civil intolerance of Catholics, by its reasons, its rules, its very nature, is in marked contrast with other forms of intolerance, which have filled history with their misdeeds, especially with those which have so often attacked Christ and His Church. How clearly, then, is shown the falseness of the charge made against Christian society, that it became a persecutor when it was no longer persecuted, and that it drowned in blood that liberty which in the first centuries it had won so gloriously at the price of its own blood!

Catholic intolerance, if the expression is permissible, is in the first place essentially different from pagan or Mahomedan intolerance. Mommsen[1] makes this judicious remark on pagan Rome, and the same observation applies (*mutatis mutandis*) to the Mahomedan Empire. The gods of Rome were virtually servants of the State. At any moment " every subject of the Empire might be called upon to believe in these gods, and to make public manifestation of that belief "; and whoever

[1] *Op. cit.*, t. 2, p. 308. M. Jordan also admits it (art. cit., t. 9, p. 37), but he attributes this measure to the desire to put an end to Christianity once for all. On the persecutions of Christians, see also Wagener, *Bulletins de l'Académie de Belgique*, 1893.

TOLERANCE AND INTOLERANCE 265

refused to do so "committed an offence, not so much against the gods as against the State," and was prosecuted for high treason. Under Christianity the crime of heresy has been compared to treason,[1] but the two, as Mommsen remarks, have never been identified. The comparison was made in order to justify the severity of the penal sanctions, and not at all to suggest that unfaithfulness to God was, as such, an offence against any mere human authority.

The Turkish Empire is essentially a theocratic monarchy, being subject in principle to the direct personal control of the Sultan, who is the successor of Mahomed, and, consequently, the spiritual head of the Moslem world, as the Pope is the spiritual head of the Christian world. Catholicism, being a universal religion, has never acknowledged the supremacy of any particular form of government. It enters into an alliance with the State, but it refuses to identify its interests with those of any State whatever.

Moreover, Catholic intolerance, though it tends effectively to preserve religious unity when it exists, refuses to introduce it by force. Non-Catholic foreigners coming into an entirely Catholic State are bound to avoid conduct or language offensive to religion,[2] but Catholic subjects alone are, within

[1] See, for example, the Constitution of Frederic II., and, later, St. Thomas and the Scholiasts.
[2] So in the secret clauses of the treaties concluded in 1604 for the Spanish Netherlands with England, and in 1609 with the United Provinces, foreign merchants are not forced to attend Catholic worship, but only to abstain from proselytism, to give no scandal to religion, and to avoid

certain limits, subject to constraint.[1] The offence which the Church punishes or permits to be punished is apostasy. Persons who are punished for heresy are those who have been subject to her legitimate authority, for St. Paul says : " I have not to judge those who are without."[2] Even in dealing with her rebellious children, she has not started from an abstract and absolute principle of intolerance and severity ; she has been guided by experience. For a long time she tried simple persuasion, and confined herself to the use of spiritual penalties ; but by degrees the experience of facts taught her that she must seek in outward coercion the means of bringing back the delinquents and preserving the rest of the flock in safety. Correction and preservation are the only two motives of her intolerance, and they also lay down the limits of her power of repression, which does not extend to the shedding of blood.[3]

Is it necessary to show how such intolerance as this contrasts with the intolerance with which Catholics have been and still are treated or threatened ?

Had the heretical, apostate, or infidel persecutors of all ages any justification for molesting Catholics in the profession of their religion ? What right,

---

public transgression of ecclesiastical precepts. See L. Willaert, *Négociations Politico-réligieuses entre l'Angleterre et les Pays-Bas Catholiques* (1598-1625); *Revue d'Histoire Ecclésiastique* for 1908, p. 102.

[1] We shall give particulars in Section II.
[2] 1 Cor. v. 12.
[3] See the proofs given in the intermediate chapter between the two sections of Part II., pp. 63 *sqq*.

TOLERANCE AND INTOLERANCE

what religious authority over the Catholic martyrs, had Henry VIII., Elizabeth, the Calvinists of the Netherlands, the Princes of Germany, the Jacobin Terror or the Communist Terror ? Amongst all these we may seek in vain for subjects in rebellion against constituted and recognized authority. Still less do we find any intention of saving and preserving, or any principle moderating the violence of their persecutions. A capricious and tyrannical will, and a material power which they abused, guided them for the most part in their arbitrary and iniquitous proceedings.

The name of intolerance is unjustly applied to the coercive action which the Church allows. The intention of tyrannizing or forcing the conscience is absent. What does the Church do ? She protects her weaker children against a deadly contagion ; she seeks to bring back the lost ones—that is her zeal ; she asks for obedience from her subjects—that is her authority. Intolerance is aggressive, and the Church acts on the defensive ; intolerance hates and oppresses, and the Church loves and desires to save. Excesses have been committed, and some men, acting in the Church's name, have been carried away and gone beyond the limits she has prescribed ; but then the voice of her faithful children has been raised in compassion for the victims, and warned her to temper justice with mercy.[1] When faith alone is at stake, violence can only momentarily be the act of Catholics ; normally and traditionally, they are the oppressed, and not the oppressors.

[1] Notably the case with certain more peaceable Lutherans condemned in Flanders under Charles V.

One last remark as to the word "tolerance." The mere use of the word implies no generosity. The true merit of tolerance, that which makes it justly popular, is its self-restraint, its modesty in judging others, its respect for their sincerity, its moderation in the use of power. Whoever insolently forces upon others his own ideas, whether religious, political, or social, has no part in this merit, although it may please him to adorn his theory with the name of tolerance ; and there are many to-day who, while boasting of their tolerance, adopt an uncompromising attitude which bears no resemblance to that of the Catholic faith or of truth.

II. THE PENAL REPRESSION OF HERESY.

SUMMARY : The repression struck heretical bonds and single heretics differently.—St. Thomas's reason for this second repression.—Argument from the promise made to the Church.—Criticism of these arguments.—The crime and the interior belief of the delinquent.—What was necessary to constitute the crime.—Just measure of punishment.—Simple abstention may be punished, but the social offence is less grave.—Difference between the unbeliever and the heretic.—Good faith much less probable formerly than now.—Why unbaptized persons were not punishable.—What is to be said of those who were brought up in heresy ?

The theoretical problem of the penal repression of heresy presents itself in an entirely different aspect —at least, outwardly—according as we are dealing with heretical factions or single heretics.

The heretical faction forms a turbulent band of agitators, aiming at nothing less than the overthrow of established institutions. It plots against the Church and the hierarchy. The Church defends

REPRESSION OF HERESY

herself against them as the Russian Empire defends itself against Nihilists; and at the time when the Catholic religion was the very foundation of society, the heretical faction was simply revolutionary. Therefore, the leaders and their followers alike were punishable under the law, though not all equally guilty, and it was not necessary to inquire into their religious convictions. That is plain common sense. Political conspirators often commit their crimes to obtain relief from some grievance, or to take revenge for some wrong, but it has never been considered the duty of judges to pay any attention to these motives.

We know, moreover, as an historical fact, that the factious combination of heretics necessitated the severe measures which were employed against them, and at a certain period the text of the law included all heretics under the same condemnation.

The question is, What would justify us in considering even an isolated case of heresy punishable as an offence against the community?

The edicts of Frederic II. contain on this subject an argument which has been developed by St. Thomas. The Emperor uses the same expressions to explain the rigorous sanctions he enacts as the prince of theologians employs to justify the severity of the punishments. A man who refuses to believe in God offers Him an insult, which is a graver offence than the crime of treason against a mere earthly Sovereign. If the crime is greater, the same punishment—namely, the penalty of death—is not too great. This appears plain, simple, and unanswerable, and this argument also satisfies many contemporary writers.

It must be admitted, however, that this reason, without some explanation, no longer appears conclusive. The argument presupposes completely formal heresy, a deliberate refusal to believe in God. But are there many men capable of committing so absurd an offence ? A man may lie in declaring that he does not believe ; but if he speaks the truth, he founds his unbelief on his ignorance of the word of God. If, in other words, he refuses to believe in the Blessed Trinity, it is because he contends that God has not revealed this mystery. This contradiction of the Catholic dogma may be accompanied by invincible ignorance, and still leave the virtue of faith intact at the bottom of his heart ; and heresy, reduced thus to purely material error, instead of being a serious crime, is innocent in the sight of God. Certainly, every time the loss of faith is formal an offence has been committed. But what offence ? Some imprudence or some sin unconnected with faith may have led to the withdrawal of the graces necessary to keep a man faithful. In short, the loss of the gratuitous gift of faith is such a mysterious matter that it offers very slender reason for penal measures.

Are the promises made at baptism, which other persons so confidently appeal to, any more conclusive ? It is said that the heretic, being bound by these promises, is guilty of treason in abandoning the Church and her teaching. It is useless to object that the promise, which the child was incapable of making, was the act of those who represented him at his baptism ; for you will be told that the Christian subsequently ratified that promise, and that in any case it binds him, as the accident of birth in a particular country imposes upon a man the duties of a citizen.

We confess that we have never been able to see the force of this argument, which seems not to bear examination. Even if it did not depend on me whether I was born here or there, my country certainly exists as a legitimate society, and my obligations towards it are so evident that they cannot be the subject of discussion. On the other hand, no promise can bind me to a Church, unless I recognize that Church as truly Divine. Consequently, in proportion as my faith is shaken, so also is the foundation of my duty to the Church. It is undoubtedly true that the heretic is wrong in denying or doubting the Church, but we cannot refuse him the benefit of this universal rule—that duty in the concrete exists only for the man who has knowledge of it.

The promises made at baptism bind the man who believes. They form an additional reason for his obligations towards God and a necessary religion—that is understood—but they cannot be used as an argument against a man who denies the truth of that religion. In our opinion, the simple absence or loss of faith cannot be cognizable by human justice. Faith is a gift of God; its birth and its loss are impenetrable to the eye of man. To command me to believe when I do not believe is to command the impossible. Now, the preceptive or prohibitive force of the law is limited to acts which it is in a man's power to do or to omit. We cannot neglect these elementary considerations, of which the highest authorities in the Church have reminded us.[1]

We must, then, try to find better reasons; and, first, let us consider the more general and very important question of the interior conviction, which is necessary to justify punishment. Are public orders or prohibitions binding only on condition that they have the inward assent of every private individual? Can a public authority punish only such persons as share its opinions on the act forbidden or commanded? The answer is clear. If we insist on such a condition, we should put public authority at the mercy of every man's individual conscience or opinion, whether truly or falsely alleged. Human authority, which cannot enter into the mind and conscience of man, cannot command or forbid whatever it pleases, and for the same reason it is not bound to inquire into the opinions of private persons on the subject of orders which are socially just; but it has full right to call on its subjects to regulate their external conduct in conformity with its legitimate commands,[2] leaving their motives to God, "who searcheth the reins and hearts."

Now, what orders are socially just? Those which

[1] See the authorities quoted on pp. 53, 54. Leo XIII. speaks in the same sense in his Encyclical *Immortale Dei*.

[2] Questions of excusable or culpable ignorance may no doubt bring about conflicts between the public authority and the private conscience. The one is as liable to error as the other. Sometimes the only practicable solution will be voluntary exile or submission to punishment. But this accidental and very rare inconvenience would be infinitely less than the harm that would be caused if the public authority were compelled to consult every private person's conscience. That would be anarchy raised to a system.

are based on a truth sufficiently recognized or admitted, and which tend to the common good. The support of truth secures the objective foundation; the approval of the general conscience gives an assurance that the law is not impracticable or oppressive; the good of the community gives to legislative measures that justification which is necessary for their validity. Such being the case, all the constituent elements of a crime will be found in an act which is objectively bad,[1] condemned as such, socially harmful, and voluntarily committed in spite of authoritative prohibition. We say *objectively* bad or reprehensible, because the social authority is not bound to submit to the subjective judgment of each individual; it is enough that the malice of the act should be generally recognized. Acts of violence, and even murder, may be committed from motives which make them meritorious acts in the opinion of the delinquent, but those opinions are of little importance. Divine grace and light, which are necessary for interior faith, are not at all required to show a man that he must not disobey lawful orders. When he has been warned that such an act or omission is illegal and punishable, he voluntarily assumes the responsibility of his act or omission, and has no right to complain if he is punished.

The gravity of the offence is in like manner estimated socially; that is to say, according to the objective malice of the act, the public scandal, and the harm done to the community.

[1] Bad, that is to say, either before the prohibition or because of it.

In other words, the punishment should not be greater than the malice of the abstract immorality; and in the second place, it should not be out of proportion to the social harm caused by the crime. When an act has been made penal by law, whoever knowingly and deliberately offends against the law becomes liable to punishment, without reference to his own personal opinion of the illegal act.

We can easily apply this reasoning to the case of heresy. In the Catholic country the true religion is normally accepted by everyone, and protected by authority as a social good of the first importance. Therefore, in accordance with the general sentiment, any contradiction of the dogmas of that religion is forbidden, as being harmful to the community. It constitutes the crime of heresy, whatever the private opinions and intentions of the offender may be. We need only add that a little good-will would be enough to show to a private individual the rashness, to say the least, of an affirmation categorically opposed to the teaching of a Church so wise and enlightened as the Catholic Church, and, in the case we are considering, generally obeyed.

It remains, then, to make the punishment proportionate to the offence. It must be regulated according to the general scale of punishments, the gravity of the offence considered objectively,[1] and

[1] To repeat. As soon as the act fulfils all the conditions required to make it a free act for which the doer is responsible, its gravity as an offence is estimated *socially*, and not individually; that is to say, in consideration of the order violated, and not according to the subjective culpability of the offender. It is impossible to admit that

the harm it is likely to cause; and the argument of St. Thomas, which we had set aside as being of no use to help us to decide the guilt of each individual heretic, recovers its force in so far as it expresses the social judgment which Christendom passed on heresy in general. Thus, even the death penalty is explained. For the obstinate contradiction of the faith of the Church was considered socially as treason against the Majesty of God, without reference to the private opinions of the heretic, just as murder was looked upon as an atrocious violation of the sacredness of human life, and theft as an invasion of another person's legal right of possession, without reference to the private opinions of the murderer and the thief. It is in accordance with these social judgments that the punishment is fixed, and the guilty person is made to understand the gravity of his offence.

An additional explanation is supplied by the fact that every heresy was certainly, or most probably, connected with some seditious heretical body. At that time these factions endangered the unity of Christendom, and finally succeeded in rending it asunder. Yet simple abstention could not have the gravity or the scandalous effects of a categorical denial. Equity itself demands less severity, and so we find that much more tolerance was shown to simple sceptics or freethinkers. "The preachers, and even Bossuet himself," says M. Jules Lemaître,

---

a personal opinion may justify a person who deliberately disturbs the public peace. Imagine him even bound in conscience to propagate his opinions. Moral impossibility would excuse him from this positive duty.

"when they are fighting against freethinkers, do it certainly with sorrow and indignation, but without a word to suggest an appeal to the law. They pity the unbelievers, they pray for them, and hope for their return to God; but they do not persecute them, provided that they keep within bounds. . . . But heretics—that is another thing. Heretics do not keep quiet. Unbelievers do not choose between dogmas but heretics do. They set up one religion against another. A heretic is one who openly and arrogantly breaks religious unity, which is an indispensable good; a freethinker is one who does not break that unity, but quietly withdraws from it for the time, and that is all. That is why the old system, which was merciful enough to freethinkers, was much less so to Protestants and even to Jansenists."[1]

Let us not forget, finally, that the plea of good faith, which we so freely admit nowadays, had formerly much less justification. In the midst of controversies on the very foundations of Christianity; while so many religions and beliefs are publicly professed; while objections are made on all sides, and the most shameless lies are circulated everywhere as to the doctrines and acts of the Church; while infidelity insolently boasts that it is supported by science, and that it is therefore sure to gain the day, and puts its secular philanthropy in opposition to religious charity, we cannot wonder that the faith of many is disturbed, and that they are led astray by a multitude of specious arguments.

[1] *Rapports de Bossuet et de Fénelon avec les Protestants.* Second Conference.

Formerly, when Europe was more isolated, there was but one form of Christianity, holding uncontested sway, to which the sciences paid homage, and which was honoured by public and private benevolence. What possible excuse was there, then, for the innovator who advanced revolutionary propositions on the sacraments, or marriage, or the hierarchy? All social life was against him, and his arguments were refuted, as the clever sophisms of modern sceptics come into collision with palpable facts and the conclusions of common sense only to be shattered. No judge would then be moved by a plea of good faith resting on such weak foundations, or feel any scruples in convicting of heresy.

We have already said that the Church had no power to extend her jurisdiction over those who did not belong to her by baptism. The reason is clear: since, according to the designs of God, faith cannot be created by force, the essence of the offence is wanting. The Church treated Christians as the State treats its civil subjects, while with regard to non-Christians her right was limited to defending herself against their attacks; and it must always be remembered that the wicked acts and words of Christians have a much more pernicious influence than any acts of those who are strangers to the Church. It is thus easy to explain why the Church treated infidels and Jews very differently from baptized heretics.

One doubt may arise here. As far as those heretics are concerned who personally abandon the faith, the distinction between them and infidels is clear; but what is to be said of those who have been brought up in schism and heresy, and therefore have never felt that they belonged to the Church ? Are they her subjects because they have been baptized, or are they strangers because since the dawn of reason they have never been in communion with the Church ? We have already[1] expressed our opinion that though, as subjects of the Church, they are entitled to the advantage of certain rights and favours and to a special solicitude, they are, nevertheless, by reason of the error of their fathers, incapable of contumacy to the Church, and therefore cannot properly be punished or molested for their religious opinions ; and we have extended this rule to children whose parents have long been separated from the Church.

The conclusion we draw is that the penal laws against heretics do not prove an intolerance which, misunderstanding the gratuitous character of the gifts of God and the voluntary character of the act of faith, would attempt to obtain conversions by force.

[1] Pp. 56, 57.

III. Consistency and Progress in the Theory of Tolerance.

Summary: Statements of M. Vacandard and Baron von Hertling.—The Church has not been dominated by two opposite traditions.—The principles on the repression and toleration of religious error have remained unchanged.—But the progress of criminal science, political science, and theological science, and the teaching of experience, suggest moderation in the application of those principles, according to existing circumstances.

" The theory of Catholic writers," says M. Vacandard,[1] " starts from the principle of absolute tolerance, and terminates in the penalty of death by fire." And at the beginning of this century Baron von Hertling shared the same opinion, when he declared in the Reichstag, " We are for the first links in the chain of tradition, not for the second."

Is it a fact that two opposite theories on the subject of tolerance have been accepted in succession by Catholic writers, and that the chain of tradition is really composed of dissimilar and incongruous links ?

Taken literally, these assertions are formally contradicted by facts. The improper use of language alone can explain or excuse them.

The principle of absolute tolerance (M. Vacandard is evidently speaking of civil tolerance) has consistently refused to the civil authority the right of securing unity in religious truth by civil sanctions. Was this principle ever accepted in the Church ? In the age of the persecutions, and even in the time of the Apostles, heresy met with the sternest repro-

[1] *L'Inquisition*, p. 250.

bation from ecclesiastical authority, and this was in a certain sense a denial of tolerance. Certainly, the Church, in launching her spiritual thunderbolts, abstained from coercive measures, which were not then within her power; and her writers held that the same gentle means should be used to bring men back to the faith as to obtain first conversions, but no authorized declaration absolutely condemns all use of force in the service of religion.

On the contrary, as soon as the question arose in practice, Catholic writers admitted that the violence of heretics should be punished by retaliation, and that the propagation of their errors should be effectively stopped. St. John Chrysostom formally proclaimed the lawfulness of such constraint as was necessary to protect the true faith; and St. Augustine, an advocate at first of entire liberty, and afterwards of moderate repression, had never questioned the justice, but only the expediency, of such repression.

It cannot be denied that experience and altered circumstances have caused a change in the methods and the practical attitude of the Church, but this change does not extend to the theory. Two principles are deduced from the writings of the Fathers and the Acts of ecclesiastical authority: the penal repression of heresy is in itself lawful; the Church does not shed blood. These two principles remained in force during the following centuries, and neither has been abandoned. In the thirteenth century a phase of civil legislation suggested a new question, Can the State suppress heresy by capital punishment? The reply of authors, appro-

THEORY OF TOLERANCE

priate to the circumstances of the time, was in the affirmative; and, without wishing for a return to such severity, we can only say, having regard to the circumstances and the penal legislation of the period, that such an answer was inevitable.

Some theologians of the sixteenth or a century later claimed also for the Church the right to strike with the sword; and they, as M. Vacandard would say, finished with the penalty of death by fire. But their opinion is not enough to constitute a tradition, any more than the theologians who opposed the dogma of the Immaculate Conception, or the advocates of the direct temporal power of the Pope, could trace their opinions back to the Apostles or to Jesus Christ. In our humble opinion, those authors were wrong. We read the true tradition in the canonical collections, where we find attributed to the Church the right of a medicinal and preservative constraint by means of reparable penalties, and, as a last resource, the right of excommunication.

The Church has not contradicted herself in her principles; she has not been dominated by two contrary traditions in succession; her doctrine on the subject of tolerance has not essentially changed, but under the guidance of God, who gives her in successive centuries new light to know herself better, her doctrine has developed and taken shape in a clearer and more complete formula of expression.

The Church is not merely conservative: she is also progressive.

Since the Middle Ages the right to punish has been fully discussed, and the distinction between the two powers and their respective jurisdiction has been more clearly laid down. We understand better now the work of grace and its essential necessity for the act of faith, as well as the frequent disappointments and the grave mischief resulting from ill-timed severity ; and we are therefore better able to define the exact purpose of repression, its extreme limits, and the conditions of its expediency. The new aspect of religious controversy, which is gradually narrowing itself to a conflict between religion and complete unbelief ; the small measure of success that new heresies can ever hope for ; the general improvement of manners, and the desire and the need of souls to be won by kindness, are not lost sight of by the ministers of the Church or by her writers ; and if they were called upon to formulate practical rules for the use of a believing people, freely and without fear or respect of persons, they would be able to secure a form of protection of truth in harmony with public sentiment and the true progress of civilization.[1]

[1] The conduct of German Catholics is, from this point of view, extremely significant. On November 23, 1900, the German Centre presented a Bill to provide for liberty of the practice of religion throughout the Empire. It was known as *Toleranztrag*, and gave rise to lively discussion in the Press. The respective attitudes of Catholics, Protestants, and Erastian Liberals, give one more proof that the truest friends of reasonable liberty are to be found within the Catholic Church. See Laurentius, S.J., *Freiheit der Religionsübung im deutschen Reiche* (*Stimmen aus Maria-Laach*, 1905, t. 68, pp. 21 *sqq.*).

IV. The Scientific or the Religious Ideal.

Scientific and Religious Liberty: Their Alleged Antagonism.

SUMMARY: Is the scientific ideal opposed to the religious?—Error of M. Bouché-Leclercq.—Exact notion of scientific theories: their object and their ambition.—The complete work of the scientist. — Though not disregarded by religion, scientific theories can neither confirm nor contradict it.—Impossibility of conflict between religion and natural sciences.—Objection founded on the alleged conflict with history and philosophy. — Incomplete answer. — Science is not the supreme good.—Sacrifices often asked of it.—Insignificance of those which religion asks of it accidentally.—Abundant compensation. — Parallel functions of science and religion. — The habit of faith not inconsistent with the scientific spirit.—Humanity needs both science and religion.—The problem of their reconciliation difficult, but important.

The copious literature of Tolerance has been recently enriched by a book written in France by a professor of the Sorbonne, entitled *L'Intolérance Religieuse et la Politique*. We have already quoted it. Its author, M. Bouché-Leclercq, is one of the survivors of rationalistic Liberalism. Though he repudiates religion, he does not approve of the open war between the Church and the State; and he even proposes a *modus vivendi*, pressing rather heavily, it is true, on Catholics. However, he augurs very ill for the future of the faith and positive religions. No reconciliation between science and revelation appears to him possible, for he declares that there is " an essential contradiction between the scientific ideal, which is the unremitting pursuit of truth through a succession of temporary or provisional theories, and the ideal of positive religions, which is the preservation of truth already acquired, and henceforth unassailable."[1]

If the conflict between science and positive religions were as implacable as he declares, the modern world, which is entirely on the side of science, and the State which represents it, instead of begging concessions of tolerance from religion, would set to work to persecute it; or at most they would grant a temporary and, so to speak, compassionate tolerance to the Church and to Catholics, as to a set of old-fashioned persons, clinging to a transitory expression of religious sentiment : their good-nature would go no farther.

Happily this is not the case—the essentiality of the contradiction is imaginary ; so, indeed, is the contradiction itself, as we shall endeavour to prove.

M. Bouché-Leclercq is mistaken, both as to religion and as to science.

What does he mean by his provisional theories ? Is he using unsuitable and inexact language ? Does he wish, in the interests of science, to associate himself with M. Payot[2] in proclaiming the necessity of the relativist principle ? He cannot do it without falling into that absolutism of statement which he so unreasonably condemns. Relativism is no more a postulate of science than stagnation is a postulate of religion.

Does M. Bouché-Leclercq speak of the provisional theories of the natural sciences in the proper sense of the word ? The ideal of these sciences does not by any means consist in the pursuit of a truth which

[1] *Op. cit.*, p. 354.   [2] Quoted above, p. 232.

RELIGION AND SCIENCE

is continually escaping from our grasp; and, on the other hand, the religious ideal is not the mere preservation of acquired truths. The acquired truth of religion is composed of a limited number of dogmas, derived from Divine revelation; but their clear understanding has sometimes taken centuries of work and preparation. Similarly, every science has its acquired truths [1] and its provisional theories. But these do not imply any attitude with regard to truth, different from the attitude of revealed religion, for the good and sufficient reason that, being entirely directed to the exact representation of external phenomena, they do not aim at the acquisition of absolute truth.

Formerly, no doubt, and even fifty years ago, scientists put forward their theories as explanations, some certain and others conjectural, of the real truths concealed beneath the phenomena whose laws they recorded. Acoustics asserted and demonstrated the undulations which produce sound; with reference to the propagation of light, various hypotheses were made, the most important of which were the emission or corpuscular theory and the undulatory theory. According to the

[1] Such are the results derived from experiments; and such, also, is a part, very difficult to define, of physical theories, of which M. Duhem says: "By a continuous tradition, every theory of physical science transmits to that which follows it that part of natural classification which it has been able to construct" (*La Théorie Physique, son Objet et sa Structure*, p. 48. See also *Physique de Croyant*, p. 41).

Poincaré similarly says: "At first sight it seems as if theories lasted only for a day; but there is something in them which survives. If one of them has enabled us to discover a real relation between two things, that relation is finally acquired, and we shall find it again in a new form in the later theories which follow to take the place of the former" (*La Valeur de la Science;* Paris, 1905).

latter, all bodies were supposed to be filled by an extremely subtle elastic medium called ether, through which waves of light were constantly throbbing; but since then modern scientists, tired of fruitless strife and defeat, have ceased to look to their methods of observation for what those methods cannot teach them. Their theories are constructed, not to explain phenomena, but to represent and classify and generalize them, and to foresee the conditions of their recurrence, and thus to group them into rational systems, by which much mental labour is saved and the investigators are put on the track of new discoveries. They do not go deep enough to discover real causes, but in their places put symbols between which the same relations exist as would exist between the realities which are represented by those symbols in their statements and calculations.

For example, the theory of luminous vibrations does not assert any real motion, but it provides an excellent basis to express in figures the experimental laws of light. Its *value* consists in the precision with which it represents a great number of laws. It establishes between luminous phenomena a logical connection which gives it its *beauty*, and it exhibits its *fecundity* in the various deductions which are drawn from it. Though superior to other theories less simple, less complete, or less exact, it does not profess to exclude them as false, so long as they remain in sufficient correlation with the phenomena of which they are the signs and symbols; for the vibratory theory, like the electro-magnetic theory, which tends to replace it, not pretending to tell us anything of the real causes of the luminous phenomena, does not present itself as objectively true or objectively false. " The object of Fresnel was not to know whether there is such a medium as ether, whether it is formed of atoms or not, or whether these atoms move in this or that direction: it was to foresee the optical phenomena."[1] This conception of scientific theories attracts scientific men of the sceptical school like H. Poincaré,[2] and of the Christian school like M. Duhem.[3] The scientific ideal ceases, then, to be the pursuit of ontological truth, and becomes the reduction of all partial theories to unity; and these succeed one another provisionally, because they are symbolical, and they must necessarily be continually modified and completed to fit in with new discoveries.

With these remarks, we may take leave of M. Bouché-Leclercq. His assertion holds good only as long as he[4] clings to an antiquated scientific ideal,

[1] H. Poincaré, *La Science et l Hypothèse*, pp. 189, 190. Before this he had said : " We are not concerned whether ether really exists ; that is the business of metaphysicians " (*Leçons sur les Théories Mathématiques de la Lumière*, Preface ; Paris, 1889).

[2] See *Sur la Valeur Objective des Théories Physiques* (*Revue de Métaphysique et de Morale*, 1902, p. 263). "The scientific fact," says Poincaré, "is nothing but the bare fact translated into appropriate language." And again : " Science is principally a classification, a way of connecting facts . . . a system of relations " (*La Valeur de la Science*, pp. 231, 265, 266).

[3] See the work, *La Théorie Physique, son Objet et sa Structure ;* and the pamphlet, *Physique de Croyant*, written in answer to the article of M. Rey, quoted below, p. 288.

[4] In company with M. Le Dantec, who, with thorough Breton tenacity, seeks to know from biology what life is, and so puts forward his *Biologie destructive* in opposition to religion. See his Conference, *Biologie Constructive*

now almost abandoned. But modern conceptions furnish us with new material, which may be utilized to put an end to the old quarrel between science and religion.

Science is one thing, the scientist another. In practice the latter oversteps the limits of the former; for who is there who does not yield to what M. Rey[1] calls the common temptation to do a little metaphysics? And so we may say that the scientist proceeds by three stages, which we may compare to the three stories of a building. In the first we have the exact observation of facts and experimental laws—facts and laws which have their phenomenal reality, and communicate their objective value to the statements in which they are expressed; in the second, we come to the rational classification of these facts and laws—the theoretical interpretation. Without expressing any opinion on the real facts, this interpretation supplies a logical, convenient, and suggestive representation by symbols. This is the work which properly belongs to science, and secures all its benefits. Lastly, these same theories, and sometimes also extra-scientific prejudices, lead scientists to set up a second series of hypotheses concerning the reality underlying the phenomena, so much the

---

et Biologie Destructive, given at the jubilee of the University of Brussels (*Revue de l'Université de Bruxelles*, 1909-10, pp. 308-318). "When a scientific theory professes to tell us what heat is, or what electricity is, or what life is, it is condemned beforehand" (Poincaré, *Le Valeur de la Science*, p. 267).

[1] *La Philosophie Scientifique de M. Duhem* (*Revue de Métaphysique et de Morale*, 1904, p. 699).

more clearly cherished because they seem as if arising spontaneously from the representative theories founded on experience. The scientist will thus become an atomist or a dynamist in cosmology ; a materialist or a determinist in natural history ; a transformist in biology. But we must remark that not one of these hypotheses is strictly contained in the physical theories or their manifold applications. They are formulated only by the aid of metaphysical principles or postulates, and the philosophic scepticism of many scientists leads them to neglect the prudent counsels of this other branch of human knowledge. They hope to deduce everything from experience, but unconsciously they overstep its teaching, and for want of philosophic discernment they proceed by guesswork to fill up the gap, which is sometimes very wide, between the theories and their hypothetical conclusions on man and the universe.

Take, for example, the naturalist, and watch him at his work. He will apply himself in the first place to the careful consideration of actual organisms and reproductions. Comparative studies of living beings will lead him to a theoretical systematization, in which all the species observed by him will occupy their logical place, in which compartments will be reserved even for intermediaries not yet discovered, but which the series of beings seems to demand, as the calculations of Leverrier postulated a new planet. That is strictly scientific work—the only work indispensable to progress in scientific discovery. The naturalist, however, following his natural inclination to announce as an established fact what is really only a hypothesis, will easily discover ontological relations between species which seem logically to be connected, and will proclaim that one is derived from the other. He will declare himself a transformist, but he will make this declaration, not as a scientist, but in the name of a parasitic philosophy which he has grafted on his science.[1]

These preliminary explanations suggest a very important question: At what stage are those contacts produced which are so incorrectly called the conflicts between science and religion?

On the first story of our scientific building peace and good understanding prevail. Nothing appears possible beyond a little friction, a slight temporary and accidental irritation. In fact, no philosophical or religious doctrine could for long deny or contradict observations founded on palpable evidence. Poincaré wittily observes that Galileo and the Grand Inquisitor were not at issue on a question of fact;[2] but the same scientist is wrong in saying that a man, when he puts on his working clothes and enters his laboratory, must leave his faith behind him.[3] It will be a delicate task to discover the points of intersection

[1] It is much less as a scientist that M. Le Dantec declares that he "abandons the language of humanity in the strictest sense" and reduces man, soul included, to a mere piece of automatic machinery. He boasts of his *destructive biology*, which, as he says, does not teach him to live well, but only to live without the fear of death (*Biologie destructive, Biologie constructive*, Conference quoted above). There is neither science nor philosophy here. The two preceding speakers, Poincaré and M. Lanson, had used much more reserved and more scientific language.

[2] *La Valeur de la Science*, p. 231.

[3] *Le Libre Examen en Matière Scientifique*, Conference at the Jubilee of the University of Brussels (*Revue de l'Université de Bruxelles*, 1909-10, pp. 285-295). The reference is specially to p. 288.

between observation and the scientific theory which accompanies it, for the proposition which formulates a scientific fact or law " is generally a mixture of experimental discovery, possessing objective importance, and of theoretical explanation, simply symbolical, without any objective significance."[1] M. Duhem adds that if a natural philosopher desires to speak of an optical phenomenon, he will speak of the vibrations of ether; in other words, he will express the phenomenon in the language of his favourite theory.

On the second story — that is, in the stage of theories—science and faith cannot come into conflict, because the scientific theory affirms nothing concerning objective reality. " By its own nature and essence every principle of theoretical physics is useless in metaphysical or theological discussions."[2] And in this sense we may assent to the statement of M. Lanson : " If there is not a German science, or a French science, or a Belgian science, but one science common to all nations, still less is there a science of a party, a monarchist or Republican science, a Catholic or Socialist science."[3]

Does this mean that the philosopher or the theologian can despise scientific theories ? Poincaré would perhaps condemn the pretensions of metaphysical research, for, according to him nothing can enable us to know the nature of things.[4] As for ourselves, who give its due place to philo-

[1] Duhem, *Physique de Croyant*, p. 27.   [2] *Ibid.*, p. 19.
[3] *L'Esprit Scientifique et la Méthode de l'Histoire littéraire*, Conference at the Jubilee of the University of Brussels (*Revue de l'Université de Bruxelles*, 1909-10, pp. 296-307; see p. 306).
[4] *La Valeur de la Science*, p. 266.

sophy, we believe also in a harmonious correspondence of the classifying genius with the Spirit which has created that genius and all other things. We admit instinctively and, as it were, necessarily between the reality of things and their ideal classification certain analogies, closer and more probable according as the classification is more comprehensive and perfect. The plan which is formed as the result of scientific observations tends to reproduce the original plan on which all things were created. " Every branch of learning appears to me a praiseworthy effort directed towards knowledge of the order which presides over a determinate category of phenomena."[1] Thus the scientific theory creates a prejudice favourable or unfavourable to a philosophical or religious doctrine, but nothing more. We remember that in these scientific theories the scientist treads ground on which he is independent, in which he need not hope for or fear any clashing with religion.

The highest story only is the stage on which science and religion are brought into contact and relation, and sometimes into conflict.

This is enough to reassure mere unscientific mortals. This upper story, as we have seen, is not one of discoveries or inventions; the scientist has not constructed it as a scientist. Even if the atmosphere there is troubled, and a wind of discord blows through, there is no reason to tremble for that earthly happiness or progress about which human nature shows such eagerness and anxiety.

It is never with science properly so called that

[1] A. de Lapparent, *La Recherche Scientifique, et la Foi*. Letter to the *Revue Pratique d'Apologétique*, t. 2, p. 267.

RELIGION AND SCIENCE

religion can find itself in conflict, but with something that we may call *meta-science*. The pretended conflicts of science and religion have never existed, except between religion and a certain philosophy that calls itself scientific.

This is enough to show that impiety has only misused the popularity of science in order to attack the faith or to make unlimited tolerance an essential condition of progress. Neither the act of faith nor submission to doctrinal authority need disturb the scientist in his truly scientific work.

There remains, it is true, his metaphysical work. For those branches of natural science which are devoted to the exploration of the material world with such valuable results, this is negligible, or of only secondary importance. It engages the attention principally of conceited inquirers, who hope to bring out of the facts of science either speculative answers on the nature and origin of life, ideas, and morals, or practical rules for the direction of our individual and social energy, the formulæ of our duties, the key to our happiness.[1] Certainly, in all departments of knowledge strictly scientific inquiries and objective perceptions remain independent of metaphysical or religious doctrines. This remark applies also to psychology, and even to mysticism, in so far as they are experimental.[2]

---

[1] To this class belong those attempts to form a so-called "scientific" code of morality, which professes to do without the help even of philosophy. But these are no longer in fashion, and at present M. Durkheim is almost the only person to plead the cause of a moral code founded exclusively on science.

[2] "The object of experimental psychology," Father

Nevertheless, hitherto the interest of observations of the psychical order has been identified with that of spiritualist or determinist teachings, and of supernatural or naturalistic explanations which inquirers rightly or wrongly professed to deduce from them. Few biologists or psychologists, and perhaps no sociologist, have confined themselves within the special limits of science.

There remain also history and historical criticism, in reference to which Rénan says: " Religions present themselves as facts, and must be discussed as facts."[1] How can we gainsay this ? The speculative, moral, or social conclusions of certain writers who have a great reputation as philosophers or scientists, and also their historical conclusions, frequently come into contact with religious dogmas or assertions which necessarily depend on those dogmas, or at least with theories, beliefs, and opinions which

---

Maréchal forcibly remarks, " is to deduce the laws of the relations of mental phenomena, but not to discover the ontological causes of the phenomena themselves " (*Le Sentiment de Présence, chez les Profanes et les Mystiques*). Speaking of mystical phenomena, the Abbé Pacheu adds: " The observation and description of facts, if men are well informed, cannot but be the same for all (*L'Expérience Mystique et l'Activité Sub-consciente*, p. 301). M. Delacroix, the secular writer who has the reputation of being the best informed on these sacred matters, writes to the author: " As you say, it is not the part of psychology either to acknowledge or to deny the supernatural " (*ibid.*, p. 305).

[1] Discourse in answer to Pasteur's discourse on admission to the French Academy. M. Bouché-Leclercq similarly says: " However high they soar, revealed religions take their standing-ground on the earth, and they are bound to show the time and place at which the revelation they assert was made. And it is on this point that they have to justify themselves before historical criticism."

are accredited and in favour in the Church, and these contacts are by no means always friendly.

Full liberty of expression and diffusion is claimed for every formal declaration put forth in the name of science, and the intolerance of the Church refuses it to science. Every scientist is called upon to give up preconceived ideas. The Catholic has his freedom of thought limited by his faith. Here is intolerance, here is slavery, which furnish the modern world with weapons against all authoritative religion.

Is it sufficient, in order to dispose of the first objection, to answer that a true dogma cannot contradict a truth of reason, and that therefore the religious barrier forbids nothing to scientists but error ? There is a double reply at once. Man can only make progress by groping his way. He fails before he succeeds ; he passes through error to arrive at the truth ; he must be allowed freedom to make unsuccessful attempts, or even wrongly to contradict articles of the Creeds. And, on the other hand, religious authority does not impose dogmas alone. It blocks the way by propositions not yet defined, but which it considers important to its cause ; it makes us subject not only to an infallible Pope, but also to Commissions and Congregations which are liable to error ; and in this connection men will triumphantly point to a small number of censures passed upon propositions which are nowadays universally accepted.

The page which bears the names of Catholic men of science is very glorious to the Church, and very useful for our argument ; but it is going a little too far to profess that it supplies a complete refutation of the objection. Certainly, we thoroughly appreciate the warning which Poincaré gave to an assembly of freethinkers: " Do not imagine that I wish to deny science to men of faith, and especially to Catholics. God forbid! I should not be such a fool as to deprive humanity of the services of a Pasteur." And we are glad to hear him admit that " believers have as much of the critical spirit as any other men." " I know many," he added, " and Pasteur is only the most illustrious among them."[1]

Again, it may be asked whether these Christians were not scientists in spite of their religion; whether they have not had to overcome difficulties and obstacles in order to gain their reputation; whether they do not owe their distinction to the emancipating influence of their environment. Perhaps, also, they are famous in those branches of science which have nothing to do—at least, at the present day—with religious questions, such as pure mathematics and astronomy. In such matters there would be no possibility of conflict with religion.

For this reason these answers appear to us incomplete, though we do not say that they are entirely devoid of truth. Some concession seems to be required, and our mind cannot be satisfied except by rising to a plane higher than that in which the difficulty lies.

It may be that in some departments of science in which the interests of religion are directly involved religion requires from scientists precautions which may entail sacrifices. It may call upon them to move slowly and carefully, and not to throw things into complete disorder; and thus it to some extent

[1] Conference quoted, p. 288.

RELIGION AND SCIENCE

hampers their investigations, and puts some restriction on their movements. Will it never go farther than is required ? Will the judgment of those who speak in the name of religion be so sound, so comprehensive, and at the same time so promptly given, as to place no unnecessary restriction on liberty ? Will their intention even be always so pure and honest as to take no counsel but from the light of reason ? We cannot expect such perfection of judgment and intention in every case without looking for a miracle which is nowhere promised, and forgetting the traditional symbol of the Church—a boat tossed on the waves of a stormy sea. The qualified representatives of the Church, and still more its self-constituted defenders, are but men. Their knowledge may be small, their prudence may be outwitted, even their virtue may fail. Their interference will sometimes be awkward, inopportune, or exaggerated. Excessive zeal, after all, should surprise us less and distress us less than the moral scandals from the pain of which God has not spared His Church.

This we grant freely and sincerely, but in making this admission we feel that we are the more justified in protesting against the absurd pretension implied in the complaint against religion and the Church. Science and all its branches and all its advances are represented as blessings so precious that they are worth purchasing at the price of any loss or sacrifice, while religion is a useless thing that is not deserving of the least attention. Unless they maintain some such proposition, our readers will admit that the famous objection as to the conflict between religion and science cannot be sustained, and that it leaves untouched our principles and our conclusions on the subject of tolerance and religion.

To explain. On a concrete question, let us reason without passion or prejudice—in other words, let us adopt what is called a scientific attitude.

If Science impersonate could appear before us, Religion and Science might well join hands, for what would religion have to fear? Science, in the full light and in peaceful possession of truth, would not sin by impatience, or be in too great a hurry to reveal her secrets; but instead of a personification, we have only the disciples of Science, the best of whom call themselves eternal beginners, always labouring at the construction of a monument which is never completed, and in which every successive course of stones is only laid finally after many fresh beginnings.

If scientists themselves (all dogma set aside) had that interior liberty of which Poincaré makes a duty; if they possessed those qualities which M. Lanson eloquently describes—" disinterested desire for information, sincere probity, laborious patience, submission to facts; if they were not too ready to believe either in themselves or in others; and if they had a continual desire for criticism, control, and verification,"[1] we should be almost ready to vote with the famous philosopher for the suppression of all barriers. Not a single barrier is raised without cost, and all are irksome. Men of the character we have just described would give to religion and to society itself guarantees of perfect security. But, unfortunately, Poincaré dare not promise us or even expect complete freedom from prejudice

[1] Lanson, Conference quoted, p. 299.

RELIGION AND SCIENCE

among scientists. He recognizes the frauds which have given Haeckel such an unfortunate notoriety;[1] while Madame Curie has shown us that scientists, in their pursuit of truth, do not necessarily forget all other desires; and the orator who followed Poincaré at Brussels condescended to go into details: "Scientists and ourselves have in common all the same human weakness, the same short sight, the wavering attention, the blind passions, the same inability to put ourselves in another person's place, the perpetual risk of deceiving ourselves and of being deceived."[2]

There is no close corporation of scientists: the first comer is permitted to usurp the title; and these are the men who claim entire freedom to write or say anything they please.

It must be admitted that entire freedom is no longer insisted upon with the same distinctness, and when to the question whether there are doctrines which are socially dangerous, and of which society can get rid as it gets rid of criminals, Poincaré replies, "No lie can be ultimately advantageous,"[3] he practically assumes without any justification that all doctrines are so many truths.

We also think that no lie can be ultimately advantageous, and precisely for that reason we would not refuse to the civil power the right to protect itself against the propagation of falsehood and error.

Is not the remark which M. Lanson makes as a literary critic equally applicable in other matters? He says: "We have been too much inclined to

---

[1] Conference quoted, p. 290. [2] *Ibid.*, p. 298.
[3] *Ibid.*, p. 290.

believe that it was sufficient to have ideas, and have not fully realized that literature, like everything else, requires ideas that have been proved to be true."[1]

But if this is the fact, and if it is really impossible to identify scientists with science and ideas with truth, then all the liberty which Poincaré claims for science and all the good that he says of harmless truth unfortunately does not apply, even from the scientific point of view, to those who call themselves scientists or to what they call their ideas.

It is perfectly natural and intelligible that a Government anxious for the public welfare should be disturbed by the social repercussions of so many fanciful theories, that are labelled " scientific " just as easily as London merchants used to label their English goods " *made in* Germany," because German goods were in fashion. And how much more is the prudent and even protective action of the Church justified ! Charged with the spiritual interests of a multitude easily scandalized and easily led away, is she wrong in taking care that scientific novelties shall not be introduced without any control or examination ? Is she wrong in refusing to risk the higher life of souls for an advantage which is always less important, and sometimes problematical ? The personal dignity of every man forbids that dangerous experiments shall be made even on the vilest bodies in the interests of medicine or surgery. Is it not the part of a wise democracy to forbid the dangerous experiments in social or educational

[1] *L'Esprit Scientifique et la Méthode d'Histoire Littéraire*, p. 304.

matters which modern sociologists or educators would like to try, as it were *in anima vili*, on the people or their children ?

This argument is not weakened by the optimistic view which prophesies a final victory for truth, for, while we are waiting for that victory to be won, error will have disturbed many souls, driven many more to utter ruin, and produced irreparable disasters.

But do not the restrictions of liberty tend to embarrass and retard the progress of science ? Granted ; but even then they are not necessarily condemned, unless we regard the least important scientific discovery as the supreme good of humanity.

However highly we may value science, we cannot consider it the highest good. All men are agreed on this point, even the scientist who steals time from his scientific studies to devote himself first to the interests of his home and the duty he owes to his family. No State will risk the issue of a war or even of a single battle for the sake of the interests of science, and the public prosecutor who suspects a scientist of having committed a crime will not hesitate to drag him from his study in order to put him in gaol. The French Revolution sent Lavoisier to the scaffold, and masonic fanaticism is incapable of respecting a monastic library.

We see, then, that the most enthusiastic admirers of science rate it as less important than family life, or national defence, or the suppression of crime, or even the gratification of political or antireligious passion—all things of the earth, earthly. Is faith only, which is heavenly, to be unable to ask the least sacrifice from science ? To make it a grievance against religion that it is opposed to the teaching of certain scientists is to prejudge it as false, and that is not scientific. It is to proclaim it useless, and that is to contradict the teaching of experience and the testimony of the human heart.

But we must not exaggerate the mischief. We must remember that it is confined to certain branches of science, whose votaries are divided by internal quarrels, and none of their conjectural discoveries have ever been considered indispensable to the happiness of the human race.

Let there be no mistake. Far be it from us to underrate the nobility of every intellectual effort, or the value of the services that may be rendered to the human race by historical discussion or philosophical speculation. Critical science has its rights. But in opposition to what has been called "hypo-criticism," which is ridiculous if not inactive, there is an arrogant hyper-criticism, the object of which is not so much to examine and record facts as to interpret them in its own fashion and obtain notoriety. As Fustel de Coulanges justly remarks, it substitutes for the real aspect of the past its own personal and modern point of view.[1] So others than ourselves have spoken of history as a "mere conjectural science";[2] and others, again, looking at the inordinate but disappointed pretensions of biological and philosophical sciences, have summed them up in one word—"bankruptcy."

It is not even true that every science is hampered by ecclesiastical restrictions, for the action of the

---

[1] *Questions Historiques*, p. 408.
[2] Lanson, Conference cited, p. 300.

RELIGION AND SCIENCE

Church does not affect all scientists. How much scientific labour and study is carried on outside the Church and without any regard for its decrees![1] It follows from this that if there have been individual restrictions laid upon such and such students, no science has lacked air and liberty. In calmer and perhaps happier times the Church allowed a wide liberty of speculation to its members; the Congregation of the Index and the regular condemnations of suspected propositions date from the sixteenth century only. When the revolutionary proceedings of the Reformation compelled the Church to take vigorous measures for the protection of the true faith, science found in the secessions of those troublous times that latitude of study and research which it might have obtained at less cost from legitimate authority. Thus God knows how to bring good out of evil. Heresies, like all revolutions, may be an occasion of progress. It is not impossible that, in spite of their erratic course, they may discover new ways useful to human progress outside the beaten tracks.

How slight, then, is the scientific sacrifice which religion incidentally asks of science, and what immense benefits it confers upon science in return!

It is hardly correct to speak of sacrifice, and we should more properly rejoice over the services which religion and science mutually render to each other.

The conflicts of religion and science are in reality

[1] We do not say " in complete independence," for that would imply something that we do not believe—namely, that in the unbelieving scientific world there are no lay dogmas, no fashionable prejudices, no victims of human respect.

the conflicts of the men who represent them, or, at least, profess to represent them. They arise in part from a solicitude which no one can blame, and which calls upon the worker to exercise that reserve, that modesty, and that circumspection, which are so appropriate in delicate and complicated matters, in which over-confident assurance is often followed by disappointment; they arise also from an excessive zeal, which fancies that it has discovered a fact opposed to some dogma, or a dogma opposed to some scientific assertion. There is no conflict between religion and science; the only conflict is between two specimens of human infirmity and weakness. Infirmity and weakness are visible in everything with which man has to do, in institutions the most necessary to humanity, and therefore we may well say that no institution is without its drawbacks. But these disputes have their advantages. They make men more precise in their proofs, more guarded in their language, and they lead to a more complete and more lasting agreement than would have been possible if there had been no discussion. If they make men go more slowly afterwards, there is no harm in that; much more mischief is caused by over-haste than by caution.

A narrow and suspicious faith may produce a diffidence that paralyzes all a man's faculties, and dogma, especially dogma imperfectly understood, may embarrass the Catholic worker. But this is not its natural influence. The true believer draws from the depth of his convictions all the confidence necessary for the most impartial research. No final result can make him uneasy, for none can shake a religion which might, perhaps, be better understood, but which can never be convicted of falsehood. In the duties which are imposed upon him by his faith he finds energy for honest and scientific labour, and courage to put aside all personal spite and animosity. The higher principles by which his faith is guided lead him willingly to undertake labour of which other men will reap the fruits; they moderate that feverish hurry after success which is so fatal to true science. The brain of the scientist cannot, like an observatory, be isolated from all disturbing influences. The scientist is human, and his first enemies are his own fancies and passions. Religion helps him to overcome them. Let us imitate M. Lanson[1] in his distrust of an excessive liberty which " makes science the slave of individual caprice." If liberty is necessary, so also is discipline; and the best is that of an enlightened religion. If dogma is a weight, it weighs like a ship's ballast, which it is very dangerous to throw overboard.

Let us take note of the eloquent testimony of the famous geologist, M. de Lapparent: " I am glad to say that not only has my faith as a Catholic never been a hindrance to me in my scientific researches, but I have been strengthened by it both intellectually and morally, and that in the special sphere in which I have been employed I have received from it the most powerful encouragement to fulfil my duty as a man of science."[2]

While religion thus gives the scientist courage to

[1] Conf. cited, p. 306.
[2] *La Recherche Scientifique et la Foi*, letter to the *Revue Pratique d'Apologétique*, 1906, t. 2, p. 266.

persevere in his work, it receives in its turn undeniable benefits from science. We speak of that impartial science of which Poincaré paints such an attractive picture.

More modest, because he knows more, the true scientist, in whatever rank he may be found,[1] uses his irrefragable authority to expose the frauds and impostures of shallow sciolists. How many false oracles on our origin or our nature would be produced against religion, and would even obtain credit, if the true man of science were not there to bar the way by his decisive contradiction! We need not hesitate to place to the credit of science those discoveries which have modified our ideas as to the antiquity of the world, its construction and its motion. Instead of looking at these as so many rebuffs, we may see in them new aids to the progress of religion. No scientific discovery has thrown any doubt on the existence of God as the primary cause of all things. Every new one, on the contrary, has shown us more clearly how wonderful He is in all His works. By showing us how imperfectly we have hitherto understood those works, these discoveries make us more humble, and therefore more religious. By correcting our erroneous ideas, they purify the homage which we offer to God, and we offer it more acceptably because He is no longer unknown; by enlightening us on certain arguments hitherto drawn from Holy Scripture, they enable us to understand more fully the manner in which the Holy Spirit of God has co-operated in the work of

[1] We except the rabid fanatics; they, however, only attack religion when they leave the branch of science in which they have earned distinction.

RELIGION AND SCIENCE

men; and there is still a further service which science renders to theology in warning those who are engaged in the latter study to approach with the greatest care all matters which touch upon human science.

In the Conference which we have already referred to, Poincaré declares that Pasteur's faith was as fresh and vigorous in the normal school as in surroundings most antagonistic to scientific culture.[1] He congratulates Pasteur on having given enlightened minds to the service of humanity, and, speaking of the Catholic pupils of the famous chemist, he says: " Whatever may be their opinions, they are our friends; and if all the rest were like these, we could live on good terms with them."[2] It could not be more clearly admitted that there is no reason why science should break with religion, and we may well return the compliment, and say of the scientists that Poincaré describes: " In spite of their opinions, these men are not our enemies; and if all the rest were like them, we could live on good terms with them."

In their final results science and religion cannot contradict one another; and instead of having to be limited one by the other, due freedom is given to each, so that they may render each other mutual help.

A superficial glance may lead us to imagine an antagonism between the religious ideal and the scientific ideal, but a more careful examination will reveal them to us as parallels. True science and true religion alike call for the judicious use of our intellectual powers, the one on the natural

[1] Conf. cited, p. 288. [2] Conf. cited, p. 298.

phenomenal world—that is to say, the world which is perceived by the senses—the other on what we might call the supernatural phenomenal world, the word of God, which is contained in the double treasury of the Scriptures and tradition, and to which we give the assent of faith. By the aid of superficial observations the ordinary man, like the scientist, gathers a first stock of ideas and impressions, like the fruits of the earth, which we gather with our hands. The supernatural world is similarly revealed with its dogmas to all believers. Scientific observation of the natural world enriches our minds with the knowledge of forces and laws which are called new, not because they have only just come into existence, but because they have hitherto escaped our notice. Scientific study, applied to the supernatural world, and here specially aided by God, brings to light truths hitherto hidden in the Divine deposit. These are the new dogmas. Thus is fulfilled the desire expressed in such eloquent language by the declaration of the Vatican Council (Sess. iii. *de fide*, cap. 4) : " Let knowledge, science, and wisdom grow with the course of times and centuries, in individuals as well as in the community, in each man as in the whole Church, but in the proper manner—*i.e.*, in the same dogma, in the same meaning, in the same understanding." In the natural world, the scientist constructs his logical theories, his catalogue, as M. Poincaré would say, in which various phenomena are shown to be so connected as to form one harmonious whole ; but he cannot give to his classifications the force of objective truth.

RELIGION AND SCIENCE

In a similar manner the theologian looks to philosophy for a rational system to co-ordinate dogmas. If he does not deny the objective value of his deductions, he nevertheless refrains from making them articles of faith : they are not new dogmas. But for those mysteries which are beyond his reason he gives up, like the scientist, the objective explanation, and is content with analogical images and symbols, which do away with the objection that faith is opposed to reason. After a period of hesitation between various systems of philosophy, the theologian ended by adopting the system of Aristotle, as being the best adapted for his purpose. Does not the scientist in the same manner choose the theory which promises to be of most use to him ? But while his theory is being perfected, and new laws are discovered to confirm it, the scientist is conscious that he is making progress ; he feels, not without emotion, that he is approaching that solid ground of absolute reality which is in no way cognizable by him: for at that point there would be an end of progress. In the same way the theologian, elaborating and perfecting his explanations, feels that he is drawing nearer to a truth which is altogether beyond the bounds of human cognition. The succession of theological systems on the Real Presence, the causality of the sacraments, etc., shows clearly that there is a process of development in religious science.

The last complaint against religion—at least, against positive religion—may also receive a complete answer. Religion, we are told, imposes an act of faith, and habits of faith produce intellectual degradation. But are the attitude of the believer and the attitude of the scientist necessarily opposed, and does one destroy the other? Let us set aside the immense difference there is between an act of Divine faith and an act of human faith, more or less strictly understood, as this difference is hardly relevant to the present issue; and let us note what are the characteristics of the attitude of the believer and the attitude of the scientist. In the former we find a disposition to accept, on the word of another, something that the believer cannot verify personally; the latter is a tendency to inquire and see for oneself.

Thus understood, each attitude is the complement of the other, and humanity cannot do without either. Every man, being at the same time an independent individual, and a member of the human race, must both see for himself and also make use of the eyes of another. If he refuses to see for himself, he is false to his rational nature; if he refuses to believe, he is false to his social nature. The child must believe in his father, his mother, his masters; the sick man must obey his physician; the people must listen to men who are better informed than themselves.[1]

No man can refuse to the knowledge and honesty of some other man that trust which is dictated by the act of faith; and scientists are bound to believe in one another, for they take up the work left unfinished by others. If they wish to proceed farther with it, they must accept the results already arrived at; and what enormous proportions their faith

[1] Too often, unfortunately, they follow leaders who are not at all trustworthy.

assumes in certain branches of science, especially in that of history!

Science discovers, faith retains; science is the element of progress, faith is the element of stability; science presents us with new facts, faith represents tradition; strict science, which is personal and individualist, and only desires to see for itself, would divide men; faith keeps them together, grouped round a central authority. But science cannot exist without the co-operation of many, and consequently requires mutual faith. Faith, being more receptive in its acquisition of knowledge, reserves its activity for works; it makes use of the discoveries of science, and applies the lever at the fixed point which science indicates; it procures for the scientist the honour due to him, and the disciples who encourage him in his labour. Science seeks to create faith, for every scientist desires to be believed; and so human nature goes on, constantly sustained by science and faith.

Moreover, at the very basis of scientific researches there is a conviction which is incapable of proof, a belief without sight, which resembles the act of faith, strictly so called. Poincaré and M. Duhem are agreed on this point. The former says: " Every generalization presupposes, in a certain measure, a belief in the unity and the simplicity of Nature ";[1] and the latter: " It is all very well for the natural philosopher to be convinced that his theories have no power to grasp the reality . . . he affirms his faith in a real order, of which his theories have an image which every day grows clearer and more like

[1] *La Science et l'Hypothèse*, p. 172.

the reality."[1] And what a support it is for the true believer in the course of his labour, while so many sceptical voices are raised to scoff at his pains and deny the necessity for them, to feel that his scientific efforts are made under the ægis of convictions which cannot fail![2] Lastly, faith tends to be changed into knowledge. The child, as he grows up, believes less and sees more; and his sight often confirms, but sometimes corrects, the teaching of an authority which is fallible, as all human authority must necessarily be.

God, then, has not done violence to our nature, but has satisfied its most intimate aspirations by teaching us, like a father who can never deceive us, vital truths which we could not acquire for ourselves. This faith, also, will one day be changed into sight, a sight which will justify it in the most perfect happiness; but that sight is reserved for that ripe and perfect age which we shall attain in the other life. And in the meantime this faith calls science to its aid to explore its object, to verify its sources of information, and to discriminate better between what is Divine and what is human; and in exchange it gives to science a force and an extension of activity, and counsels of prudence which preserve it from a crowd of errors.

Human science and faith, human as well as Divine, are given to us that we may receive light from both; and it is our own fault if they seem to contradict each other. These imaginary conflicts are not

[1] *La Théorie Physique, son Objet et sa Structure*, p. 38.
[2] A. de Lapparent, *La Recherche Scientifique et la Foi*, in the *Revue Pratique d'Apologétique*, t. 2, p. 269.

imputable to science or to faith, but to ourselves, who are too ready to say, *I believe*, or *I know*. Reason affirms this, and experience proves it ; and the more reality there is in science, and the more purity in faith, the rarer will be these conflicts, and the easier of solution. Counterfeit science presumptuously sets itself up in opposition to the Church and Divine faith. The liberty of true science has neither the will nor the power to harm them.

Man, in his intellectual and moral life, as in his physical life, must combine the use of the different forces of which he is composed. The alliance of science and faith is imposed upon humanity as a difficult problem, it may be, but one that is necessary, and fruitful in glorious results. As it realizes this alliance, the human race makes progress towards perfection, for it cannot give up either the one or the other. Our intellectual curiosity is too lively to be satisfied without science, and the world only rejects faith to fall into credulity. The first falsehood that it blindly accepts is the dogma of its emancipation ; and what a tissue of incoherent absurdities is put forward as the creed of the world by the false prophets of the school, the Press, and the senate !

Let us do justice to both science and faith ; and as we are obliged so often to believe in men, let us not, under the pretext of science or scientific liberty, refuse to believe in God, or to reject *a priori* a faith which comes to us as the gift of the Author of Divine Revelation.

V. The Genesis of Civil Tolerance.

SUMMARY : Effective tolerance is much more a concession made to necessity and to material or political interests than a fruit of philosophic or religious doctrines.—Influence of humanism, of the school of natural law, and of scepticism.—Is tolerance a fruit of the Protestant Reformation ?

Tolerance exists as a *fact*, more or less extended, but real ; as a *right*, recorded in codes of law and even in constitutions ; and as a popular *ideal*. It will, then, be convenient to investigate its origin, or, rather, to put it in evidence, for the preceding pages, in describing doctrines and events and the order of their succession, have already given a substantial account of it.

In the New World, as in the Old World, treaties of tolerance have been concluded, edicts have been published, and laws enacted, as an inevitable consequence of the divisions which have separated the peoples into different Christian bodies, and have necessitated the recognition and regulation of various forms of worship on the same territory. Christians have had to live with Jews ; henceforth Christians of different denominations must live in peace together. Material interests, too, the voice of which is almost always listened to, plead the cause of tolerance. We must also add political considerations. Merchants of different nationalities and beliefs must be enabled to meet in the same markets ; and in North America it became necessary for the different religious bodies, established side by side on the same territory, to come to an understanding,

GENESIS OF CIVIL TOLERANCE

in order to obtain political unity, and finally complete independence. For the Old World we may mention, as an example, the secret treaties admitting heretical merchants into the Spanish Netherlands; for the New World it will be enough to quote the testimony of Hägermann. In a study specially intended to show the influence of the religious factor on the libertarian movement in America, that learned writer comes to the distinct conclusion that decrees of toleration have often had economic or political circumstances as their first cause.[1]

Considered as satisfying a right of man, civil tolerance does not originate from any desire to promote peace, or any process of intellectual reasoning. It was only in 1776 that America proclaimed the right to religious liberty; but this liberty had already found its way into public life, as a means of settling disputes entirely unconnected with religion. Thus we sum up the observations of M. Adalbert Wacht.[2]

We must not, however, neglect to make allowance for the rise of new ideas on the subject of religion, or underrate their influence. When supernatural faith and life grow weaker, concepts of religion are formed which contain the germ of a more radical tolerantist doctrine, and the exigencies of facts at the same time become more and more pressing.

From our point of view we can thus distinguish

---

[1] *Die Erklärungen der Menschen- und Bürgerrechte in den ersten Amerikanischen Staatsverfassungen;* Berlin, 1910 (*Historische Studien herausgegeben von E. Ebering*, No. 78).

[2] *Zur Geschichte der Menschenrechte* (*Historische Zeitschrift*, 1909, t. 103, p. 82).

three periods or stages, corresponding to medieval Catholicism, the modern Renaissance, and the contemporary Revolution.

For ages after the triumph of Christianity, all education was given and all edification perfected on the basis of Revelation. Only one religion was known—the religion given by God. It reigned in undisputed sovereignty, and sciences and politics alike took their inspiration from it.

As long as this faith was supreme in men's minds, it was impossible to speak against religion without offering an outrageous insult to God ; and the idea of putting human error and Divine truth on an equality was rejected as blasphemous. Faith would have incited even the believer to violence and fanaticism if the meekness of Christ had not intervened, as it always does in true Christianity, to forbid hatred, to moderate anger, and to prevent violent excesses.

In the second period of pagan renaissance, cultivated minds took their stand on human reason rather than on faith, moulded their style on classic models, and sought to establish on the principles of natural law the rules of political government, and the rights and duties of Sovereigns and subjects. Without precisely denying revealed religion, they compared its claims with those of natural religion ; they endeavoured to define the authority in religious matters that the Sovereign would have exercised if it had not been for the institution of the Church, and to show the influence of that institution on the juridical position of Governments.

Natural religion is no longer Divine, except in its

object. It is human in its developments; and the mind, in taking natural religion for its base, by degrees becomes accustomed to consider different religions as so many human constructions springing from the religious foundation laid in our hearts. The idea of giving equal treatment to different forms of worship meets with less resistance, and soon the religion which asks for favours or privileges, or a monopoly, will be looked upon as giving way to jealousy and setting up an unjust claim.

On the other hand, the duties of the Sovereign with regard to religion are no longer estimated according to revealed commandments, but according to the indications of Nature. He protects religion less for God or for its own sake than for the sake of society; and thence it begins to be discussed how far a single religion—that is, a State religion—is necessary. Men write on the mutual rights of the conscience and the Sovereign, and easily end by restricting the authority of the latter to outward and public worship. Men no longer trouble themselves so much about truth or about social unity, and so heretics come to be defined as " Christians who obstinately refuse to join in the profession of faith officially received and approved in the State."[1]

This indifference shown to the various forms of religion—at least, to those which are called " Christian "—is, in fact, a mild form of scepticism; and partial scepticism bears within it the germ of more complete scepticism, which degenerates from diluted

[1] Karl Fuhrmann, *Dissertatio inauguralis juridica de Tolerantiæ religiosæ effectibus civilibus;* Halle, 1762.

Christianity into philosophic Deism, only to end in simple atheism.

Political tolerance is obliged to enlarge the scope of its concessions, for men are not agreed even as to the existence of God. Atheists claim to be recognized, and even those who are not atheists desire to establish society on a purely human foundation. That was the spirit of the French Revolution. With it all reason for intolerance had disappeared. By that we mean the intolerance which was exercised in favour of religion; but a new form of intolerance remained possible, and its first edicts were signed by the French Revolution. This is the intolerance which persecutes religion, and specially the Catholic Church, in the name of a vague secular dogma, which is sometimes dignified by the honourable name of "progress."

Such, in short, it seems to us, is the genesis of civil tolerance. An unfortunate event made it necessary, and an increasing contempt for religion made an idol of it. Its history, or three-fourths of it, is the history of religious decay.

The tolerance which is admitted and professed by Catholics is a matter of necessity; but it is, nevertheless, sincere and loyal and constant.

And what of Protestantism, it will be asked? The leaders of the Reformation were certainly anything but tolerant. They persecuted wherever they had the power. Some of them, like Zwingli and Calvin, hankered after a pitiless theocracy modelled on that of the Old Testament, and all the more terrible because it gave up everything to the head of the State. As late as the second half of the

GENESIS OF CIVIL TOLERANCE

seventeenth century, Thomasius continually taxed the Protestant ministers with continuing the traditions of Popery.[1]

They certainly can take no credit for the spread of tolerance ; but did they not help it unconsciously ? Was not civil tolerance a necessary result of Protestant teaching ?

Opinions on this point are divided; and in the Catholic camp, as in the Protestant, some persons admit and others deny that tolerance is a logical postulate of Protestantism.

It is not, say some ; and they appeal to the theocratic concept of the Reformers and their acts.[2] Others say that it is, and point to the principle of private judgment, which Protestantism substituted for the principle of authority, even in religion.

There is something to be said on both sides. Nothing in orthodox Protestantism, which retained a belief in Christ and Holy Scripture, logically contained a dogma of absolute tolerance ; but a limited tolerance seems necessarily to follow from the individualist principle of private judgment. This principle inevitably led to the disruption of Christianity into rival sects, no one of which had any claim to supremacy over the others. It produced a diversity of opinions, which was afterwards, with great inconsistency, denounced and condemned.

[1] See, for instance, his Dialogue, *An Hæresis sit Crimen;* and he frequently returns to this idea in his other works.

[2] See this opinion very seriously defended by Nicolaus Paulus in *Protestantismus und Toleranz im 16 Jahrhundert,* n. 25. The author specially quotes the recent words of Eberhard Gothein, *In den neuen evangelischen Konfessionen lag an sich kein Element der Toleranz* (*Die Kultur der Gegenwart,* part ii., p. 194; Berlin, 1908).

Thus we soon see Protestant writers rising against the oppression of one sect by another, and showing that they are of one mind on essential points.

This tolerance, which was limited to Christian sects without being extended even to all of them, was opposed by reasons of State, the rights of the Sovereign, and that alienation of personal rights which was implied by a theory much in favour with the jurists of the Reformation—the theory of the *social contract*.

But complete tolerance is not by any means the result of Protestantism. Friedberg expresses himself in these terms : " In tolerance, as we understand it, we must, before all things, recognize a product of the school of natural law, of the period of the *Aufklärung*,[1] and, to some extent, of religious indifference in general."[2] In short, it is rooted in humanism, rationalism, and irreligion. Döllinger wrote in 1861 : " Historically there is no greater mistake than to consider the Reformation as a movement in favour of liberty of conscience. The exact opposite is the truth."[3]

---

[1] The Germans use this word to denote the rationalistic renaissance of law and philosophy which took place in Germany in the eighteenth century.

[2] *Deutsche Zeitschrift für Kirchenrecht*, 1905, xxxvii. 477.

[3] *Kirche und Kirchen*, p. 68.

VI. WHAT AGREEMENT IS POSSIBLE ?

SUMMARY : Modern maxims of liberty.—They do not disclose any new political principle : their application is not even constant.—Their popularity depends on another appreciation of the common good.—But it is with a view to this good that men now, as formerly, grant or restrict civil liberties.—Between believers and unbelievers the conflict is not political, but religious.—On what basis can a mutual understanding be promoted ?—On a convention of practical tolerance, inspired and sustained by charity.—Ephemeral reign of doctrinal liberalism.—What it has taught Catholics.

" No one shall be molested on account of his opinions, even his religious opinions, and no one shall incur any incapacity or disability on that account. Everyone is at liberty to express and spread his opinions, even his religious opinions, and to associate himself with others, provided that they conform to the laws relating to associations, and do not disturb the public peace."

Do these provisions, which are found in many laws and constitutions, prove the existence of that radical antagonism between the political principles of Catholics and those of the modern State which is alleged by many persons, and to which they even appeal as a reason for excluding Catholics from power and official position, or for inducing them to withdraw voluntarily ?

Our study of doctrines and facts since the French Revolution has shown us that they do not. If these formulæ are intended to indicate a new policy, they should be derived from a principle both absolute and new, which we cannot find anywhere—certainly not in the conscience, the inviolability of which has always existed without any such declaration of liberty, for throughout the ages no one has defended it more eloquently than the Church by the blood of her martyrs and the voice of her most illustrious doctors ; not in the Declaration of the Rights of Man, "which no one has ever applied, which its authors were the first to contravene, and which on the least pretext is put aside altogether."[1]

In more than one country Catholics are left to hope that some day they will see a more liberal and more equitable application of these provisions in their favour ; and they learn to their cost the unsubstantial character of the sacrosanct principle that gives liberty to every opinion. There are other significant exceptions to the rule. The idea which suggests the commission of a crime is an opinion, but who will justify the propagation of that opinion ? And what are we to think of the attacks made upon principles considered as essential to existing society ? Ought the civil power to disregard them ? " The question remains open, and in practice is not susceptible of any but temporary solutions." Such is the astonishing but instructive reply of an authorized representative of contemporary rationalistic politics, M. Bouché-Leclercq. Ten lines earlier the same author had written that the State "condemned nothing but acts!"[2] The question remains open, in spite of the natural rights of man and their immortal Declaration, in spite of the much-vaunted abolition of the crime of opinion. And would not many vote against liberty

[1] Victor Jacobs, *Les Droits Naturels de l'Homme*, p. 681.
[2] *L'Intolérance Religieuse et la Politique*, pp. 354, 355.

of discussion of the general policy of laicization and of laws proclaimed unalterable ? To prove this, see the discourses of French Members of Parliament. And what would become of liberty of opinions and their public expression in days of revolutionary effervescence, when tribunals are set up to search for suspected persons ?[1] Is not the fact that a palpable material interest is in danger enough to make the rationalist Press and the accredited organs of modern politics complain of mischievous and dangerous theories ; to make them use the language of former days, and show themselves ready to ratify the most violent measures of proscription ?[2] If anyone ventured to express astonishment, they would reply by appealing to social necessities.

And now they come round to the Catholic point of view, which considers civil liberties valuable in proportion as they conduce to the public good. Men have varied in the idea of what is good, but all honest policy is directed to the attainment of that end. Modern philosophers and politicians, on the one hand, considering religion as a thing of no value to the community, and, on the other hand, intoxicated with evolutionism and relativist opinions, were led to look for the principles of a new order in ideas now considered subversive of all order, and to make free discussion an essential condition of progress ; and they naturally declared for liberty of opinions and their expression, and the most absolute

[1] Let us remember 1793, and let us observe what is actually going on in Portugal.
[2] To be convinced of this, we have only to read some of the articles published in certain newspapers of the Left at the time of the French railway strikes in 1911.

religious tolerance. But for what reason? For the sake of some right of man or some new philosophy? It would seem so at first sight, but this is not the case really. The true reason was that they looked upon all religious tolerance as socially inoffensive, and the tolerance of opinions as socially useful. Thus, when facts speak too loudly, and an opinion seems to endanger social order as they imagine it, their declarations are ignored, and their dogma of absolute tolerance is entirely forgotten.

The policy of the modern State, then, has no supreme positive principle peculiar to itself, for the principle of the rights of man is neither supreme nor even effective. Society may be deceived as to its foundations and its essential principles; but it remains true that "every society is intolerant in regard to what attacks its foundations," and absolute liberty in religious and philosophical matters is " a system of anarchy which never has existed, and never will exist anywhere."[1] "Absolute liberalism is a sociological heresy, for it misunderstands the essential conditions of social life; and for that very reason it is an impossible and purely Utopian idea." M. L. de la Vallée-Poussin thus concludes the reflections suggested by M. Goblet d'Aviella's work on the congresses of religion.[2]

Between believers and unbelievers the discord is not political, but religious. If unbelievers were converted to-morrow, if they looked upon religion as we look upon it, the dogma of religious tolerance

[1] V. Jacobs, article above quoted.
[2] *Revue Pratique d'Apologétique*, December 1, 1910.

POSSIBLE AGREEMENT

would have no more adherents, and all men would understand tolerance as we do.

But while we are waiting for this conversion to take place, will not the irreconcilable religious conflict necessarily put citizens on a footing of mutual hostility? How can we imagine civic peace among people who, while disagreeing as to the foundations of social order, are, nevertheless, agreed on the necessity of defending them? If the first disagreement were complete, peace and fraternity could not exist at all. At present they are only rendered more difficult of attainment. A more fragile and more superficial peace may be established on a basis of ideas remaining common to both parties, and on a certain natural sense of honour and morality, which are admitted by all persons to be necessary, provided that Catholics do not seek to force upon others their ideas on religion, nor unbelievers their evolutionist doctrine, and consequently their dogma of tolerance, which is the fruit of that doctrine. This peace admits, and, indeed, peremptorily demands, a practical rule of tolerance, but a tolerance founded upon a principle of charity, and not upon a religious theory, which would be the negation of Catholicism. Still less does it demand the recognition of an absolute dogmatic tolerance, which is a myth, an idol without worshippers. Such a peace, immediately made and loyally observed, may ultimately lead to the restoration of religious unity.

Catholics have always been willing to conclude such a peace, and to observe its conditions, and so were the Liberals of the Belgian Constitution.

But the death-knell of that Liberalism has sounded, and radical extremists claim to monopolize the idea of true progress, to set the pace for society, and so to proceed methodically and pitilessly, even by way of confiscation and banishment, to the elimination of the religious idea. Liberalism has passed away. False in principle, it has fallen into ruin, dragging with it its bigoted followers into the mire of irreligious demagoguism. But, like all error, it has left its portion of truth as a heritage to the Church and to Catholics.

God, indeed, who protects His Church, does not exempt it from the conditions of human life and progress, nor does He preserve it from all liability to failure. Infallible in her teaching authority, but not in her practical politics (at least, there is nothing to prove it), she learns from experience, which is sometimes happy and sometimes painful, how best to direct her steps towards her glorious end. And thus all ages, even the worst, have been fruitful in teaching for the Church.

Born on Calvary, hunted down and persecuted for more than three hundred years, the Church has retained from the first period of her history that aversion to bloodshed that we claim as her chief honour; and she has proclaimed in the face of the whole world that faith must proceed from the will moved by the grace of God.

A second period showed her the lawfulness and expediency of outward coercion—not to produce convictions, but to preserve them, and sometimes to give them liberty; less to force than to permit people to believe. Public authorities, under the

POSSIBLE AGREEMENT

pressure of circumstances, proceeded to measures of extreme severity, which received the approval of the heads of the Church. Then appeared the uselessness and impotence of severity. Neither wars nor courts of justice were able to prevent a disruption, but for which a wholly Catholic Europe would have formed a Christian universe. The Church had to pay very dearly for the services of the secular arm ; and, however lawful and necessary its intervention may have been, it has left behind it a prejudice and distrust from which we are still suffering. St. Augustine wrote in 512 : " In times of turbulence and danger, moderation is looked upon as a sign of weakness or indifference ; but when once the excitement has passed away, the beauty of mercy is recognized, and men take pleasure in reading the annals in which it is recorded."[1] Noxious germs are always swarming in the air that surrounds our globe, and cause to feeble organisms harm that sometimes requires heroic remedies, while healthy bodies are able to resist their influence. If the reforming Council of Trent had been assembled a century earlier, it might have saved Christianity from that religious disaster which is still the greatest misfortune of the world.

A third period thus begins in the midst of rebellions and apostasies, in the course of which the Church devotes her attention to herself, applies herself with all her power to beautify and strengthen her inward position, and displays the immense resources that she possesses in the purity of her doctrine, the exemplary life of her ministers, the

[1] Letter to Marcellinus (M.P.L., t. 33, p. 535).

virtues of her faithful children, the enlightenment of her preaching, and the sweet unction of her sacraments. When outward help fails, she feels her own inward vigour increase; when civil Governments refuse to stand by her, she pursues her own course unaided; and what she loses in the prestige of physical force, she gains in a prestige of moral force more sublime, more impressive, more successful in winning hearts that long for enlightenment and peace.

Formed thus in the school of twenty centuries, that Church is now preparing, by the gentleness and the virtues of her mature age, to win back from anarchy that same world, now mad with licence, which, by the gentleness and the virtues of her infancy, she delivered from the degrading despotism of Cæsar.

SECOND SECTION: HISTORICAL VIEW

I. The Past.

1. *General Conclusions.*

SUMMARY : Danger of books which treat of one particular point—for instance, the Inquisition.—Ill-informed and partial authors.—Reasoned appreciation of the past in general, of heresy, the procedure against heresy, and its severe repression.—The principles were just, the intentions generally honest.—Testimony of Paulsen as to the probable necessity of this severity.—Indulgence necessary for our own age.

It is difficult to get a true impression of facts from works which treat of one special point only in a long controverted subject, especially if this subject embraces facts and theories in which human passions and weakness are concerned. The difficulty arises from the specialism of the authors, who confine their attention to one period and one country, and therefore can only give a very brief account of anterior events and the circumstances of neighbouring countries. The opinions and practices they describe are too much detached from the events which led up to them, and which explain and perhaps justify them. Facts scattered through different centuries and countries are crowded together as if they belonged to the same time and place, and the appeal to general custom does not sufficiently explain the use of methods and procedure adopted for one special purpose. We have a realistic picture of which the details, taken singly, are true, but the general effect is false and misleading. To correct these optical errors, impartial authors have endeavoured to use a kind of perspective, with the result that their readers have distrusted the accuracy of their recital. In short, as the wars of a monarch do not show the real character of his reign, in the same way we cannot judge of the Church's tolerance by the Inquisition alone.

What shall we say of authors who write without any qualification for the task; of ignorant persons who, for want of complete information, cannot form an accurate judgment; of prejudiced persons who exploit the past only for the purpose of exciting hatred; of " pragmatists " who, by their concessions and admissions, seek to create for themselves a reputation for impartiality, and to give the Church the benefit of extenuating circumstances?[1]

The wide scope of our inquiry saves us from any danger of this kind, and as in our review of events and doctrines facts and theories have been presented in their proper historical order, we naturally have a true picture of the long struggle of the Church and the civil powers against heresy; and without any need of accidental and imperfect excuses, suggested by the personality of the heretics or the acts of intolerance laid to their charge, the Catholic doctrine and the action of the Church are shown in a more favourable light than would have seemed possible without the study and examination that is now brought to a close.

To sum up the results of our inquiry. No preconceived idea impelled the Church to demand the punishment of heretics, or to have recourse to any but ecclesiastical penalties; but little by little the

[1] See G. Sorel, *Réflexions sur la Violence*, p. 393.

THE PAST : GENERAL CONCLUSIONS

violent conduct of certain sects, and the force used by them to retain their disciples, led to special repressions which prepared the way for a more general proscription.

Heresy in our Western countries did not present itself merely as a platonic or speculative contradiction of doctrine ; it set up a revolutionary principle in opposition to the Church. Theoretical discussion, if there was any, was a secondary weapon, which served it to support a movement subversive of ecclesiastical authority and often of social order.[1] We need not, then, imagine a new theological controversy, cut short by the sword ; the retractation of error was insisted upon less for its own sake than as an indication of submission to lawful authority. The Church did not desire so much to attack men's convictions as to organize her own defence.

Laws of exceptional severity may be meant simply to terrify, and the most elementary honesty obliges us to judge of legislation, not only by the text of the laws, but also by their application. As we have seen, this was the object of the terrible laws of Theodosius ; and M. Pirenne, speaking of the cruel proclamations of Charles V., tells us that " most of them [the échevins] regarded the proclamations as mere bugbears designed to frighten the

[1] M. Jordan, in his articles frequently quoted, quoting M. Giraud, admits this for the end of the Middle Ages. " In a time when human thought was most commonly expressed under a theological form, doctrines of socialism, communism, and anarchy, were preached under the form of heresy. . . . The great heresies of the end of the Middle Ages, such as those of the Fraticelli, the Lollards, Hussites, and Anabaptists, were social or national revolts almost as much as religious innovations, and were the cause of trouble and bloodshed."

people, but that they were to be applied with discretion, the punishment being made proportionate to the crime ";[1] and, according to the testimony of Lea,[2] the Inquisition did not take proceedings against all persons who were liable to prosecution under the laws then in force.

In short, the repression of heresy was not signalized by any increase of judicial severity, but, on the contrary, its influence on the penal system was rather favourable than otherwise.[3] In occupying itself with the reformation of the criminal, it drew an attention to one object of punishment which was at that time very little considered ; and in introducing the practice of imprisonment,[4] it made possible all the humanitarian reforms of criminal legislation.

But, for all that, we cannot reconcile the institutions of the past with our present ideas : these

[1] *Histoire de Belgique*, t. 3, p. 355.
[2] " There was one class of offenders who would have afforded the Inquisition an ample field for its authority had it been disposed to take cognizance of them. By the Canons anyone who had endured excommunication for a year without submission and seeking absolution was pronounced suspect of heresy. In 1301 the Council of Rheims directed that proceedings should be commenced, when it next should meet, against all who had been under excommunication for two years, as being suspect of heresy, and in 1303 it called on all such to come forward and purge themselves of the suspicion ; but the Court in which this was to be done was that of the Bishops, and not of the Inquisition " (*op. cit.*, t. 2, p. 122).
[3] On this subject see the pamphlet of M. Labrocquère already quoted, *De l'Influence de la Législation Canonique sur la Législation Criminelle;* Bastia, 1877.
[4] This punishment was then called *emmuraillement*, or walling in ; and sectarian misrepresentation has not failed to make use of this unfortunate word for the purpose of showing that prisoners were buried alive with walls built round them.

THE PAST : GENERAL CONCLUSIONS

ideas require to be enlarged. In order to understand thoroughly the severe punishments prescribed and sometimes inflicted for heresy, we need to have the lively faith of the Middle Ages, and to attach the same importance as the men of that time to religious unity for the good of civil society. We need to take careful account, on the one hand, of the revolutionary conduct and language of many heretics, and, on the other hand, of the disorder and agitation produced by heresy in the whole community. In short, we need to put ourselves in the place of men whose thoughts and sentiments and judgments were suggested by a civilization ruder than our own, and, above all, infinitely more cruel in its measures of repression.

Our own conclusions—even those which are most reasonable and just, and practically true, though based on unchangeable principles—are, at the same time, influenced to some extent by accidental circumstances, by which posterity will not be affected. Thus it is that, because they cannot make allowance for circumstances, men condemn without reserve the public opinion which called for the death of heretics, the laws which sanctioned it, and the magistrates who administered the law. They judge the past and lay down the law for the future as if the past, the present, and the future, occupied the same plane on the scene of history ; as if political and social problems presented themselves at different times in the same conditions.

This irresponsible criticism of the past is just as absurd as the infatuation of some people who see absolute perfection in our existing institutions, as if no further progress were possible. But it is easy to declaim against the prejudices of the past; would it not be more practicable to be on our guard against the prejudices of the present?

We take so much account nowadays of the relativity of knowledge that we ought to make a double allowance for our ancestors. Let us explain. We consider our own convictions and environment, and we condemn such-and-such a method or system of former days, such-and-such a law or decision, and are quite ready to express an opinion as to what ought to have been done. Perhaps our advice may be the best *to-day;* but would it have been the best in the former circumstances? And if the answer is not already negative, let us ask ourselves a further question: Would the advice have been possible or practicable, regard being had to the opinions prevalent at the time? The principles of justice are absolute, but we learn by experience how to apply them better and better; and can we blame our predecessors for not having learned the lessons taught by subsequent events? At this rate the physicians of former days deserved to be criminally prosecuted, and our magistrates ought to be ashamed to occupy a bench disgraced by the bloodthirsty judges of old times.

If we wish to be fair in our estimate of past legislation and jurisprudence, let us look at the principles that were applied, and the intentions of those who applied them. Were those principles just? Were those intentions honest? Men may have been mistaken, but they cannot be condemned for their mistakes.

We must be careful not to say lightly, or without a sufficient consideration of their circumstances, that they were mistaken. As we have seen, the repression of heresy cannot be better described, from its dominant character, than as a political and social defence organized according to the science and art of the time for the preservation of institutions which were esteemed essential—religion, family, property—and more especially to establish the principle of authority in the Church and the State. We may regret the severity of this defence, and condemn its excesses and abuses, but we cannot blame the principle or deny the inevitable necessity.

The following remarks of the Protestant moralist Paulsen supply us with matter for reflection :[1] " The Middle Ages are blamed for having burned heretics and sorcerers, for having put accused persons to the question, and for having put to death thousands of criminals. It must be admitted that such manners are wanting in elegance and refinement, but it does not follow that a ruder age than our own was wrong in adopting such measures. It may be that frequent abuses occurred, but it may also be true—though the nature of things renders it difficult to prove—that the methods employed were appropriate to the times, and therefore necessary. Perhaps in the disciplinary formation of character the Church[2] fulfils such an indispensable condition of progress towards a higher civilization that history will justify the Middle Ages in having resisted, in the most

[1] *System der Ethik*, fifth edition, p. 21. Paulsen died in 1909, while a professor in Berlin.
[2] It must be remembered that the most rigorous part of the education was not the work of the Church.

resolute manner, all attempts to escape from that discipline ; and that was the object to which every heretical movement was most generally directed. The whole criminal procedure of the period, with its cruel methods, was, perhaps, temporarily necessary, to permit the transition to the complicated social life of the cities of the Middle Ages. We may congratulate ourselves that the organization of our law-courts and our police has been made perfect, and that they succeed in obtaining as good, or better results by more humane methods ; but that does not prove that our methods would have been able to preserve the peace in the Middle Ages. The Middle Ages might well reply to our criticism : ' If such mild repression is enough for you, you are indebted to us for the fact ; our labours, continued through several centuries, destroyed the elements which were incompatible with social order. It was not an agreeable task, but it is hardly fair to make it a grievance against us, and, moreover, no one knows how long your own procedure will suffice to save you from trouble.' "

If we remember also that heresies had for their declared adversaries saints and men whom even Lea[1] describes as " men of the kindliest tempers, the profoundest intelligence, the noblest associations, the purest zeal for righteousness, professing a religion founded on love and charity," shall we not see in their attitude a new and grave reason for being very careful before we absolutely condemn what they practised and approved ?

We might, moreover, pay dearly in the future for a too inflexible severity of judgment. The Bulls

[1] *Op. cit.*, t. I, p. 234.

THE PAST: GENERAL CONCLUSIONS

and Edicts issued against heresy, and the courts and tribunals established to *exterminate* it,[1] were machines which may be compared to those tremendous armaments which different nations of modern Europe find necessary to insure peace and order within and respect to their frontiers from without. If those laws and tribunals are comparable to our engines of war by their object, they were much less destructive of human life, and were even capable of preventing greater bloodshed. A day will perhaps come when wars will seem absurd and criminal, and when countless tears will be shed over the millions of innocent men who have fallen on the battle-field for some national cause. Let us show the wisdom we should wish our descendants to possess if ever tribunals of arbitration succeed in bringing back a sort of golden age; let us judge of past deeds by the light of former days; let us appreciate present necessities by the light we now possess. Thus, without doing injustice to those who have gone before us, we may adopt new practical rules for new situations, and apply our unchanging principles to changing circumstances. The wave of events has swept away the Inquisition and extinguished the fires of the stake. We may bid farewell to them without regret, and without any desire to see them rekindled, but we must not assume that their use was to be entirely condemned.

[1] This is another word which has been much misused. *Exterminare* means literally to drive out, to expel, to banish. The Fourth Council of the Lateran obliged Sovereigns to *exterminare* heretics; but if we translate the Latin word by the English *exterminate*, we make it appear that the Council and Pope Innocent III. wished to make a bloody sacrifice of all heretics.

2. *The Inquisition in Particular.*

SUMMARY: Points to be remembered in connection with the nature of the institution and the number of the victims.

Many persons speak and even write of the Inquisition who would find very great difficulty in stating exactly what it was.

On this subject it is important to remember—

That there were several Inquisitions, greatly differing in their constitution, their character, and their severity.

That, as a full and impartial history of the tribunals of the Inquisition has not yet been written, their action, especially since the sixteenth century, still remains wrapped in obscurity.

That the Inquisition did not introduce either capital punishment or the stake,[1] but that it regularized the procedure against heresy. The stake is an invention of the secular power, a legacy of the Pagan Empire, and of customs resumed in the eleventh and twelfth centuries. This legacy was first accepted by an enemy of the Papacy, a Prince who has the reputation of having been a freethinker—Frederic II.

That the use of torture revived with the revival of the popularity of Roman law, and any Pope who

[1] " We might thus write all the history of penal legislation against heretics . . . almost without referring to the Canons which instituted the Inquisition. Certainly these Canons kept close to the penal laws, and sometimes even encroached upon them ; but their object was different, and their history should remain distinct " (Maillet-Hanquet, *op. cit.*, p. 87).

THE INQUISITION

ventured to reject this means of investigation would most probably have been taxed with bigotry and narrowmindedness.[1]

That the executions of heretics were ordered from the point of view that such persons were a source of danger to the community.

The number of persons condemned to death cannot be exactly stated, but it is interesting to observe how remarkably the figures are reduced when we turn from the works of prejudiced writers to those that are more impartial and better supported by evidence.

Take one remarkable example with reference to the Spanish Inquisition. A French school reader, bearing the signature of " Primaire " (a pseudonym), attributes to this Inquisition two millions of victims in ten years. A. Rambaud, in his *Histoire de la Civilisation Française* (t. 1, p. 327), gives the number as three hundred thousand for three centuries and a half. Llorente, who was very ill-disposed to the Inquisition, brings it down for the same period to thirty thousand.[2] According to Mgr. Landrieux,[3] recent German investigations reduce this still further to ten thousand ; and, finally, Gams puts it at four thousand only.[4]

---

[1] " The use of torture is evidently derived from the Roman law. It was first employed by the secular authority, and later was applied by the subordinate agents of the Inquisitors, under the orders of the latter " (Hinschius, *System der Kath. Kirchenrechts*, t. 5, p. 485).

[2] T. 4, p. 271. Exactly 31,912, to which he adds 17,659 persons burned in effigy.

[3] *L'Inquisition*, etc., p. 147. We have taken from this author the quotation from "Primaire."

[4] *Die Kirchengeschichte von Spanien*, vol. iii., sec. 2, l. 13, p. 76. The figures are disputed after p. 68.

II. The Present and the Future.

1. *The Present.*

SUMMARY : Tolerant unbelievers and fanatical unbelievers.—Testimony of Balmès, of MM. Barrès, Piou, and Picard.—Moderation of Catholics in their acts, their speeches, and their writings.

Balmès[1] well divides into two classes those men who follow no religious banner.

Some simply have no faith ; they are sceptical rather than irreligious, and freely admit the services that religion has rendered, and still renders, to society ; and the Church receives from their lips honourable testimony, which we gladly use in her defence. Tolerance is easy and natural to them, though there is little merit in it.

Others, on the contrary, profess a hatred of religion, or, rather, as they say, a hatred of the Church. " These men," says Balmès, " are intolerant in the extreme, and their intolerance is the worst of all, for it is not accompanied by any moral principle capable of restraining it." Certainly, they pride themselves on being preachers of tolerance, and make that the pretext of their war against the Church. But, as we have known liberalism which was merely another name for religious indifference, so in the mouths of these men " tolerance " may be translated as " free-thought," and of this free-thought they make a dogma, the only one they recognize—a dogma which they impose on others by all the means that the modern State places at their dis-

[1] *Le Protestantisme*, etc., t. 1, p. 167.

THE PRESENT

posal : the dispersion of religious associations, pressure put upon an army of office-holders, official teaching rendered practically obligatory by a monopoly, in fact, if not by law.[1] " You are now on the way," said M. Barrès to the freethinkers who now tyrannize over France—" you are now on the way to try a new kind of religion—a haphazard religion, which you wish to raise to the dignity of a religion of State, of which the schoolmasters are to be the beneficiaries ; and you exact penal laws against the heretics who venture to criticize your school manuals and the propositions of your schoolmasters."[2] Another representative of unbigoted unbelief, a Belgian, formulated his judgment in these terms : " They call this ' government,' but it ought rather to be called ' tyranny,' and that the worst and most odious kind of all—not tyranny by a stranger, but by compatriots ; half the nation seizing the other half by the throat, and hustling it off to the lock-up. Oh, what an abominable crew are these fanatics ! It is, I will not say a freethinker, but a thinker free from unreasoning prejudice, who cannot help proclaiming the truth."[3]

To anyone who will keep his eyes and ears open, it must be evident that, since the French Revolution, or, rather, since the advent of rationalism, and

[1] Even in Belgium M. Janson proposed to reserve all public offices for those who had made their studies in the State schools. And will not liberty be made so onerous to Catholics that the poor children in the cities will have no other but the official schools at their disposal?

[2] Educational debate in the French Chamber, January, 1910.

[3] Picard, weekly article in the *Chronique*, March 4, 1911.

even since the legists, true Catholics have not been on the side of the persecutors, but of the persecuted. It is not for the power of oppression, but for freedom, that they have fought—at one time against the despotism of Cæsar, at another against that of the sects and the Masonic lodges. The attitude they adopt everywhere to-day is described by this eloquent peroration of M. Piou : " We challenge you to fight on the field of liberty ; for if the stronger party insists on using the State, the budget, the administration of government, all public authority, merely to secure its own advantage, to crush its adversaries, and persecute them even in their consciences —this is tyranny of the most odious description. There are issues between us on which we are irreconcilably divided ; but at least let us come to an understanding, and live at liberty and peace together."[1]

Such appeals, unfortunately, are made to no purpose, when a Catholic minority finds itself opposed to an irreligious majority ; and, on the other hand, when Catholics are in the majority, according to the famous saying, " they astonish the world by their moderation." " It is time," wrote M. Goyau, " that the hateful and lying accusation should, once for all, be withdrawn—viz., that Catholics in power would refuse to others that liberty which Catholics in the minority ask of others for themselves. Belgium bears witness to the contrary."[2]

These acts, which speak more strongly than words,

[1] Educational debate in the French Chamber, 1910.
[2] *L'Œuvre du parti Catholique Belge*, in *Correspondant* of September 10, 1911. The expression was attributed to Louis Veuillot, who always denied having used it.

only confirm the unanimous declarations made by all Catholics who have taken part in public affairs in any position whatever. If some Catholic treatise, published for the use of theological students, contains a platonic dissertation on the theoretical power which the Church possesses over heretics, and contains statements which the enemies of religion seize upon with avidity,[1] no Catholic author, even in Latin, ever thinks nowadays of suggesting such persecuting measures as the enemies of religion would not hesitate to employ, however loudly they may protest their hatred of persecution.[2] Neither in Pontifical encyclicals,[3] nor in parliamentary speeches, nor books, reviews, or newspapers published by Catholics, can we find a suggestion of oppressive measures. In this matter the German Centre party is at one with the French Catholic parties and the Belgian Right. " I have said over

[1] How eager they are to find an opportunity of declaring that they are in fear of their lives! A literary man, Dr. Demade, proposed in a review to erect a statue to the Duke of Alva, for having placed at the service of Catholicism a sword which so many other men had turned against it. What an excitement there was in the Press of the Left! " These Catholics want to cut our heads off!" And yet the enemies of religion will name one of the streets in Brussels after Ferrer, one of the ringleaders of the odious and bloody revolt at Barcelona; and Catholics are told they have no right to protest against the proceedings of Ferrer's admirers. The intentions of the man himself may be gathered from the following words: " In order to show my contempt for the prejudices of religion, patriotism, and authority, I refuse to show any respect for the dead. I will not attend any funeral, or take off my hat before a dead body" (*Huelga General*, November 25, 1901; words quoted by *L'Anarchiste*, November, 1911).

[2] For instance, in reference to the persecutions in France and Portugal.

[3] See Encyclical *Immortale Dei*.

and over again," said M. Woeste,[1] " that Belgium needs to become more Christian. Can this end be attained by oppression ? No ; it is by liberty that we hope to reach it." Catholic University teaching is on the same lines. The Rector of the Catholic faculties at Toulouse, Mgr. Breton, wrote recently : " Montalembert believed, and we may believe with him, that liberty of worship, as at present established in modern nations, is a necessary consequence of the division of opinions on the subject of religion, and that the interests of the Church make tolerance a duty."[2] He had previously quoted these other words from the same author : " Accept the free fight of error against truth ; there is no life henceforth except in complete liberty for all, the same for all."[3]

2. *The Future.*

SUMMARY: Objection against Catholics : their moderation is only impotence.—Reply.—Catholics have no persecuting principle.—What they would do if they had a majority ; what they would do if religious unity were once more a fact.—Words of Lamennais.—Notorious defect of our existing institutions.—They cannot last for ever.—Conjectures as to the distant future are idle. —At present, as in the near future, tolerance is not called in question except by the Jacobins of the twentieth century.

There was once a reformer who thought himself a philanthropist. His reflections on the evil consequences of brawls and contentions led him to invent and disseminate a doctrine which absolutely forbade

---

[1] Belgian Chamber, December 1, 1910.
[2] See *Bulletin de Toulouse*, 1910, p. 422.
[3] *Ibid.*, p. 414.

THE FUTURE

the use of force on any pretext whatever, even in legitimate self-defence. One day, when walking on the highroad, he met someone who contradicted him. Being the stronger of the two, and having no hope of convincing the other man, he rushed upon him and knocked him down. When his victim, who was utterly amazed at his behaviour, ventured to protest, he explained : " I knock you down because I am sure that, so long as you do not share my opinions, you will some day try to knock me down." In this way the professor of forbearance parried by real blows in the present the problematical blows of the future, and it must be admitted that in substituting his own system for the old rules on the subject of self-defence, our philanthropist did not lose much by the exchange.

This little fable serves to illustrate the position and conduct of Catholics and the anti-Church party respectively. On the subject of tolerance the latter professes absolute ideas which the former do not share, and do not intend to share at any price ; the anti-Church party therefore claims the right to exclude them from the general truce, of which it is the self-constituted herald, and it starts against them a relentless campaign, which stops at nothing. As this anti-Church party has no other adversaries but the Catholics, it earns a very cheap reputation for magnanimity ; its tolerance, which is universal in theory, is in practice reserved for its friends.

Has this party any right to put forward its alleged fear for the future as an excuse for its violence in the present ? Has it any justification for the suggestion that the generosity of Catholics is the generosity of impotence? If we were masters, would our principles compel us to become persecutors?

We may put out of question the torture and the stake, for the more honest of our opponents are quite willing to admit that they do not suspect us of any bloodthirsty intentions. But there may be persecution without bloodshed; it is persecution when men are punished for professing any particular form of religious belief, and that is what Catholics are accused of wishing to introduce. The charge is false, as we can easily prove from Catholic doctrine.

Pagan or Jacobin reasons of State permitted violence and oppression, but what reason of Church can exist for the same? The Catholic statesman can have but one point of view—that of the public good, which demands respect for all rights, fidelity to all promises, and the Gospel in which he believes is not to be preached by violence.

Let us suppose the Catholic party with a political majority, by which we mean such a crushing majority as to make them secure against all attacks. They have in opposition a coalition of Protestants and unbelievers, whom they are bound to protect in the enjoyment of all their civil rights equally with all the citizens of the State. These non-Catholics have not, as such, committed any offence which permits them to be deprived of it; they have not failed in any social obligation. Therefore their personal liberty is unassailable; their rights must remain intact.

But let us go farther. What would Catholics do if the whole country returned to the true faith?

THE FUTURE

They would certainly endeavour to preserve the immense blessing of religious unity. But would it be their duty for this purpose to make heresy a crime, to punish it by fire and imprisonment? There is nothing to prove it. We have already quoted the admirable words of Victor Jacobs: "If ever religious unity returns, it will be reflected in the laws; but it will be equally reflected in the spirit of the age."[1] Lamennais was right when he said: "It is not given to any man to foresee what will be the exact relations between Church and State when the time comes; but it is certain that there will be a close alliance, spiritual and political, between the two societies, though we cannot tell what form it will take"[2]

We have no absurd dream of a return to the past. The true Catholic is not the reactionary that he is represented to be; he recognizes the providentially destructive influence of time, which swept away the Inquisition, as it swept away feudalism and the old Roman Empire. If he believes in the resurrection, he knows it will only give him back his body transfigured. Every age receives from the preceding ages some good which it is bound to add to and hand on to the age that succeeds. The good is handed on like a jewel in its setting; the setting, indeed, wears out, and is replaced by a new one, which, in its turn, is also discarded. Such is the law of progress, which forbids us to look too much behind us, but at the same time warns us against believing in the permanence of our existing institutions. And

[1] Article quoted, p. 672.
[2] *Dès Progrès de la Révolution*, ch. 3.

certainly an end must be put to that unrestricted licence of misrepresentation,[1] still permitted to the corrupters of the multitude, while truth possesses no practical means of stopping the mouths of the liars.

In this we see the one disadvantage under which the Church labours to-day. She has nothing to fear from honest controversy, but she has to be always on her guard against a shameless calumny which misrepresents her doctrine, travesties her worship, and throws an unmerited discredit on her ministers. But even for the preservation of religious unity it is not necessary to make heresy an offence punishable under the penal code. Catholics have only, as we think, to hope for the disappearance of that hateful and immoral habit of lying, which common sense and the instinct of social self-preservation will be forced by events to repudiate and destroy.

We think we have said more than enough to dispose of the objection, and reply to the question. The latter is only serious when it takes this form: in modern society, in the situations which we are able to understand and appreciate, would Catholics in power suppress a single one of the liberties which are so dear to the present generation ? A categorical

[1] Many persons besides Catholics see the impossible situation into which we are drifting. The opinion of a former French Minister, published in the *Action* of October, 1911, is worthy of note : " The evil which is destroying our fleet is the same which is devouring our army, our public administration, our public services, our system of parliamentary government, our whole society. This evil is anarchy—that is to say, such a disordered condition of minds and affairs that nothing is done as reason demands that it should be done, and no man behaves in accordance with the dictates of his professional or moral duty."

THE FUTURE

negative is the answer given by their acts, their words, and their very principles.

If in the course of time new social necessities arose, they would be guided by circumstances. We need not here explain what measures would then be adopted; but we may be sure that they would be such as would be necessary for the public welfare, and would be generally approved, and would not then, any more than they can now, give any reason for attack or complaint. And why should we be afraid of what would satisfy everyone?

We may add, however, that, unlike the principles of their opponents, Catholic principles contain nothing suggestive of tyranny or persecution, nothing which need alarm the most convinced advocate of reasonable liberty.

Let us have done with hypocrisy and shams. The opposition to tolerance comes, not from Catholics, but from their enemies. The Church has no desire to persecute, but she has good reason to fear persecution.[1]

[1] Probably not bloody persecution; the stake is not in fashion nowadays, though others have very gloomy views of the future. According to Dr. Gustave Lebon, " M. Georges Sorel very reasonably prophesies that the first proceeding of triumphant Socialism would be to massacre all its adversaries without mercy" (*Les Opinions et les Croyances*, p. 236).

CONCLUSION

CHRISTIANITY THE RELIGION OF LOVE

SUMMARY: Frontispiece of the manifesto of the Marnix Committee.—M. Payot's criticism: Christianity has failed as a religion of love.—Absurdity of deciding on imperfect examination.—The benefits of every good institution on earth must be weighed against accidental evils.—Blessings conferred by the Christian religion.—If the teachings of Christianity were better obeyed, many murders would be prevented in modern society.—Christianity is a religion of love, for it has made men love one another.—Religion alone can do this.—As a religion of love, it must be victorious.—Duties of Catholics: to set an example of charity and all Christian virtues; to draw men by the teaching of steadfast, intelligent, and enlightened faith; to multiply initiatives for the multitude.—The hopes of Leo XIII.

THE Marnix Committee for the Diffusion of Ideas of Justice and Liberty[1] issues manifestoes pompously entitled *Against Intolerance*. On the title-page is reproduced the famous picture of Debat-Ponsan, *Christ on the Mount*. This represents several Crusaders, an Inquisitor, a Pope, and three Kings of France,[2] surveying a pile of dead bodies lying at their feet. Most of the bodies are naked, but some clothed and recognizable—De Coligny, a shepherd of the Cévennes, and perhaps John Huss.

---

[1] As far as we know, this Committee has never defended any but Jews and Protestants.

[2] Francis I., Charles IX., and Louis XIV.

THE RELIGION OF LOVE

Behind, on the hill, stands Christ, His features wearing an expression of meekness and resignation, His hands hanging down as if in sadness and despair. Below is the legend: " And I commanded you to love one another, as I have loved you." M. Payot says more plainly: " Christianity has failed as a religion of love."

To represent in this manner, without comment, soldiers and their fallen enemies, judges and the criminals they have condemned, to display the sword without saying anything of the provocation or the threats which have necessitated its use, to point to its victims without counting those whom it has protected and saved, to charge it with accidental abuses without mentioning its benefits—this is the way to foment discord and hatred, but by calumny. In this way we might lay the responsibility for countless murders and assassinations on the noblest and most necessary institutions, and charge infinite misfortune and suffering to the family and property.

Man has always two voices speaking within him, persuading him to good or evil. Opposed as they are to each other, they divide humanity into two hostile armies. Thus law and authority cause insurrections; marriage produces adulteries; property excites the cupidity of the thief; human life offers a temptation to the assassin; the mention of God and religion irritates the impious and the proud. Some unruly rebel, some enemy of all that is good, will rise against every kind of order and authority; and the more essential the good, the more seriously does its assailant disturb the peace of society.

But is it fair to judge of an institution by the disorders caused by its adversaries? Is it reasonable even to make it responsible for the abuses committed by its defenders? Can we lay to the charge of religion proceedings in which it had no part, or number among its victims those criminals who would have been condemned under any penal code in the world? And, above all, do not the benefits which flow from religion as from their natural source more than counterbalance occasional evils? For one war declared on account of religion, how many treaties of peace has religion brought about? for one outburst of fanaticism, how many reconciliations? for one act of injustice, how many reparations? for one person placed under restraint, how many have been set free? This is not the place to describe all that the Church has done for the pacification and civilization of the pagan world, the barbarian world, the savage world, nor all the benefits of the Church's intervention in favour of slaves, of women, and of children. The reverence, and protection, and love that Christianity has secured for children alone should be enough to wipe out from the minds of sensible men the remembrance of punishments and struggles in which faith has been concerned, and make them proclaim the inestimable value of the religion of the Cross.

Let us not dispute the value of those services by sharing the opinions or believing the lies of those who attribute the softening of manners to irresistible evolution or necessary progress. What becomes of rights in the present day in societies which have lost the faith? What shall we say of the abominable practices introduced to prevent the birth of

THE RELIGION OF LOVE 353

children—fœticide and artificial sterility—which not only exist, but have become fashionable, and have found apologists and defenders? An official census shows that eight hundred thousand children are born alive in France every year; and friends of the atheist Republic calculate that miscarriages are more numerous than births! Thus, in a single year and in a single country the number of innocent victims of theoretical or practical irreligion is ten times greater than the number of heretics ever sent to the stake on account of religion. It is true that the murders of those little beings, who cannot even complain, are committed in secret, and therefore make no sensation; but is the fact any less deplorable? And when we see the cruel and sanguinary instincts that are developed with unbelief, and the deeds of violence that increasing selfishness[1] leads men to perpetrate, sometimes on savages who cannot defend themselves, sometimes on honest people who stand in the way of their passion; we may well ask ourselves whether a civilization which has filled Paris, the City of Light, with Apaches will go on long without some terrible bloodshed. Napoleon said of nations without religion: "They are not to be governed by ordinary means; the only way of dealing with them is by a charge of grape-shot."[2]

[1] "The melancholy results of the neutral education which is now being introduced are only too visible. Unscrupulous greed and selfishness are its bitter fruits. It becomes difficult to induce citizens to care for anything but their own selfish material interests" (Picard, in the *Chronique* of Sunday, June 4, 1911.)

[2] Quoted by M. Louis Ollivier in the French Chamber on April 12, 1905, in the discussion of the law of Separation of Church and State.

CONCLUSION

Has the Catholic religion failed as a religion of love ? If you would know, ask if it has made men love one another ; and what an eloquent answer will you receive in its name from the innumerable heroes of charity, who form and lead what has been recently called " the square battalion of sacrifice and devotion ;"[1] from the Sisters in charge of its lazarets, its hospitals, its orphanages, and its old men's homes ; from its missionaries, who have at times been the authorized peace-makers between hostile nations, and whose whole life is one long act of self-sacrificing love ! The Catholic religion might answer you by pointing to its penal justice itself, the salutary influence of which we have described ; it might answer you by all its saints and those very men who were conspicuous for their zeal against heresy. Even Lea admits that cruelty to heretics was sometimes accompanied in the same minds by an infinite love for men.[2]

Let us remember this, that all the repressive action of the Church is justifiable only if it proceeds from love for men. Fanaticism and bitterness may sometimes have been accidentally mixed with it, as a result of human weakness ; but, unlike other forms of religion, Christianity forbids us to hate, and only permits us to punish in order to save—to save, if possible, those who are punished ; to save at least those who would otherwise be corrupted by them.

Christianity has not failed as a religion of love ; it has made men love. Nay, more : religion alone

---

[1] Henri de Lavedan, in his discourse on the rewards for virtue (French Academy, December 7, 1911).

[2] *Op. cit.*, p. 239.

can produce real love, for how can love be produced by negation or scepticism ? How should the seeds of generosity and love be sown by an unbelief which directs all its aspirations and all its desires to those visible goods for which men quarrel and fight ? " Priest, how I hate you !"-" And how I love you !" This little dialogue, which took place in the street between a priest and a rabid Socialist, summarizes the sentiments inspired by a faith which is called " intolerant," and a free-thought which prides itself on its tolerance.

Christianity has not failed as a religion of love : as a religion of love it is destined to triumph.

When the true religion cannot rely on the secular power or on any purely human support, it still retains in charity its great power of expansion and conversion ; and our first duty as Catholics is to secure for that power its fullest development, and at the same time to practise generous and sincere tolerance in private life. Let us declare ourselves opposed, on the one hand, to that overweening erudition which magnifies its flimsiest conjectures into irrefutable arguments against religion ; and, on the other hand, to that narrow-minded orthodoxy which, by exaggerating the purport of authoritative definitions and explanations of the truth, throws suspicion on the loyalty of others. Let us not make of religion an obstacle to serious and honest work; but, while we refuse to listen to pretentious charlatanism, let us give free scope to real science, Let a delicate consideration for all acquired rights and a scrupulous fidelity to all conventions show that the very principles of our religion engender a sincere, practical tolerance, and that we need not sacrifice a single truth for fear of offending any conscience.

Let us do our best to bring men nearer to us; let us give them what they need—a *clear and honest statement* of our principles, without either boasting or diffidence; *conduct* in accordance with the lofty rules of our faith, so that in their intercourse with us they may confidently seek rest for their minds and their hearts. Let scrupulous veracity in our words, strict justice in our actions, and considerate kindness to all,[1] show what moral vigour and nobility religion gives to men; and thus let our intelligent and enlightened faith dissipate the prejudices of ignorance.

The unique position of the Catholic Church must strike every thinking person. That Church stands alone, to excite the jealousy of every despotism, to withstand the attack of every heresy. Notwithstanding their almost infinite diversity, all forms of impiety are united in the endeavour to bring about the downfall of the Catholic hierarchy, and so of religious society. They are all united against what they call " clericalism." Dogma irritates them less than authority in religion.

All sects are united for the attack upon Catholic unity. The civilized world has been tending, not since yesterday only, but for a long time, to separate into two divisions—the Church and anti-Church. The latter is the common name of all heresies, all

[1] Gentleness, prudence, and patience " were the only weapons of Christianity in its first days; they should be the only weapons of Christianity under trial " (Letter of Lamartine, 1829, to M. De Marcellus at Rome. See Maréchal, *Lamennais et Lamartine*, p. 177).

THE RELIGION OF LOVE

schisms, and all apostasies. The oldest heresiarchs discussed dogma only to find a pretext for rebellion; the Councils only assembled to cement the Church built upon Peter by Jesus Christ. Opponents of every class, deceived by intellectual illusions and dazzled by the prospect of innovations, have had one cry against the Church, which has re-echoed from age to age, from Donatism to Catharism, from Catharism to the Reformation, from the Reformation to the Revolution, from the Revolution to Anarchy. But this unity shows another common character of all these revolts against the Church's authority: their positive elements have been absorbed in the progress of the theandric work; the revolts themselves have ended in utter ruin. The same thing happens always: when man gives up God, he finds only nothingness.

This constant opposition to the Church will strike all men, at least those who preserve the elements of moral vigour and sanity; for when they examine the claims of the Church they cannot but feel that attraction which is so powerful at a time when so many men are foundering in a sea of doubt; the attraction of that supernatural certitude which the Church alone is able to give without interfering with the work of science. Man has need of both reason and faith, of movement and equilibrium; and that religion is true which gives him faith and equilibrium, which invites him to movement, and leads him to God.

The special dangers of the people, on whom our Lord looked with such loving pity, call for the zealous efforts of prudent and well-instructed teachers. Everywhere, we may say, the civil Government, even when it is not actively hostile, allows a free hand to all doctrinal attacks upon faith and morals. We are further removed from the Middle Ages by the opinions that find favour than by the centuries that have intervened ; and we can no longer count on the silent preaching of the Christs and Madonnas at the corners of our streets, nor on the calls to prayer that echoed of old, even in the dead of night, nor on official care to save men from seduction. The images and statues that meet the eyes of poor and rich alike, as they leave their homes, are full of indecent suggestiveness. Newspapers and other publications are offered for sale whose very titles are sometimes filthy or blasphemous ; and the worst of it all is that calumny is added to the insult—calumny against dogmas, so distorted as to be unrecognizable ; calumny against persons, with circumstantial details invented to make it more readily believed.[1]

The men who are deceived by these things are our brothers, and it is our duty to give them, by the vigour of our initiative, the constancy of our efforts, and the development of our generosity, the support, the encouragement, and the protection, which the law refuses them.

If the general situation has its shadows, yet it offers to the man of faith a magnificent work, worthy of his best efforts—the work of bringing about the victory of religion by the only weapons which

[1] For instance, a charge is made against a priest ; no name is given, but an alleged photograph of the incriminated priest is produced. No one can be recognized, and so refutation is made impossible.

liberty allows. The work is both Divine and human —Divine by grace, without which no man can come to Jesus Christ ; human by the labour which that grace generally demands, and to which it gives inspiration.

Let us give ourselves wholly to the accomplishment of this great purpose; let us be persuaded that in the present crisis lukewarmness is almost as bad as irreligion. Let our faith refuse no light, let our hearts be open to every virtue, let our hands be ready for any good work. Two futures are entrusted to us—that of the civilized world and that of worlds that are still barbarian.

Weary of their unhappiness, tired of being the sport of false hopes and the victims of selfish and ambitious leaders, men will turn to the truth they have so long refused to acknowledge ;[1] they will consider it with a calm and unprejudiced attention ; and they will be surprised to find so near them in the Church what they have so vainly and so laboriously sought for outside.

Who are we, it may be asked, to use such language as this ? It is not ours ; it is the language which came eighteen years ago from the heart of an illustrious and venerable Pontiff—a heart always full of generous ideas and desires. This is what Leo XIII. said and prophesied in his memorable Apostolic Letter to the Princes and people of the

[1] " We have not found in the Republic either work, or peace, or justice, or the security we counted on finding there ; we will return to the Church." M. Colly, a Socialist Deputy, thus interprets the sentiments of many French railway employés (French Chamber : debate on the reinstatement of railway workers, 1911).

whole world. He, too, longed for a social and political restoration of all things in Christ, and in the contemplation of that sublime prospect he wrote those burning words of prayer and hope with which this work shall be concluded :

" With these thoughts in Our mind and ardent yearnings in Our heart, We see from afar what would be the new order of things that would arise from the earth, and nothing could be sweeter to Us than the contemplation of the benefits that would flow from it. It can hardly be imagined what immediate and rapid progress would be made all over the earth in all manner of greatness and prosperity, with the establishment of tranquillity and peace, the promotion of studies, the founding and the multiplying on Christian lines, according to Our directions, of associations for the cultivators of the soil, for workmen and tradesmen, through whose agency rapacious usury would be put down and a large field opened for useful labours.

" And these abundant benefits would not be confined within the limits of civilized nations, but, like an overcharged river, would flow far and wide. It must be remembered, as We observed at the outset, that an immense number of races have been waiting all through the long ages to receive the light of truth and civilization. Most certainly the counsels of God with regard to the eternal salvation of peoples are far removed above the understanding of man ; yet, if miserable superstition still prevails in so many parts of the world, the blame must be attributed in no small measure to religious dissensions. For, as far as it is given to human reason to judge

THE RELIGION OF LOVE 361

from the nature of events, this seems, without doubt, to be the mission assigned by God to Europe, to go on by degrees carrying Christian civilization to every portion of the earth. The beginnings and first growth of this great work which sprang from the labours of former centuries were rapidly receiving large developments, when all of a sudden the discord of the sixteenth century broke out. Christendom was torn with quarrels and dissensions, Europe exhausted with contests and wars, and the sacred missions felt the baneful influence of the times. While the causes of dissensions still remain, what wonder is it that so large a portion of mankind is held enthralled with barbarous customs and insane rites ?

" Let us one and all, then, for the sake of the common welfare, labour with equal assiduity to restore the ancient concord. In order to bring about this concord, and spread abroad the benefits of the Christian revelation, the present is the most seasonable time, for never before have the sentiments of human brotherhood penetrated so deeply into the souls of men, and never in any age has man been seen to seek out his fellow-men more eagerly, in order to know them better and to help them. Immense tracts of land and sea are traversed with incredible rapidity, and thus extraordinary advantages are offered, not only for commerce and scientific investigations, but also for the propagation of the word of God, from the rising of the sun to the going down of the same.

" We are well aware of the long labours involved in the restoration of that order of things which We desire ; and it may be that there are those who consider that We are far too sanguine, and look for things that are rather to be wished for than expected. But We unhesitatingly place all Our hope and confidence in the Saviour of mankind, Jesus Christ, well remembering what great things have been achieved in times past by the folly of the Cross and its preaching, to the astonishment and confusion of the wisdom of the world."[1]

[1] Letter *Præclara Gratulationis*, June 10, 1894.

BIBLIOGRAPHY[1]

Acta Conciliorum, Ed. Harduin, Parisiis, 1814-15.
AMPHOUX, H.: Michel de l'Hôpital et la liberté de conscience au xiiie siècle, Paris, 1900.
ARNETH, A. VON: Maria Theresa und Joseph II. Ihre Correspondenz, 3 Bd., Wien, 1867 (R. Br.).
BALMÈS, J.: Le Protestantisme comparé avec le Catholicisme, dans ses rapports avec la civilisation européenne, 3e éd. Revised by De Blanche-Raffin, 2 vols., Bruxelles, 1854.
BARBEYRAC, J.: Traité de la morale des Pères de l'Église Amsterdam, 1728 (Berl.).
BARBEYRAC, J.: Du Pouvoir des Souverains et de la Liberté de Conscience. In two lectures, translated from the Latin of M. Noodt, Professor of Law in the University of Leyden. With notes by John Frederick Gregorovius and the translator.
BARONIUS: Annales ecclesiastici (cum continuatione Raynaldi), éd. Theiner, 37 vols., Bar-le-Duc, 1869-1883.

---

[1] The Bibliography is limited to the books quoted, and in order to facilitate reference, a note is added to show where the older and rarer works are to be found.

(Berl.): Royal Library, Berlin.
(Bonn.): Royal University Library, Bonn.
(R. Br.): Royal Library, Brussels.
(Boll. B.): Bollandists' Library, Brussels.
(Gand): University Library, Ghent.
(Br. M.): British Museum, London.
(U. L.): University Library, Louvain.
(C. T. L.): Jesuit Theological College Library, Louvain.
(Mün.): Royal Library, Munich.

BARTHOLOTTI, J. N.: Exercitatio politico-theologica, in qua de libertate conscientiae et de receptarum romano-theutonica religionum tolerantia), Viennæ, de Kurtzbek, 1782 (Berl.).

BARTOLO, ABBÉ SALVATORE DI: Nuova esposizione dei criteri teologici, Roma, 1904.

BASNAGE, H.: Tolérance des religions, Rotterdam, 1684 (Berl.).

BAYLE, P.: Œuvres diverses, La Haye, 1727, t. ii. (C. T. L.).

BIANCHI DE LUCCA (O.F.M.): Della potestà e della politia della chiesa, 5 vols., Roma, 1746 (C. T. L.).

BILLOT, L. (CARD., S.J.): Tractatus de Ecclesia Christi, t. ii., De habitudine Ecclesiæ ad civilem societatem, Prati, 1910.

BODINUS, J.: Colloquium Heptaplomeres de rerum sublimium arcanis abditis, e codicibus manuscriptis bibliothecæ academicæ Gissensis cum varia lectione aliorum apographorum nunc primum typis describendum curavit Ludovicus Noack, Philosophicæ doctor, in universitate Gissensi Professor extraordinarius. Suerini Megaloburgiensium, 1857 (Gand).

BOEHMERI, I. H.: Ius ecclesiasticum Protestantium, Halæ, 1717 (C. T. L.).

BOUCHÉ-LECLERCQ: L'Intolérance religieuse et la politique, Paris, 1911.

BOURDALOUE: Pensées sur divers sujets de religion et de morale, Louvain, 1823.

BOUTARD, CH.: Lamennais, sa vie et ses doctrines, 2ᵉ vol., Le Catholicisme libéral, Paris, 1908.

BRANDI (S.J.): Del potere coattivo della chiesa (Civilta Cattolica, 18ᵉ série, vol. vii., 1902, pp. 1 et suiv.).

BRUNNER, S.: Die theologische Dienerschaft am Hofe Joseph II., Wien, 1868.

BUSHER, L.: Religious Peace; or a play for liberty of conscience (in a volume entitled " Tracts on the Liberty of Conscience "), London, 1646 (Br. M.).

CARTELLIERI-STECHELE: Chronicon universale anonymi laudunensis, Paris, 1909.

DE CAUZONS, ABBÉ THOMAS: Histoire de l'Inquisition en France. Les origines de l'Inquisition, 1ᵉʳ vol., Paris, 1909.

BIBLIOGRAPHY

Cavagnis (Card.) : Institutiones iuris publici ecclesiastici, 3 vols., Romæ, 1906.

Choupin, L. (S.J.) : L'Inquisition. La responsabilité de l'Église dans la répression de l'hérésie au moyen âge, Tournai, 1909.

Chowancz, J. : Die Inquisition ; was und wie sie wirklich war, Aachen, 1857.

Comte, A. : Cours de philosophie positive, 6 vols., Paris, 1830-1842.

Comte, A. : Système de politique positive, 4 vols., Paris, 1851-1854.

(Anonymous): Contre l'intolérance (Manifesto of the Marnix Committee, Brussels), Bruxelles, 1901.

Corpus iuris canonici, Ed. Friedberg, 2 vols., Lipsiæ, 1881.

Damoiseaux, M. : La Formation de la Société politique belge, Bruxelles, 1907.

Dargaud, J. M. : Histoire de la Liberté religieuse en France et de ses fondateurs, 4 vols., Paris, 1859.

Descamps, Ed. : Études sur les fondateurs de la science du droit, I. Hugo Grotius et le droit naturel, Louvain, 1883.

De Stoop, Em. : Essai sur la diffusion du manichéisme dans l'empire romain (No. 28 of a collection of works published by the Faculty of Philosophy and Letters in the University of Ghent), Gand, 1909.

Döllinger, Ign. : Kirche und Kirchen, Papsthum und Kirchenstaat, München, 1861.

Douais, Mgr. : L'Inquisition, Ses origines, sa procédure, Paris, 1906.

Duhem, P. : Physique de Croyant (extrait des Annales de Philosophie Chrétiennes), Paris, 1905.

Duhem, P. : La Théorie Physique, son objet et sa structure, Paris, 1906.

Duplessis d'Argentré, C. : Collectio iudiciorum de novis erroribus, etc., t. ii., Parisis, 1728.

Eymericus, N. (O.P.) : Directorium Inquisitorum, Romæ, ædibus populi romani, 1585.

Febronius, J. (de Hontheim) : De Statu Ecclesiæ et legitima potestate romani Pontificis ad reuniendos dissidentes in religione christianos compositus, ed. altera. Bullioni, 1765 (U. L.).

FOUILLÉE, A. : L'idée moderne du droit en France (Revue des Deux Mondes, 1878).

FOURNIER, P. : H. Charles Lea. Histoire de l'Inquisition au moyen âge (Revue Hist. Eccl., t. iii., Louvain, 1902, p. 708 ss.).

Fragmenta Vaticana. Mosaicarum et romanarum Legum collatio, ed. Mommsen-Krüger, Berolini, 1890.

FRÉDÉRIC II. DE PRUSSE : De la superstition et de la religion, Works, vol. i., Berlin, in folio, 1846 (R. Br.).

FREDERICHS, J. : Robert Le Bougre, premier inquisiteur général en France, Gand, 1892.

FREDERICHS, J. : De Kettervervolgingen van Philips Van den Elzas, Gent, 1890.

FRÉDÉRICQ, P. : Corpus documentorum Inquisitionis hæreticæ pravitatis Neerlandicæ (1025-1528), 1899-1903, 5 vols.

FRIEDBERG, AEM : Die Grenzen zwischen Staat und Kirche, Tübingen, 1872.

FROMMEL, G. : Les destinées de l'individualité morale et religieuse à travers le développement du christianisme catholique (Collection, Foi et Vie), Paris-Genève, 1903.

FUHRMANN, C. H. : De Tolerantiæ Religiosæ effectibus civilibus, Halæ, 1726 (Berl.).

FUSTEL DE COULANGES, N. : Questions historiques, Paris, 1893.

Gaï Institutiones, ed. Krüger and Studemund (Collectio librorum iuris anteiustiniani, t. i.), Berolini, 1905.

GAMS : Kirchengeschichte von Spanien, 5 vols., Regensburg, 1862-1879.

GÉNIER, R. (O.P.) : Vie de S. Euthyme le Grand, Paris, 1909.

GIRON, A. : La liberté de conscience à Rome (Bulletins de l'Académie Royale de Belgique, 63rd year, 3rd series, t. xxv., p. 113), Bruxelles, 1893.

GLANVILL, J. : The Vanity of Dogmatizing, etc. (or Confidence in Opinions manifested in a Discourse of the Shortness and Uncertainty of our Knowledge and its Causes ; with Some Reflections on Peripateticism, and an Apology for Philosophy), London, 1660 (Br. M.).

GLANVILL, J. : Scepsis scientifica or confest Ignorance. the Way to Science (in an essay of the vanity of dogmatizing and confident opinion, with a reply to the exceptions of the learned Thomas Callius), London, 1665 (Br. M.).

GLANVILL, J. : Scir^e tuum nihil est, or the Author's Defence to the Vanity of Dogmatizing, against the exceptions of the learned Thomas Albin in his late scire, London, 1665 (Br. M.).

GRAEZ, H.: Geschichte der Juden, 2 vols., Leipzig, 1868-1878.

GOYAU, G.: L'Allemagne religieuse, tt. iii. et iv., Le catholicisme, Paris, 1909.

GOYAU, G.: L'œuvre du parti catholique belge (Correspondant [Brussels], t. ccxliv., 1911, p. 1016 ss.).

GROTIUS, H.: De Imperio summarum potestatum circa sacra, Neapoli, 1780 (C. T. L.).

GUIDO, B. (O.P.): Practica Inquisitionis Heretice Pravitatis (Publié par Mgr. Douais), Paris, 1886.

GUIRAUD, J.: Cartulaire de Notre-Dame de Prouille, preceded by a study of Albigensianism in Languedoc in the twelfth and thirteenth centuries, 2 vols., Paris 1907.

HAEGERMANN: Die Erklärungen der Menschen- und Bürgerrechte in den ersten amerikanischen Staatsverfassungen (Historische Studien herausgegeben von E. Ebering, 78stes Heft, 1910).

HARRINGTON, JAMES: Political Aphorisms, London, 1659 (Br. M.).

HAUCK, A.: Kirchengeschichte Deutschlands, 2 Theil, Leipzig, 1900.

HAVET, J.: L'Hérésie et le Bras séculier au moyen âge jusqu'au treizième siècle (Bibliothèque de l'École des Chartes, t. xli., 1880, p. 488 ss. and p. 570 ss.), Paris, 1880.

HINSCHIUS, P.: System des Katholischen Kirchenrechts mit besonderer Rücksicht auf Deutschland, 6 vols., Berlin, 1869-1897.

HUYTTENS DE TERBECQ, E.: Discussions du Congrès national de Belgique en 1830-1831, 5 vols., Bruxelles, 1844-45.

JACOBS, V.: Les droits naturels de l'homme (Revue Générale, 46e année, 1880, p. 663 ss.).

(ANONYMOUS) : Jefferson's Notes on the State of Virginia, with the appendices complete (to which is subjoined a sublime and argumentative dissertation on M. Jefferson's Religious Principles), Baltimore, 1800 (Br. M.).

JORDAN, E. : La Responsabilité de l'Église dans la répression de l'hérésie au moyen âge. See Annales de Philosophie Chrétiennes, tt. iv. (1907), vi. (1908), viii. (1909), ix. (1909), Paris.

JURIEU, P. : Des Droits des deux souverains en matière de religion, la conscience et le Prince (written to destroy the dogma of the indifference of religions, and of universal tolerance, against a book entitled " Commentaire Philosophique sur ces paroles de la Parabole ' Contrainsles d'entrer ' "), Rotterdam, 1687 (Br. M.).

KISSELSTEIN, G. (ABBÉ) : Étude sur " L'attitude du Clergé français dans la longue lutte de l'Église et de l'État au sujet du mariage " (Séminaire historique de l'Université de Louvain, Rapport sur les travaux de 1908-09), Louvain, 1910.

LABERTHONIÈRE, L. (ABBÉ) : Dogme et Théologie (Annales de Philos. Chrétienne, 4th series, t. iv., sept. 1907 et ss.).

LABROQUIÈRE, A. : De l'Influence du Droit Canonique sur la législation criminelle, Bastia, 1877.

LACORDAIRE, H. : Mélanges (Œuvres du R. P. Lacordaire, t. ix.), Paris, 1886.

LAMENNAIS, F. DE : Des progrès de la Révolution et de la guerre contre l'Église, Paris, 1829.

LAMY, ÉT. : La psychologie d'un révolutionnaire, Le conventionnel André Dumont (articles written for the Correspondant, t. ccxxxix., 1910, pp. 345, 347 ss.).

LANDRIEUX, MGR. : L'Inquisition, Les Temps, les Causes, les Faits, Paris, 1911.

LANSON, G. : L'esprit scientifique et la méthode de l'histoire littéraire (Revue de l'Université de Bruxelles, 1909-10, pp. 296-307).

LAPPARENT, A. DE : La recherche scientifique et la Foi (Revue Pratique d'Apologétique, t. ii., p. 266 ss.), Paris, 1906.

LAVISSE, E. : Histoire de France, depuis les origines jusqu'à la Révolution, Paris, 1903.

BIBLIOGRAPHY

LEA, H. CH. : A History of the Inquisition in the Middle Ages (3 vols., New York, 1888). A French translation by Salomon Reinach, with preface by Paul Frédéricq, was published in Paris in 1900 (3 vols.), and a German translation by Hansen (Bonn, 1905).

LE BON, H. : Les Opinions et les Croyances, Genèse-Évolution, Paris, 1911.

LECANUET (PR. OR.) : L'Église de France et la troisième République, 2 vols., Paris, 1910.

LECANUET (PR. OR.) : Montalembert, 3 vols., Paris, 1898.

LE DANTEC, J. : Biologie constructive et Biologie destructive. (Revue de l'Université de Bruxelles, 1909-10, pp. 308-318.)

LEMAÎTRE, J. : Fénelon, Deuxième conférence, Paris (s.d.), 8th édition.

LEO XIII. : Lettres Apostoliques, Encycliques, Brefs, etc. (edited by the "Maison de la Bonne Presse"), Paris.

LÉPICIER, A. M. (O.S.M.) : De Stabilitate et Progressu Dogmatis, Romæ, 1908.

LESSING, G. : Nathan der Weise, Lessings Werke, Kurz Ausgabe, Leipzig, Bd. ii., 1875, pp. 261-417.

L'HOSPITAL, M. : Œuvres complètes, 2 vols., précédées d'un essai sur sa vie et ses ouvrages, Paris, 1824. (Boll. Br.).

LIPSIUS, JUSTUS : Politicorum sive civilis Doctrinæ libri sex qui ad Principatum maxime spectant. De una religione adversus Dialogistam liber, Opera omnia, 4 vols., Vesalicæ, 1675, tomus iv.

LOCKE, J. : The Works of John Locke, 4 vols., 8th ed., London, 1777 (C. T. L.).

LOENING, EDG. : Geschichte des deutschen Kirchenrechts, 2 vols., Strassburg, 1895.

LONCHAY, H. : Les édits des princes-évêques de Liége en matière d'hérésie au xvie siècle (P. Frédéricq. Travaux du cours pratique d'histoire nationale, Université de Liége, Gand et La Haye, fasc. ii.), 1884.

DE LUCA, MAR. (S.J.) : Institutiones Iuris Ecclesiastici Publici, 2 vols., Romæ, 1901.

LUCHAIRE, A. : Innocent III., La croisade des Albigeois, Paris, 1905.

BIBLIOGRAPHY

MACAULAY, LORD : The History of England, London, 10th ed., 5 vols., 1854.

MAILLET-HANQUET : L'Église et la répression sanglante de l'hérésie (Bibliothèque de la Faculté de Philosophie et Lettres de l'Université de Liége, fasc. xvi.), Liège, 1909.

MARÉCHAL, CH. : Lamennais et Lamartine, Paris, 1907.

MAULTROIT : Voy. TRAILHÉ.

MAZELLA, E. (CARD.) : De Religione et Ecclesia, éd. ii., Romæ, 1880.

MEYHOFFER, I. : Le martyrologe protestant des Pays-Bas, 1523-1597, Nessonvaux, 1907.

MILTON, JOHN : Thoughts on True Religion, Schism, and Toleration (by John Milton, Author of the " Paradise Lost," and other works. To which are added remarks on essentials in religion, charitableness, and uncharitableness, extracted from the writings of Isaac Watts, D.D.), Harlow, 1811 (Br. M.).

MILTON, JOHN : Areopagitica : A Speech for the Liberty of Unlicensed Printing, with notes for the use of Schools, by T. S. Osborn, M.A., London, 1873 (Br. M.).

MILTON, JOHN : Of True Religion, Heresies, Schism, Toleration, and what Best Means may be used against the Growth of Popery. The author, G. M., London, 1673 (Br. M.).

MOLINIER, CH. : L'Église et la Société cathares (Revue Historique, tt. xciv. et xcv., 1907).

MOLINIER, CH. : L'Inquisition dans le Midi de la France au xiiie et au xive siècle, Paris, 1881.

MOMMSEN, TH. : Le droit pénal romain, trad. Duquesne, 3 vols., Paris, 1907.

MONIN, (ABBÉ) : L'Inquisition (étude citée dans le rapport sur les travaux du séminaire historique de l'Université de Louvain en 1904-05), Louvain, 1905.

MONTESQUIEU, CH. DE : De l'Esprit des lois, 4 vols. in 24mo., Amsterdam-Leipzig, 1759.

NEWMAN, J. H. (CARD.) : Open Letter to His Grace the Duke of Norfolk (Difficulties of Anglicans, vol. ii.), London.

NOODT, G. : Dissertatio de religione ab imperio iure gentium libera, Lugduni Batavorum, 1706 (Br. M.).

BIBLIOGRAPHY

Parisis, Mgr. : Instruction pastorale sur le droit divin dans l'Église, Bruxelles, 1846.
Paulsen, Fr. : System der Ethik, 5e éd., Berlin, 1900.
Paulus, N. : Protestantismus und Toleranz im 16. Jahrhundert, Freiburg i. B., 1911.
Philipot, J. : Les Justes Bornes de la Tolérance, avec la défense des mystères du Christianisme, Amsterdam, 1691 (Br. M.).
Pilati, C. : Di una Riforma d'Italia, Ossia dei mezzi di riformare i più cattivi costumi e le più perniciosi leggi d'Italia, 2e éd., Villafranca, 1770 (Br. M.).
Pirenne, H. : Histoire de Belgique, 4 vols., Bruxelles, 1902, suiv.
Poincare, H. : Sur la valeur objective des théories physiques (Revue de Métaphysique et de Morale, x., 1902, pp. 263-293).
Poincaré, H. : La valeur de la science, Paris, 1905.
Poincaré, H. : La science et l'hypothèse, Paris (sans date).
Potter, F. de : L'union des catholiques et des libéraux dans les Pays-Bas, Bruxelles, 1829.
Poullet, Ed. : Histoire du droit pénal dans l'ancien duché de Brabant (Mémoires de l'Académie de Belgique, etc., tt. xxxiii. et xxxv.), 2 vols., in-4e, Bruxelles, 1867-1870.
Proudhon, P. G. : De la justice dans la Révolution et dans l'Église, Nouvelle édition, revue et corrigée, 12 fascicules in-8e, Bruxelles, 1860.
Rambaud : Histoire de la civilisation française, 2e éd., Paris, 1887.
Pufendorf, Sam : De Habitu Religionis Christianæ ad vitam civilem, Bremiæ, 1687, (Berl.).
Reiffenstuel, A. (F. M.) : Ius canonicum universum, 7 vols., Paris, 1864-1870.
Reinhardt, J. G. : Meditationes de jure principum Germaniæ, cum primis Saxoniæ, circa sacra ante tempora reformationis exercito, Halæ, 1717 (Berl.).
Rousseau, J. J. : Du Contrat social, Œuvres, 18 vols., in-4e, Paris, 1739.
Rousselot, P. : Les yeux de la foi (Recherches de Science Religieuse, t. i.), Paris, 1910.
Rube, J. C. : Problema iuridicum, voyez Thomas.

Rube, J. C. : De Iure Principis circa hæreticos (Thèses inaugurales), Halæ, 1697 (Berl.).

Ruffini, Fr. : La libertà religiosa, vol. i., Storia dell' idea, Torino, 1901.

Sabatier, A. : Esquisse d'une Philosophie de la Religion d'après la psychologie et l'histoire, 5e éd., Paris, 1898.

Sacrorum Conciliorum nova et amplissima Collectio, ed. Mansi, Florentiæ, 1759-1798.

Anonymous : Sammlung (vollständige) aller Schriften die durch Veranlassung der Allerhöchsten kaiserl. Toleranz und Reformations-Edikten, auch anderer Verordnungen, 5 vols., Wien, 1782 (Berl.).

Sexter Band, Strassburg, 1786 (Bonn.).

Saurin, E. : Réflexions sur les droits de la conscience, etc. Utrecht, 1697 (Bonn.).

Simon, J. : La Liberté de Conscience, Paris, 1857.

Sorel, G. : Réflexions sur la Violence, 2e éd., Paris, 1910.

Taine, H. : Les origines de la France contemporaine, Paris, 1876-1894.

Tamburinus, P. : Prælectiones de Ecclesia Christi et universa iurisprudentia ecclesiastica, quas habuit in academia Ticinensi, 2 vols., in-8° (Opus posthumum), Lipsiæ, 1845 (Br. M.).

Tanon, L. : Histoire des Tribunaux de l'Inquisition en France, Paris, 1893.

Taparelli, Luigi (S.J.) : Saggio teoretico di Dritto Naturale, 2 vols., Roma, 1855.

Tarquini (Card., S.J.) : Iuris ecclesiastici publici institutiones, 13e éd., Romæ, 1890.

Taylor, Jeremy : Treatises of (1) The Liberty of Prophesying ; (2) Prayer ex Tempore ; (3) Episcopacie (together with a sermon preached at Oxon, on the anniversary of the 5th of November), London, 1648 (Br. M.).

Theodosiani Codicis libri xvi. cum Constitutionibus sirmondianis et leges novellæ ad theodosianum pertinentes, ed. Mommsen et Mayer, 3 vols., Berolini, 1905.

Thomas (Abbe) : Voyez de Cauzons.

Thomasius, Chr. : Problema iuridicum an Hæresis sit crimen ? Halæ, 1697 (Berl.).

BIBLIOGRAPHY

THOMASIUS, CHR. : Vollständige Erläuterung der Kirchen-Rechtgelahrheit, oder gründliche Abhandlung vom Verhältniss der Religion gegen den Staat, über Sam. Puffendorffii tract. De Habitu religionis christianæ ad vitam civilem (Erster Theil.), Franckfurth, 1738 (Berl.).

THOMASIUS, CHR. : De Iure Principis circa Hæreticos, Halæ, 1697 (B. Berl.).

THOMASSEN, CHRIST. U. BRENNEYSEN, R. : Das Recht Evangelischer Fürsten in theologischen Streitigkeiten, Halle, 1713 (Berl.).

TRAILHE ET MAULTROIT (ABBÉS) : Questions sur la tolérance, 2ᵉ vol., Genève, 1758 (Boll. Br.).

TRAUTMANSDORFF, CHAN. DE : De la Tolérance ecclésiastique et civile (Work written in Latin by Thaddeus Trautmansdorff, Count of the Roman Empire, Canon of the Metropolitan Church of Olmutz, and pupil of the Germano-Hungarian College of Pavia), translated by Citizen P. S. S., Paris, 1796 (Br. M.).

Ulpiani liber singularis Regularum. Pauli libri v. sententiarum. Fragmenta minora, sæc. p. Chr. nat. ii. et iii., ed. Krüger, Berolini, 1878.

VACANDARD, E. (ABBÉ) : Vie de Saint Bernard, 2ᵉ éd., Paris, 1910.

VACANDARD, E. (ABBÉ) : L'Inquisition (Historical and critical study on the coercive power of the Church), 2nd ed., Paris, 1907.

VACANDARD, E. (ABBÉ) : Études de Critique et d'Histoire religieuse, 2nd series, Paris, 1910.

VIOLLET, P. : Histoire du droit civil français, Paris, 1905.

VOLTAIRE : Œuvres complètes, Politique et législation, t. xxxviii., 2nd ed., Paris, 1827.

WACHT : Zur Geschichte des Menschenrechts (Historische Zeitschrift, t. ciii., 1909, p. 82 ss.).

WAGENER, A. : La Liberté de conscience à Rome (Bulletins de l'Académie Royale, 63rd year, 3rd series, t. xxvi., Bruxelles, 1893.

WATTS, ISAAC : Remarks on Essentials in Religion, Charitableness, and Uncharitableness (published in Milton's " Thoughts on True Religion "). See MILTON.

BIBLIOGRAPHY

WILLAERT, L. (S.J.) : Négociations politico-religieuses entre l'Angleterre et les Pays-Bas catholiques (1598-1625), (Revue d'Histoire Ecclésiastique, t. viii., p. 81 ss.), Louvain, 1907.

WILLIAMS, R. : The Bloudy Tenent of Persecution. Publications of the Narragansett Club, vol. iii., Providence, 1867 (Berl.).

WILLIAMS, R. : The Bloody Tenent yet more Bloody, by Mr. Cotton's endeavour to wash it white in the blood of the Lamb ; of whose precious Blood, spilt in the blood of His servants ; and of the blood of Millions spilt in former and later wars for conscience' sake, that most Bloody Tenent of persecution for cause of conscience, upon a second Tryal, is found now more apparently and more notoriously guilty.
    I. The nature of persecution.
    II. The Power of the civil sword in spirituals.
    III. The Parliament's permission of dissenting consciences, in-4e, London, 1652 (Br. M.).

ZWIERLEIN, FR. J. : Religion in New Netherland (1623-1664), Rochester, 1910.

OTHER WORKS BY F. VERMEERSCH

MANUEL SOCIAL: LA LÉGISLATION ET LES ŒUVRES EN BELGIQUE, avec la collaboration du R. P. MULLER, S.J., docteur en sciences politiques et sociales et avec une préface de M. G. COOREMAN, ancien Ministre de l'Industrie et du Travail, 3e édition, Louvain, Uyst pruyst, 1909, 2 vol. in-8. Prix, Belgique, 12.50 fr.; étranger, 15.00 fr.

LA QUESTION CONGOLAISE. 1 vol. in-12 de 375 pp. Bruxelles, De Wit, 1906, avec carte. Prix 3.50 fr.

LES DESTINÉES DU CONGO BELGE. Supplément à *La Question Congolaise*. 1 vol. gr. in-8 de 90 pp., 1906. Prix 1.25 fr. Les deux volumes réunis, 4.50 fr.

LE BELGE ET LA PERSONNE CIVILE. 1 vol. in-8 de 95 pp. Bruxelles, De Wit, 1908. Prix 1 fr.

POUR L'HONNÊTETÉ CONJUGALE. 3e édition. Louvain, Fontaine, 1909, 1 vol. in-8 de 125 pp. Prix 1.25 fr.

LE PROBLÈME DE LA NATALITÉ EN BELGIQUE. Bruxelles, Action Catholique, 1910. Prix 0.50 fr.

DE RELIGIOSIS INSTITUTIS ET PERSONIS. Tractatus canonico moralis, ad recentissimas leges exactus. Tomus I ad usum scholarum, editio altera. Bruges, Beyaert, 1907. 4/5 rel., 6/-. Tomus II ad usum profes. Supplementa et Monumenta. Editio quarta, Ibidem, 1910, 12/10—rel. 14/5.

QUAESTIONES DE JUSTITIA, AD USUM HODIERNUM SCHOLASTICE DISPUTATÆ, altera editio. Bruges, Beyaert, 1904, 1 vol. in-8, xxvi-758 pp. Pretium 5/6.

QUAESTIONES DE RELIGIONE ET PIETATE. 1 vol. in-8, xv-282 pp. Ibidem, 1912. Pretium 2/5.

DE PROHIBITIONE ET CENSURA LIBRORUM. Editio 4. Romæ, Desclée, 1906, 1 vol. in-12, viii-217 pp. Pretium 2/-

DE FORMA SPONSALIUM AC MATRIMONII, POST DECRETUM "NE TEMERE." Editio 5. Bruges, Beyaert, 1912. Pretium 8d.

DE CASU APOSTOLI seu fidei privilegio. Bruges, Beyaert, 1910. Pretium 8d.

PRACTICAL DEVOTION TO THE SACRED HEART. For the use of the Clergy and the Faithful. By A. VERMEERSCH, S.J. Translated by Madame CECILIA. Morocco grain, imitation leather, red edges, 3/6 net. (Postage 4d.)

MEDITATIONS AND INSTRUCTIONS ON THE BLESSED VIRGIN. By A. VERMEERSCH, S.J. For the use of the Clergy and the Faithful. Translated by W. HUMPHREY PAGE, K.S.G. Vol. I. Feasts of Mary. Month of Mary. Vol. II. Meditations for the Sundays of the Year. Morocco grain, imitation leather, red edges, 3/6 net each. (Postage 4d.)